Modern Terrorism and Psychological Trauma

Edited by

Brian Trappler, M.D.

Gordian Knot Books
An Imprint of Richard Altschuler & Associates, Inc.
New York

Modern Terrorism and Psychological Trauma.
Copyright©2007 by Brian Trappler. For information
contact the publisher, Richard Altschuler & Associates,
Inc., at 100 West 57th Street, New York, NY 10019,
RAltschuler @rcn.com or (212) 397-7233.

Library of Congress Control Number: 2007933885
CIP data for this book are available from the Library of
Congress

ISBN-13: 978-1-884092-72-5
ISBN-10: 1-884092-72-1

Gordian Knot Books is an imprint of
Richard Altschuler & Associates, Inc.

Cover Design and Layout: Josh Garfield

Cover Art, "The Fence," by the late Zalman Kleinman,
Reprinted with permission of his Wife, Rosa Kleinman,
And the Chasidic Art Institute

Printed in the United States of America

Distributed by University of Nebraska Press

Dedication

This book is dedicated to my father, Leon Trappler, who fostered the spirit of inquiry, and the Lubavitcher Rebbe, who revealed the secrets.

Contents

Brian Trappler
Editor's Preface   ix

Section I: Single Trauma Incidents

Behzad Hassani
Trauma and Terrorism: How Do Humans Respond?   1

**Sandro Galea, Jennifer Ahern, Heidi Resnick, Dean Kilpatrick,
Michael Bucuvalas, Joel Gold and David Vlahov**
Psychological Sequelae of the September 11 Terrorist Attacks   14
In New York City

**Mark A. Schuster, Bradley D. Stein, Lisa H. Jaycox, Rebecca L.
Collins, Grant N. Marshall, Marc N. Elliott, Annie J. Zhou, David
E. Kanouse, Janina L. Morrison and Sandra H. Berry**
A National Survey of Stress Reactions After the September 11, 2001, 25
Terrorist Attacks

Brian Trappler and Steven Friedman
Posttraumatic Stress Disorder in Survivors of the Brooklyn Bridge   39
Shooting

**G. James Rubin, Chris R. Brewin, Neil Greenberg,
John Simpson and Simon Wessely**
Psychological and Behavioural Reactions to the Bombings in   46
London on 7 July 2005: Cross Sectional Survey of a
Representative Sample of Londoners

Carmelo Vázquez, Pau Pérez-Sales and Georg Matt
Post-Traumatic Stress Reactions Following the March 11, 2004,   61
Terrorist Attacks in a Madrid Community Sample: A Cautionary
Note about the Measurement of Psychological Trauma

Peter S. Curran
Psychiatric Aspects of Terrorist Violence: Northern Ireland   88
1969-1987

Section II: Continuous Trauma Paradigm

Nadežda Savjak
Multiple Traumatisation as a Risk Factor of Post-Traumatic   101
Stress Disorder

Avi Bleich, Marc Gelkopf, Yuval Melamed and
Zahava Solomon   113
Mental Health and Resiliency Following 44 Months of Terrorism:
A Survey of an Israeli National Representative Sample

Arieh Y. Shalev, Rivka Tuval, Sarah Frenkiel-Fishman,
Hilit Hadar and Spencer Eth
Psychological Responses to Continuous Terror: A Study of   136
Two Communities in Israel

Brian Trappler and Arieh Y. Shalev
The Continuous Trauma Phenomenon: Psychological   152
Responses To Continuous Terror—An Exchange Between
Dr. Trappler and Dr. Shalev

J. David Kinzie, James H. Boehnlein, Crystal Riley and
Landy Sparr
The Effects of September 11 on Traumatized Refugees: 157
Reactivation of Posttraumatic Stress Disorder

Section III: The Enduring Effects of PTSD

Joel Sadavoy
Survivors: A Review of Late-Life Effects of Prior Psychological   167
Trauma

Brian Trappler, Jeffrey W. Braunstein, George Moskowitz
and Steven Friedman
Holocaust Survivors in a Primary Care Setting: Fifty Years Later   190

Dov Shmotkin, Tzvia Blumstein and Baruch Modan
Tracing Long-Term Effects of Early Trauma: A Broad-Scope   201
View of Holocaust Survivors in Late Life

Zahava Solomon and Edward Prager
Elderly Israeli Holocaust Survivors During the Persian Gulf War   232

Permissions   241

Editor's Preface

The U. S. State Department (2007) defines terrorism as "premeditated and politically motivated violence perpetrated against non-combatant targets," i.e., innocent civilians. Such violence is the quintessential culmination of the traumatic phenomenon in the modern era. The goal of terrorism extends beyond damage to a specific victim, since its ability to violate traditional boundaries enables it to produce overwhelming psychological and behavioral shock-effects that also are capable of disrupting socio-economic functioning and destabilizing society.

At the community level, one could define terrorism as the source of *the* ultimately effective psychological trauma, since it violates any human sense of safety and integrity, replacing order and stability with fear and immobility. Unlike in the past, such as during the Holocaust, modern terrorists usurp the technology of civilization and use the vast network of mass media, satellite TV, and instant Internet as an effective weapon to dissipate trauma imagery and disseminate fear across communities.

An especially vivid example of modern terrorists using communication technology to dissipate trauma imagery and, thereby, instill fear in society at large, is the deliberately videoed brutal beheading of Daniel Pearl, among other Western civilians, and the distribution of the videos to Western media outlets. The purpose of this method, which imprints barbaric and terrifying imagery in the minds of viewers, is to inflict dread on all civilized communities. Civilian contractors and journalists thus serve both as human sacrifices and as vehicles for the dissipation of horrific violence to a wide audience of collateral targets, i.e., media consumers, who are exposed to such terror imagery. Portraying graphic trauma imagery on a world stage violates the individual's boundaries by personalizing the experience for the viewer, who identifies with the victim but is, at the same time, deprived the opportunity of being debriefed and reassured about his or her own personal safety.

Given that terrorist activities today are chronic, modern terrorism has profound consequences for the mental health of tens of millions of people everywhere, both directly and indirectly. For these reasons, it is vitally important that psychotherapists of every kind, as well as politicians and all concerned citizens, understand the psychological consequences of modern terrorism in as much detail and depth as possible.

Towards this end, the primary purpose of this book is to attempt to address the impact of modern terrorism on the entire spectrum of humans' psychological functions, including the effects of psychological trauma on individuals' behavior and affective functions. To fulfill this promise, I have divided this rich collection of articles into three conceptually distinct, but inter-related, sections, discussed immediately below. As will be seen, they reflect the varied nature of psychological trauma, including Type I Trauma, Type II Trauma (a more complex constellation of symptoms that arises in victims subjected to continuous threat), and the effects of terrorism in exacerbating symptoms in cohorts of previously traumatized populations.

Before discussing these sections, I want to emphasize that, although the articles chosen for this book do not focus on therapeutic approaches to treating psychological trauma, I nonetheless feel it is important to address this issue, which I have done both in the ensuing discussion at appropriate places and at the end of this Preface. There, I also propose a theory of the *caretaker role,* which looks beyond the victim to the role of caretaker failure in contributing to the problem of systemic terrorist assaults on innocent civilians.

Organization of the Anthology

Section I includes articles that focus on solitary terrorist attacks, such as recently occurred in Madrid, London, and New York, and the consequent Type I Trauma responses related to a single terrorist event, especially post-traumatic stress disorder (PTSD). These terrorist events are often shocking or catastrophic, and usually totally unanticipated. Survivors of these events may suffer a wide array of symptoms, including intense fear, or even dissociation, where the individual's awareness and ability to engage psychologically in the present is usurped by traumatic material or defenses. As a result, consciously or unconsciously, the world freezes at the trauma scene and ceases to unfold in a spontaneous, cohesive way. The subject is left in a state of insidious dread, and others objectively experience him or her as being distracted, detached, and emotionally absent. These symptoms are frequently associated with sleep disturbance, anxiety, and distressing trauma recollections (flashbacks).

At the epicenter of a terrorist attack, 90 percent of surviving victims may exhibit some adverse psychological reaction in the hours and days following the critical event. While the frequency of psychological distress dissipates as one moves in time or distance from its epicenter, a small but significant percentage of previously healthy individuals continue to bear significant distress. These findings have been demonstrated in demographic studies conducted with local and national populations exposed to trauma imagery. Following the September 11th terrorist attacks, for example, national surveys of stress reactions identified substantial symptoms of stress in Americans across the country (Schlenger et al., 2002; Schuster et al., 2001).

Most follow-up studies of trauma survivors demonstrate that victims, over time, "habituate," or develop a certain tolerance towards such symptoms. A small but significant percentage of such individuals, however, remain in a state of hyper-vigilance and distressed by the visitations of traumatic recollections or flashbacks. Furthermore, in an unconscious attempt to shield themselves against further trauma triggers, such victims continue to engage in a variety of avoidance behaviors. This, in itself, can become disabling.

Multiple factors will influence the recovery process. Younger persons, for example, are more vulnerable than older persons. The amount of damage done to the individual, the amount of death or devastation that he or she has witnessed, the extent of exposure to the event, the absence of social supports, or the disruption of the continuity of the individual's life may all impact negatively on trauma recovery. Yet for many victims there is an inner yearning for a life that exists beyond the trauma—one that is safe, secure, peaceful, and calm.

At the time of this writing, spring 2007, America and countries in Western Europe have been spared the shock-frequency for the citizenry to be symptomatically affected by the tally of cumulative psychological damage. Following a single traumatic event, most healthy individuals will naturally regain the capacity to self-soothe and function as they had previously. The limited, available data appear to indicate that persistence of disabling symptoms decades beyond a single terror occurrence is very unusual for Type I traumatic incidents.

Section II contains articles that illustrate "Type II" or "complex trauma" proposed by Dr. Judith Herman in *Trauma and Recovery* (1992; for more detail see *The PTSD Workbook* by Williams and Poijula, 2002). In the context of this book, this trauma model is referred to as the "continuous terror" paradigm, especially as proposed by Shalev et al. (2006) in "Psychological Responses to Continuous Terror: A Study of Two Communities in Israel." The uniqueness of the psychological effects of complex trauma that derives from this situation is not in its acute stress symptoms but in its ability to shape (and distort) how the victims think about themselves and the perpetrator, e.g., in the same way one often hears how an abused child believes he or she is "bad," not the abuser. Such ongoing trauma, which creates a pervasive feeling of terror and helplessness in its victims, is described in the literature as a Type II Trauma.

While identical to Type I Trauma in its intensity and shock-effect, Type II Trauma is applied frequently and unexpectedly over an extended period. The predator (in this case the terrorists) uses the fear of impending death or mass-genocide as a weapon to ferment political change by creating a culture of terror. The constant fear of violation, the uncertainty of one's future, the disruption of normal social functioning, and the political instability constitute the building blocks of the Type II Trauma paradigm. With it, the objective is the application of a multitude of fear triggers without the respite required for psychological reconstitution or physiological habituation. Through the application of fear, combined with the seduction of safety in exchange for political capitulation, this type of terror becomes an extremely powerful political tool.

Included in Section II on "continuous trauma" are case studies that demonstrate multiple traumatization that result from terrorism against civilians, compounded by the effect of governmental failure to protect its citizens from injury, separation or displacement. The examples in this section include the genocide in the former republics of Yugoslavia, and the current Intifada in Israel. As regards Israel, for example, Bleich et al. (2006), in "Mental Health and Resiliency Following 44 months of Terrorism," point out that by 2004, 0.1 percent of the Israeli population had been killed or wounded by 13,000 terrorist attacks. This would represent an equivalent per capita of 300,000 American casualties. In addition, 47 percent of the Israeli population sampled continued to feel a sense of life-threatening danger. Following the subsequent unilateral evacuation of Gaza, hundreds of Israeli families remain "housed" in trailers, consisting of modified Formica containers. Communities have been deliberately dispersed in a brilliant military tactic of isolating the "enemy within." Terrorist missile factories that rain fear and death over the skies of Sderot, Ashdot, and Ashkelon have replaced the once-thriving Jewish agricultural center of Gush Katif. Household leaders, once gainfully employed from the produce that miraculously sprouted from the desert, beg from communal coffers. Community leaders are held indefinitely in detention lest they mobilize attention or political support. In short, Gaza and the beautiful Mediterranean Port of Gush Katif, once the strategic southern flank of Israel, have been dismantled as a social experiment of appeasing an unrepentant predator.

In my estimation, this situation demonstrates to terrorists and their supporters that the paradigm of continuous terror ultimately fulfills its goal. As the enemy hijacks the victim's ego-functions, the victim's beliefs, emotions and political actions are "split off," and he acts in concert with the thoughts, feelings, and behaviors imposed by his perpetrator. In other words, a structural dissociation sets in, as the victim unwittingly comes to identify with his persecutor, at the expense of sacrificing the "self" and isolating the "soul." This loss of agency appears to be the ultimate psychological and spiritual consequence of boundary violation characterizing Type II Trauma.

Section III contains articles that focus on the long-term consequences for individuals of early trauma, decades later, and their continued vulnerability to trauma triggers throughout the life course. Thus, this section describes the long-term, more complex Type II Trauma syndromes that appear among survivors of a prolonged, repeated, and intense trauma. While it is not yet established that the "chronic survivor syndrome" is synonymous with the long-term effects that will persist after repeated acts of terrorism, the Holocaust survivor represents an opportunity to examine complex Type II Trauma among a homogenous population. Most survivors from the Holocaust settled in New York and Israel, where they remained a protected treasure of Jewish survival. While many of these survivors have led productive lives and maintained the Jewish European culture, many did this without the joy of life. With increasing frailty, illness, and loss, their continued will to live gradually has been overshadowed by an underlying sense of survivor-guilt, loss and despair. These findings are presented in the articles written by, among others, Shmotkin et al. (2003) and Sadavoy (1997), who examines a multitude of long-term trauma victims in older populations and adds significance to the enduring effects of different trauma events on diverse population samples.

The psychological, as well as physiological and social, responses to collective terror may be predicted by examining the data on Holocaust survivors, since they represent one of the few surviving communities meticulously studied regarding the effects of cumulative terror on civilian society decades following continuous threat.

I included in this section the article by Solomon and Prager (1992) on the reactivation of PTSD in Holocaust survivors following the Scud missile attack during the first Gulf War. The article by Kinzie et al. (2002), which covers Type II, or Complex, Trauma, is included in Section II since this unique study examines the effects of the September 11th attacks on five different ethnic groups of refugees previously traumatized as civilians in their native war-torn countries. Bosnian and Somalian patients showed the greatest deterioration in their subjective sense of safety and security consistent with the continuous terror paradigm.

Therapeutic Considerations and the Role of the Caretaker

Earlier I mentioned that, although the focus of this book is on understanding the types of psychological trauma that can be expected to occur following different types of terrorist activities, I feel it is important to devote some attention to the role of the "*caretaker*" as a dynamic link between the perpetrator and victim (a "tripartite hypothesis"), in all forms of interpersonal trauma, including terrorism. While I have devoted some attention to these matters in the foregoing discussion, I now want to focus on them in some depth in the remainder the Preface.

Donald Kalsched, in his book *The Inner World of Trauma* (1996), uses a Jungian model to explain two of the most disturbing findings in the literature about trauma. His first observation is that the traumatized psyche becomes *self-traumatizing*. Trauma doesn't end with the cessation of external threat. Instead, it continues unabated in the inner world of the trauma victim, whose consciousness becomes haunted by persecutory inner figures. His second finding is the counter-intuitive observation that trauma victims continuously find themselves in life situations that are re-traumatizing. No matter how much the victim wants to change, something more powerful than the ego continually undermines progress. This corresponds to the clinical research findings of disturbed attachment behaviors in victims of childhood abuse made by Marylene Cloitre (2006), where survivors continue to invite relationships that allow the patterns of the abuse dynamic to be permanently perpetuated.

Most contemporary analytical writers are inclined to see this attacking figure as the internalized version of the actual perpetrator of the trauma who has "possessed" the inner world of the trauma victim. But, according to Kalsched, this view is only half correct. The diabolical inner figure is often more sadistic and brutal than any outer perpetrator, indicating that we are dealing here with more than just a psychological factor let loose in the inner world by trauma. Rather, it appears that we are dealing with an Archetypal traumatogenic agency beyond the psyche. By violating the victim's psychological boundaries, the terrorist is able to assert this demonic force. Its lingering metaphysical power, once unleashed, is far more sinister than that of the hostage-taker, tormentor, or physical abuser, since it is not confined to time or space. It can neither be contained nor confronted, and as it unleashes other persecutory archetypes, the victim is left without safe-haven within this repetitive trauma complex.

Primate research done by Coplan, Andrews, Rosenblum et al. (1996) has confirmed what has been observed in the complex interpersonal relationships of abused victims who perpetuate disturbed dynamics in their patterns of attachment behavior well beyond their trauma experience. These victimized patients continue to utilize intrapsychic schemas based on the understanding of a built-in expectation for ambush. Just as in the *intrapsychic* sphere—where survivors remain tormented with fear, insecurities, and the painful recollections of the traumas carried into the present—so, too, in the *interpersonal* context, survivors of childhood trauma may have left the abusive environment but, nonetheless, maintain trauma-generated expectations.

The convention of cognitive-behavioral exposure therapy, otherwise known as "narrative storytelling," creates a safe therapeutic environment that allows the patient to relocate the trauma in the past. The therapy creates a safe-haven which is orderly, logical and controllable, re-establishing the individual's sense of integrity. The recovering trauma victim begins to reformulate a safe and healthy sense of self and other, one that becomes anchored in the present, and is chronologically distinguished from the grip of the traumatic past.

In the field of cognitive behavior therapy, there is also an emerging emphasis on the pursuit of "emotionally-engaged" living. Much attention is now being paid to developing skills in social competency among trauma survivors crippled by avoidance behaviors.

The Role of the Caretaker

From an object-relations perspective, one needs to extend the study of the trauma survivor into a construct larger than that of self and other by including the behavior patterns of the designated caretaker. As mentioned above, a "tripartite hypothesis" of trauma would postulate that three parties are involved in any act of trauma: the perpetrator, the victim, and the caretaker. The role of the caretaker is mysterious; often blatant, sometimes invisible, but in either instance usually contributory. In terms of prevention or cure, caretaker functioning can be the most elusive component in the formula, but the most critical function to address. In the remainder of this discussion, I will give anecdotal examples of this hypothesis, applying it to various trauma scenarios that culminate in its relevance to terrorism.

The perpetrator, or "predator," in order to reach the victim, has to cross the barrier posed by the caretaker. In order to do so, the predator sometimes has to temporarily function as a "trickster"—a vital archetype in Jungian literature. By so doing, the predator manages to establish collusion with either the victim or the caretaker, thus allowing the predator to bypass the obstacle posed by the caretaker.

To understand this process better, especially as it pertains to modern terrorism and its victims, let us begin with a more common example of a predator from everyday life, the pedophile. The pedophile usually has some relationship with the caretaker, which allows him access to the potential victim. After the abuse has occurred, the victim may be threatened to believe that his or her survival depends on keeping the event secret, thereby allowing the violation to continue. In the mind of the victim, breaking the pact is tantamount to suicide. Collusion is established, in this instance, between the victim and the perpetrator. The child may show physical or psychological signs of injury, which he or she attempts to conceal. But the caretaker has passively colluded through his silence and inactivity. If that were not so, how could the victims' profound physical or psychological trauma continue to be undetected by the very person entrusted to safeguard their well-being?

What happens, however, when the caretaker himself or herself *is* the perpetrator? Civilized society has educated teachers, physicians, and other healthcare providers to recognize signs of child abuse and act in a definitive way, by alerting government agencies to intervene and take over the caretaking function.

In most cases where children are abused or women have been battered to death by their jealous ex-lovers, the criminal investigators uncover a trail of warnings and missed opportunities, e.g., caseworkers not reporting disturbing signs to their supervisors or judges allowing felons free access to their victims, even after the victims have exhausted their efforts in crying out to their caretakers to be rescued. Such cases force one to assume that the predator has exploited or outwitted the cracks in the system that allow him or her—as trickster—to outwit the negligent or indifferent caretaker, thereby reaching the helpless victim.

Why is this concept so critical to trauma management? From a preventative point of view, society needs to be reassured after a tragic event that life is still safe, or safer, not less so. A lesson has been learned so that potential victims will be better protected. Society will pay for improved resources, but it will not tolerate repeated betrayals by appointed caretakers.

Mental health professionals involved in trauma healing have to, before anything else, begin the process of allowing the victim to believe that the world is safe again. The empathic bond established early in the relationship may constitute the first building-block in replacing the patient's sense of chaos and danger with one of order and predictability. The microcosm of safety in the therapeutic relationship, however, can only be effective if it is mirrored by a safe, social infrastructure or "holding environment."

In the case of terrorism, governments often assume the role of caretaker. The British Government, for example, during the civil war in Ireland over the past several decades, fulfilled the caretaker role effectively. The article by Curran (1988) in Section I, which covers terrorist violence in Northern Ireland over a 17-year period, documents the limited long-term trauma-related symptoms on the civilian population. This is not a coincidence. Terrorism only works if it creates a pervasive feeling of fear, disrupts the functions of the social infrastructures, and impairs safe travel and access to help. Using the tripartite model of trauma presented above, it can be said that, in its quest for autonomy, the IRA, or "predator" in this case, remained within certain parameters in its methodology, never resorting to the barbaric savagery of radical Islam. In its response, the British Government (caretaker) never left an iota of doubt regarding its efficacy in the caretaking function. Thus, despite the attack on civilians, social order was not disrupted, damage was contained, and healing could begin. This was mirrored by the caretaking role exhibited by

Mayor Giuliani after the attack on the Twin Towers, where he was able, through "compassionate articulation," to provide emotional containment to a city in chaos (Korn, 2001).

In contrast, consider the case of Bosnia and Herzegovina, where one-third of the population became displaced, and the threat to life was compounded by the governmental failure to accept or deliver disaster relief to non-combatants. Critical household providers were killed or removed, information was withheld as to their whereabouts, and relief agencies were denied access to disaster areas. No leadership (caretaker) function was provided. This chaotic effect of state-sponsored terrorism on psychological function is discussed at length in the article by Savjak (2003), in Section II of the anthology. Similar compounding of traumatic effects of personal horrors in the face of breakdown of civil order are described among Cambodian and Afghan refugees, even when studied many years post-trauma in New Zealand and the United States (Cheung, 1994).

The articles by Shalev et al. (2006) and Bleich et al. (2006), previously mentioned, regarding the Intifada, speak not only to the compounding effects of continuous terror, but also to its connection to the absence of the governmental caretaking function.

At this point I will attempt to explain, using various trauma models, how the collective failure of an entire nation to maintain this caretaking function has occurred and brought the nation to the brink of annihilation.

For victims of Type II Trauma, the symptoms of PTSD are more enduring because of a process termed "neurological kindling," whereby the fear-circuitry thermostat is reset at a higher baseline level of vigilance and arousal. While intending to serve a protective function, this state of chronic apprehension drains and depletes the individual emotionally, preventing him or her from *creative engagement*.

Patients suffering from chronic PTSD, in addition to having difficulty with affect-regulation, find it hard to *stay in the present*. They may also accept the perpetrator's projections about themselves as being true. An example of a "negative introject" is when a rape victim is repeatedly told by her or his perpetrator (and comes to believe) that the *victim* "wanted this." Such victims lose their sense of faith of ever regaining a sense of personal agency in relations with others. Their interpersonal schemas become distorted into an entrapment of introjections, and they find themselves living within the belief-systems of their own internalized tyrannical masters.

The above-mentioned symptoms then dominate the psychological and behavioral functions of the trauma victim, who not only participates in but also becomes victimized by gathering forces that constellate in tandem as archetypal persecutory agents. I believe that this process can be used to describe the Israeli Defense Force who responded to a cross-border invasion and kidnapping by terrorists into Lebanon. Their efforts were undermined by their government's survivor guilt compounded by the perpetrator's propaganda in a dramatic irony and role-reversal on their victims (Israeli society and its leadership) to believe that *they* (the victims) were functioning as *persecutors*. The "cry-foul" chorus, which was led by the terrorists and then echoed by the leaders of both the Western democracies and the United Nations, illustrates the so-called "Participation Mystique," described by Carl Jung. At the epicenter of this delusion is the belief by the victims that they truly are responsible and deserving of their misfortune. This is the classic propaganda template of the terrorist paradigm: the exploitation of the unconscious willingness of the trauma victim to participate in the "repetition-compulsion" of abuse. For the abuse survivor (of terrorism), the victim-victimizer dyad is the template for relating. The terrorist is able to identify and exploit the victim's template, which, as long as it remains unconscious, lacks any strategy to free itself from participation in the abuse dynamic. My hypothesis is supported by the Winograd Commission, whose findings indicated that there never was an operational plan to rescue the kidnapped hostages, and which stated that the prime minister never inquired as to whether such an operational plan existed.

In my personal work as a psychiatrist, after treating hundreds of Holocaust survivors, I was dismayed to find how symptoms of psychological trauma returned with such voracity following a current traumatic event, such as loss of a spouse or severe physical illness. Review of the few long-term follow-up studies on survivors of solitary terrorist attacks failed to illustrate the profound pathology observed in patients 60 years after the Holocaust or after profound childhood trauma. This observation convinced me that using the perpetrator-victim dynamic was insufficient to explain how solitary trauma ("A") could lead to chronic enduring effects of trauma ("C"). In most circumstances, only complex trauma ("B") emanating from the "continuous terror" paradigm, discussed above, could lead to "C." I also propose that this occurrence requires the participation of the caretaker in an enabling role or in some form of collusion with the perpetrator.

My theory about the importance of the caretaker role is further corroborated by my personal experience treating trauma victims from both the riots in Crown Heights, New York, which occurred when David Dinkins was mayor, and the Brooklyn Bridge shooting, which occurred when Rudy Giuliani was mayor. In the former incident, the community residents perceived the mayor as being sympathetic to the rioters, and so the residents felt less safe. In particular, Lemrick Nelson was acquitted of the murder of Jacob Rosenbaum, despite being identified by the victim and making a personal confession. After the acquittal, the jurors held a dinner-party, which was attended by Mayor Dinkins. New York City, however, was forced to compensate residents for personal and property damages resulting from the police allowing the rioters to continue unimpeded for seventy-two hours. In contrast, after the Brooklyn Bridge terrorist attack on the same community, during the tenure of Mayor Giuliani, the perpetrator was rapidly apprehended and sentenced to fifteen consecutive life sentences. Despite the terrible sacrifice of having one student killed and another paralyzed by the attack, the community felt safer after the attack, and after five years none of the direct survivors showed signs of PTSD.

Traditional PTSD follow-up studies examine trauma models where the cataclysmic event occurs beyond the perimeter of the victim's safe "holding environment." In such circumstances the victim is afforded the opportunity to return to his safe world and heal, or "reconstruct," using the trusted resources of predictable caretakers and intact social agencies. In contrast, the unrecovered patient remains imprisoned by traumatic fears and memories. Certain traumatic memories can never become extinguished, and such patients are eternally held hostage by the overwhelming fear remnants that have been permanently encoded by the trauma. Such traumatic memories are easily reactivated with sufficient cuing. Examples of this proposition of trauma reactivation are the so-called "anniversary reactions," where certain environmental cues or circumstances serve as triggers and re-evoke the experience of the original trauma.

While recovered survivors of trauma develop a representational form of memory, one that is abstract and organized into a coherent picture, the unrecovered victim remains struggling with highly affect-laden sensory fragments and sensations. The intrusions into consciousness of these frightening fragments of memory produce the flashback, a terrifying image or reliving of the traumatic past. Such victims are never allowed to feel the luxury or the safety of the present. Furthermore, the unrecovered survivor remains locked in this state of dread, easily startled, never at comfort within himself, and vulnerable to the visitations of his sadistic tormentors, real or imagined. He or she is locked in the past, since life has became frozen at the point of traumatic impact. For this trauma survivor the clock has stopped. Often when meeting such victims, one is struck by their absence. Such survivors have either not been given the opportunity of recovery, or have been sabotaged by subsequent events, so that the healthy process of habituation and stress-tolerance never took place. Fear is only one of the many emotions that are generated by trauma. Others include shame, sadness, grief, or disgust. Any or all of these emotional components continue to contaminate the emotional field of the survivor, who remains captive to his traumatic experience.

In trauma recovery, the cornerstone of treatment is providing an environment that is physically and mentally safe. The survivor needs to be convinced by an empowered, benevolent caretaker or agency that he or she is currently free of physical danger, and can now safely reassume a sense of personal agency. Such conviction provides the survivor with a choice of belief systems and engagement in patterns of thinking and emoting that reflect this newly found self-awareness. The feeling of safety includes social, political and religious life, where the umbrella of protection allows trust and belief in a higher power and freedom from external threat.

At the microcosmic level of healing, i.e., during the process of healing the individual victim, the therapist replaces the perpetrator, but the power conferred to the caretaker is now devoted to healing and benevolence, where the integrity and sanctity of the individual become categorically reestablished. At the macrocosmic level, i.e., the task of healing traumatized societies, the role of caretaker has to be fulfilled by balancing the benevolent power of government agencies with the caretaking function, by establishing the integrity of boundaries while being willing to strike mercilessly at those who desecrate its inner sanctuary. These political guardians elected by democracies that were established following a century of horrendous slaughter and genocide, however, straddle on the brink of apathy and indifference. As the emboldened predator prepares in the shadows for his lethal attack, the guardian sleeps.

How apt of Behzad Hassani (2005), in the opening article of this book, "Trauma and Terrorism," to quote William Blake:

"O rose, thou art sick.
The invisible worm,
That flies in the night
In the howling storm:
Has found out thy bed
Of crimson joy:
And his dark, secret love
Does thy life destroy."

References

Bleich, A., Gelkopf, M., Melamed, Y. & Solomon, Z. (2006). Mental health and resiliency following 44 months of terrorism: a survey of an Israeli national representative sample. *BMC Medicine* 4:21, doi:10.1186/1741-7015-4-21.

Cheung, P. (1994). Posttraumatic stress disorder among Cambodian refugees in New Zealand. *International Journal of Social Psychiatry, 40*(1), 17-26.

Cloitre, M. (2006). *Treating survivors of childhood abuse: Psychotherapy for the interrupted life.* New York: Guilford Press.

Coplan, J. D., Andrews, M. W., Rosenblum, L. A., et al. (1996). Persistent elevations of cerebrospinal fluid concentrations of corticotropin-releasing factor in adult nonhuman primates exposed to early-life stressors: Implications for the pathophysiology of mood and anxiety disorders. *Proceedings of the National Academy of Science, 93*(4), 1619–1623.

Curran, P. S. (1988). Psychiatric aspects of terrorist violence: Northern Ireland 1969-1987. *British Journal of Psychiatry, 153*, 470-5.

Hassani, B. (2005). Trauma and terrorism: How do humans respond? *University of Toronto Medical Journal, 83*(1), 58-62.

Herman, J. (1992). *Trauma and recovery.* New York: Basic Books.

Kalsched, D. (1996). *The inner world of trauma.* London: Brunner-Routledge.

Kinzie, J. D., Boehnlein, J. K., Riley, C., & Sparr, L. (2002). The effects of September 11 on traumatized refugees: Reactivation of posttraumatic stress disorder. *Journal of Nervous & Mental Disease. 190*(7): 437-441.

Korn, M. L. (2001). Trauma and PTSD: Aftermaths of the WTC disaster—an interview with Yael Danieli, PhD. *Medscape General Medicine* (posted 10/08/2001).

Sadavoy, J. (1997). Survivors: A review of late-life effects of prior psychological trauma. *American Journal of Geriatric Psychiatry, 5*(4), 287-301.

Savjak, N. (2003). Multiple traumatisation as a risk factor of post-traumatic stress disorder. *PSIHOLOGIJA, 36*(1-2), 59-71.

Schlenger, W. E., Caddell, J. M., Ebert, L., et al. (2002). Psychological reactions to terrorist attacks: Findings from the national study of Americans' reactions to September 11. *JAMA, 288*, 581-588.

Schuster, M.A., Stein, B. D., Jaycox, L. H., et al. (2001). A national survey of stress reactions after the September 11, 2001, terrorist attacks. *New England Journal of Medicine, 345,* 1507-1512.

Shalev, A. Y., Tuval, R., Frenkiel-Fishman, S., Hadar, H. & Eth, S. (2006). Psychological responses to continuous terror: A study of two communities in Israel. *American Journal of Psychiatry, 164*(4), 667-673.

Shmotkin, D., Blumstein, T. & Modan, B. (2003). Tracing long-term effects of early trauma: A broad-scope view of Holocaust survivors in late life. *Journal of Consulting and Clinical Psychology, 71*(2), 223-234.

Solomon, Z. & Prager, E. (1992). Elderly Israeli Holocaust survivors during the Persian Gulf War. *American Journal of Psychiatry, 149*(12), 1707-1710.

U.S. Department of State. (2007). Retrieved from the internet July 2007 at http://www.state.gov/s/ct/rls/pgtrpt/2000/index.cfm?docid=2419

Williams, M. B. & Poijula, S. (2002). *The PTSD workbook.* Oakland, CA: New Harbinger Publications, Inc.

Section I: Single Trauma Incidents

Trauma and Terrorism: How Do Humans Respond?

Behzad Hassani, H.B.A.

The Sick Rose

O Rose thou art sick.
The invisible worm,
That flies in the night
In the howling storm:

Has found out thy bed
Of crimson joy:
And his dark secret love
Does thy life destroy.

William Blake

The Beginning

Terrorism is a reality of our time. The US State Department defines terrorism as "premeditated, politically motivated violence perpetrated against non-combatant targets by sub-national groups or clandestine agents, usually intended to influence an audience."[1] Although the statement above is a worthy attempt at defining this age-old phenomenon, it fails to encompass the grand spectrum of societal implications that terrorism creates.

Terrorism erodes, at both the individual and the community level, the sense of security and safety of daily life. It defies our natural need to conceptualize life on earth as predictable, orderly, logical, and controllable. Terrorism destroys lives, shatters families, and destabilizes societies. As such, it compromises the mental and the spiritual well-being of humans, in addition to its obvious physical and material consequences. Recent attacks—September 11, 2001, on the Twin Towers and Washington; the London and Madrid bombings; and the extensive yet chronic Israeli experience with terror, intensified following the *Intifada*—have focused the world's attention on the psychological impacts of terrorism.

This brief account strives to address the human response to terrorism from the perspective of the individual as well as the community. Needless to say, treatises can be written on such a profound topic and the present endeavour aims merely to present a brief survey outlining the far-reaching psychological implications of this bitter reality.

The Spectrum

Terrorism is a prototypic traumatic event for those whose life and physical integrity are directly threatened and for those who experience sudden loss of a loved one.[2] However, one must also consider that the ultimate goal of terrorism is to instill fear in society at large, in addition to threatening the integrity of single individuals and small groups. Thus, collateral effects develop among individuals and communities who are not directly affected by the event, particularly since such occurrences receive extensive coverage by the mass media. The burden may persist with individuals as chronic disorders for years to come, and could very well change the fabric of the society drastically. Therefore, terrorism defies the boundaries of space and time. This unique quality complicates any effort undertaken for the purpose of assessment and organization of the psychosocial impacts of this phenomenon—but we shall try.

Human Reactions

It is said that up to 90% of victims of a terrorist attack may exhibit some adverse psychological reaction in the hours immediately following the event.[2] In most instances, symptoms subside over the weeks to come, although by 12 weeks, approximately 30% of the victims may still bear significant distress. The numbers continue to drop afterwards, even though delayed responses or responses to later consequences of the incident continue to appear. In brief, most who are distressed in the first weeks will recover. This process can best be observed in the New York City experience following the 9/11 attacks.[3,4] Surveys conducted by the

New York Academy of Medicine five to eight weeks following the attacks reported a Post-Traumatic Stress Disorder (PTSD) prevalence rate of 7.5%, with those having the most severe exposure or personal loss at higher risk than others. Six months following the attacks, this figure dropped to a mere 0.6% for PTSD and an additional 4.7% for subsyndromal PTSD.

Notice, however, that the above study does not present the complete picture. First, it points to the flaws of the early assessment and estimation of PTSD prevalence based on early symptoms. In other words, early symptoms did not constitute a real clinical syndrome requiring treatment in all cases; many of the early indicators were simply a reflection of transient distress. Furthermore, the short period of time covered by the study protocol could not include the delayed-onset cases of PTSD, nor could the design distinguish between acute versus chronic distress. It remains clear, however, that strong physiological, cognitive and emotional responses to trauma exist that are simply normal reactions to extreme situations and not a sign of mental disorder or moral weakness. Nevertheless, even such benign reactions can interfere with the ability of individuals to regain control of their lives, and hence must be addressed by mental health professionals.

Now that we have confronted a few of the methodological obstacles, we can make an effort to categorize the disorderly continuum of psychosocial responses to terrorism. We can do so by conceptualizing the aftermath of a terrorist attack in terms of a series of stages or phases, each with its own unique characteristics and psychiatric profile on the individual and community level:[5]

Phase 1: Immediate Response and the "Rescue Stage"

During the first hours to days after the terrorist event, the focus lies on rescuing victims and seeking to stabilize the situation. In this stage, various types of acute emotional response are observed: heightened autonomic arousal, diffuse anxiety, fear, confusion, survivor guilt, and ambivalence about learning the truth. Furthermore, the release of stress hormones and peripheral cathecolamines following the traumatic event result in improved cognitive performance. However, as stress persists, behavioural and cognitive performance may become narrowly focused, leading to a loss of flexibility. This may give rise to disorganized thinking, which in turn results in either a fight or flight response or a freeze response (psychic numbing). Internal conflicts over acceptance/rejection of nurturance may develop, and affective instability or brief reactive psychosis and hysteria may be observed.

Contrary to popular belief, victims show little panic and often engage in heroic or altruistic acts. Many of the above behaviours are adaptive and ensure short-term survival. Such response to trauma was perhaps best observed following the 9/11 attacks, when tens of thousands of people peacefully evacuated Manhattan and thousands volunteered to care for the emergency workers and donated blood and food. Most uncharacteristically, New Yorkers stopped going to work and spoke to strangers on the streets![6] A further instance of surprising human kindness was replicated in London following the subway bombings of July 7: one London shop owner posted a sign inviting passers-by to "come in and stay as long as you like. Join us for tea, soft drinks, coffee, and soup on the house."[7]

As noted, most of the acute reactions dissipate over time, and even though they are normal responses to extreme conditions, the symptoms may be perceived by the victims as socially inappropriate, shameful, and as evidence of inadequacy. This in turn will lead to further distress. On a community level, the risk of mass panic and acute outbreaks of medically unexplained symptoms (OMUS) is at its peak. These topics will be addressed in a later section.

Phase 2: Intermediate Response—Adaptation, Arousal, and Avoidance: The "Inventory Stage"

From one week to several months after the event, the attention turns to longer-term solutions with bureaucratic forms of help replacing the heroic rescue missions. Victims may initially experience a transient "honeymoon" phase: a feeling of relief at being safe and optimism about the roads that lie ahead. Soon after, a more realistic appraisal of the lasting consequences will be performed and disillusionment may set in. Intrusive recollections of the event, heightened and persistent autonomic arousal, avoidance of stimuli linked with the trauma, and somatic symptoms (dizziness, headache, fatigue, nausea) are commonly found. Stress may even precipitate early labour and may cause fetal distress. Several psychiatric disorders develop in this stage. Anger, irritability, apathy, disordered grief, abnormal bereavement, and social withdrawal are common manifestations. Major depression, panic disorder, generalized anxiety disorder, substance/alcohol abuse (as was demonstrated in a Manhattan study),[8] and somatoform disorders are further consequences of trauma in this period.[2] Although the emphasis of the present account will be on PTSD and some culture-specific manifestations, one must note that the other syndromes may also prove terribly debilitating and cause significant pathology among the survivors.

Post-Traumatic Stress Disorder (PTSD)

As mentioned earlier, the mechanisms of natural recovery from traumatic events are strong in humans and will bring about gradual dissipation of acute post-traumatic symptoms, many of which are recognized PTSD symptoms. However, some may develop psychiatric disorders in the long term; most commonly, PTSD, which occurs in as many as 30% of individuals exposed to a terrorist attack.[6] Thus, the pathologic process involved in PTSD is a reflection of a failure of recovery from early symptoms. Studies of the Israeli experience have shown that the rate of PTSD following terrorist attacks is twice as high as that observed in other traumatic events.[9] Interestingly, the recovery course of PTSD during an era of chronic terror is similar to that of other traumatic events. Studies of 9/11 victims suggest that severity of the experience and the degree of exposure are the best predictors of PTSD.[4] Those whose lives are directly affected, who are physically injured, and who witness grotesque events are at higher risk. It is notable, however, that even indirect exposure could render individuals vulnerable to PTSD: family members and friends of survivors, rescue workers, and health care workers have been among the reported cases. The domain of influence is such that even those who watch more media coverage are also at higher risk for PTSD.[10]

Furthermore, a multi-generational component to post-traumatic reactions has been observed: adult children of Holocaust survivors with PTSD show a greater prevalence of PTSD to their own traumatic experiences compared to adult children of Holocaust survivors without PTSD.[11] The rate is also higher among monozygotic compared with dizygotic twins.[12] Further risk factors for PTSD are: family history of psychopathology, prior exposure to trauma, lower IQ, lower educational attainment, history of heavy alcohol use, female gender, and poor post-traumatic social support.[2]

It must be emphasized that a small proportion of people who experience more persistent stressors after the initial trauma (e.g. chronic experience with terror, subsequent threat of attacks, biological agents) can apparently develop PTSD after a delayed period of time (six months to years) following the initial traumatic event.[2] This quality further complicates the aetiology, detection, and treatment of PTSD in the affected population. Cardinal features of PTSD are as follows:[13]

Persistent and intrusive re-experiencing of the traumatic event via nightmares or flashbacks is a critical manifestation of PTSD. The patient may experience intense psychological distress and physiological reactivity on exposure to internal or external cues that symbolize the event. Re-enactments of the events through subtle and repetitive play may occur among children.

Persistent avoidance of reminders and cues associated with the trauma as well as persistent emotional numbing are further signs of PTSD. Patients may evade activities, places, or people that remind them of the experience, and may develop a fatalist sense of a foreshortened future without expectations of a normal lifespan or life.

Persistent symptoms of autonomic hyper-arousal, such as insomnia, anger, and hypervigilance are further manifestations of PTSD.

It is noteworthy that even though the above cluster of PTSD symptoms has been reported in every part of the world, significant cultural variations in manifestation exist. In less industrialized nations, avoidance and numbing are less common and instead dissociative and trance-like states, in which fragments of the event are relived, are more common.

Culture-Specific Disorders[13]

A comprehensive analysis of culture-specific syndromes cannot be undertaken in the present account. However, a brief synopsis is included in order to draw attention to this much-neglected, yet vital topic. The boundaries between disorders of the "mind" and the "body" are often porous and at best arbitrary. In other words, the Cartesian dichotomy of "mind vs. body" is nothing but an illusion and a futile attempt at simplifying life's chaotic reality. The interpenetration of the two spheres is most visible in the study of culture-specific manifestations of psychiatric disorders. In many cultures, depression is often experienced largely in somatic terms: complaints of "nerves", headaches, chronic diffuse pain, fatigue, trance disorders, problems of the "heart", feelings of "heat", and fears of somatic illness are merely a few examples. Some culture-specific post-traumatic syndromes with irregular somatoform presentations include: *Susto* (Latin America), *Amok* (Malaysia, Philippines), *Dhat* (India), *Latah* (South Pacific, southeast Asia), and *Khoucheraug* (Cambodia). It is axiomatic that much emphasis need be placed on the analysis of these "irregular" manifestations of the human experience in the postmodern multicultural world of today. Psychiatry must transcend its Eurocentric roots and its rigid definitions and strive to ponder the universal human condition. The courage to embrace Nature's chaos and uncertainty is at the heart of this process.

Phase 3: Long-term Response—Recovery, Reconstruction, Impairment, and Change[13]

A year or more after the traumatic event, relative stability may have been restored to the victims' lives. However, many may experience feelings of resentment and disappointment if initial hopes for assistance or restoration are not met. Symptoms of the "Inventory Stage" may persist, and a significant late onset incidence of PTSD, depression and anxiety may manifest. Rates of suicide may increase, and late-appearing somatoform symptoms may disrupt daily life. More complex syndromes may appear among survivors of prolonged, repeated, and intense trauma (chronic experience with terrorism), an example of which is *survivor syndrome.* The survivor journeys through life "without a spark."[13] The joy of life is gone and the will to live is overshadowed by despair. The spectrum of behaviour ranges from depression and guilt to chronic aggression and an "addiction to hate."[3] Family dynamics are disrupted, and on a grand scale the sense of community is weakened. The collective response of a community is peculiar in this stage and abounds with paradox and subtleties.

Communities in Distress

The disruptive force of terrorism transcends the individual. The very aim of terrorism is to create tears in the fabric of social life by instilling fear

and instituting chaos. The acute collective community response to terrorism includes symptoms of emotional distress, misattribution of somatic
symptoms, and social symptoms such as loss of confidence in the administration, resentment of authority figures, social isolation, demoralization, marginalization, and scapegoating using traditional divisions in
the society (e.g. along religious or ethnic lines).[14,15] In this section, we
will survey the general group responses to terrorism and take a closer
look at the Israeli society, the only nation-state to have had decades of
experience with this disruptive phenomenon.

Three specific collective reactions to trauma have been documented
in the literature: mass panic,[14] acute outbreaks of medically unexplained
symptoms (OMUS),[16] and chronic cases of medically unexplained physical symptoms (MUPS).[17] Furthermore, it is worthwhile to consider the
community response to biological and chemical attacks separately as
several unique features of the agents make them particularly terrifying to
the public.

Mass panic, simply phrased, is an intense and contagious fear
whereby the individual's only reference of conduct becomes the "self."[18]
Extremes of behaviour are expected: desire to escape or, alternatively,
behavioural paralysis. Chaos ensues in the community, and social organization and cultural roles are compromised. In spite of the popular
myth, mass panics are relatively uncommon. The trials of the Tokyo sa-
rin attack, the Israeli SCUD missile attacks, the Oklahoma City bombing,
and even the Hiroshima and Nagasaki nuclear attacks bear witness to this
claim. As mentioned earlier, altruistic and heroic acts (adaptive behaviours) are the norm after the trauma of a terrorist attack.[14] It is understandable, however, that factors such as feelings of utter hopelessness or
lack of confidence in the authorities could increase the likelihood of a
mass panic. Once again, extensive mass media coverage of such events
could contribute to the propagation of fear and the inducement of emotional trauma, and subsequently heighten the risk for chaos.

The human stress response is comprised of arousal, anxiety, and
vigilance: evolution's solution to trauma. However, the physiological
reactions of the survival response may be mistakenly attributed to the
effect of biological/chemical agents or medical illness. The symptoms
may manifest on a large scale and present as mass outbreaks of medically
unexplained symptoms (OMUS). Although no identifiable medical cause
can be ascertained, the condition appears contagious, spreads by sight
and sound, and presents in public places or among social groupings.

Rapid onset and remission of symptoms—such as hyperventilation, shortness of breath, dizziness, nausea, syncope, and abdominal distress—characterize this esoteric phenomenon. Often, these symptoms mimic the reported or perceived effects of an infectious or chemical agent.[19] Remarkable epidemics of such somatization have been observed in the USA and the West Bank following false reports of poisonous gas leaks.[20] OMUS may lead to significant chaos and social disruption following chemical and biological attacks, and may impose a tremendous burden on an already stressed healthcare system.

As mentioned earlier, rapid onset and remission characterize the OMUS. However, acute to chronic transition of the aforementioned enigmatic symptoms is a possibility. Although research has not yet identified terrorism-induced clusters of medically unexplained physical symptoms (MUPS), evidence from World War I and the Vietnam War is abundant.[17] It is likely that biological and chemical attacks could bring about the formation of MUPS in the affected societies. The above symptoms have often been categorized as "somatoform". This vague convention casts more shadow upon the doctor-patient relationship than light. The manifestations of MUPS are debilitating in the long run. Naturally, the patient may become convinced of the medical nature of their condition and in frustration demand a treatment. On the other hand, the physician is skeptical of any medical diagnosis for the problem and may implicitly convey to the patient that the symptoms are not "real". The tension will inevitably lead to alienation and amount to a doctor-patient standoff. Once again, the vitality of mediators such as trust, respect, understanding, empathy, and validation for patients' concerns is highlighted in practice.

In recent years, the presentation and management of chemical/biological attacks have become the topics of intense debate among healthcare professionals and the focus of dramatic coverage in mass media as well as Hollywood. Chemical/biological agents are often invisible and odourless. The symptoms may often mimic those of common illnesses and therefore evade early detection. Some agents cause gross deformities (small pox, mustard gas) and thus terrify the public and heighten the fear of contagious spread. To complicate the situation further, the agents and their symptomatology are often unfamiliar to physicians. Even our preventive response to these agents is problematic: the protective gear worn during the attacks increases social isolation, and limits intra-group interaction. Indeed, it increases the incidence of psychiatric ailments.[21] In brief, the likelihood of mass panic and occurrence of MUPS is increased following biochemical terrorist campaigns. For example, twice as many gas hysteria cases were observed during World War I as there were actual gas exposure cases.[18] On the other hand, many biological and chemical agents directly affect the central nervous system and cause symptoms such as lethargy, depression, disorientation, and psychosis.[19] Furthermore, it is likely that different behavioural responses would present for biological versus chemical agents. Each has its own peculiar onset, presentation, and aetiology and is tended to by different groups of professionals and first responders. It is due to these complicating parameters that social preparedness and structured response are even more critical during and following biological/chemical attacks.

In keeping with its peripatetic scientific roots, medicine often strives to categorize, routinize, and organize symptoms and conditions. In essence, it aims to render the unpredictable, predictable. Similar reaction is expected when exploring the human response to terrorism. However, in the realm of psychiatry, the chaos and disorderliness of life presents a genuine and insurmountable challenge to our preconceived and simplified constructs. One example of such contention is seen in the landmark study by Israeli scientists, who found that terror attacks in Israel produced a transient quiescence in light automobile accidents one day after the event, followed by a 35% spike in fatal accidents precisely three days subsequent to the attack.[22] Furthermore, public reports of decline in New York City murder rates following 9/11 attacks highlighted the broad-based, short-term societal responses to terror that cannot be easily explained.[23] Understanding such paradoxical population-wide reactions to traumatic events is critical if the medical community is to devise measures to detect and address the subtle and indirect human responses to terrorism.

Towards New Horizons

Terrorism is a blight on humanity's record. It targets innocent civilians and instills horror in populations. Terrorism carries the element of uncertainty in human life to devastating heights. It destroys lives, property and material culture. The psychiatric implications of such traumatic events have only recently become the focus of academic attention. What can be done to alleviate the pain? The best approach would be to abolish the trauma. The next best remedy would be to foster resilience and bolster support so that individuals can develop the necessary coping capacity prior to the event. In the future, academic emphasis must be placed on the refinement of risk factors, predictors, and aetiological indicators of post-traumatic disorders. Early detection and treatment of traumatized individuals would further prevent a prolonged and debilitating stress response.

Furthermore, one must not neglect to acknowledge, reclaim, and harness the grand vitality of human resilience, a hard-earned virtue and a precious gift from our evolutionary past. Perhaps the most touching embodiment of this virtue is seen in a poem written by a 16-year-old Israeli girl following a deadly suicide bombing campaign:[24]

While you were showering
A mortar fell
And three people died.
While you were sleeping
Shots were fired
And eight soldiers were wounded.
While you were eating
Terrorists infiltrated
A house where children were sleeping.
And while you were saying the grace after meals
All that remained of the children
Were pieces.
While you were playing
A terrorist entered
A hall full of people.
And while you were losing
Their souls left their bodies
The guests, the bride and the groom.
So let's hurry, let's run, let's get organized,
Let's finish, let's do as much as we can
For who knows what will happen,
The next time someone sits down to eat.

Martin Luther King, Jr. once wrote:

"Cowardice asks... "Is it safe?"
Expedience asks... "Is it politic?"
Vanity asks... "Is it popular?"
Then comes a time
When one must take a position
That is neither safe, politic, nor popular,
But one must take it because it is right."

References

1. US Department of State [homepage on the Internet]. Washington D.C.: Bureau of Public Affairs, U.S. Department of State; c2005 [cited 2005 Sept 5]. Available from: http://www.state.gov/.

2. Yehuda R, Bryant R, Marmar C, Zohar J. Pathological response to terrorism. Neuropsychopharmacology. 2005 Oct;30(10):1793-805. *Epub* 2005 Jul 13.

3. Galea S, Ahern J, Resnick H, Kilpratric D, Bucuvalas M, Gold J, *et al.* Psychological sequelae of the September 11 terrorist attacks. *N Eng J Med.* 2002 Mar 23;346:982-7.

4. Galea S, Vlahov D, Resnick H, Ahern J, Susser E, Gold J, *et al.* Trends of probable post-traumatic stress disorder in New York City after the September 11 terrorist attacks. *Am J Epidemiol.* 2003;158:514-24.

5. Ursano RJ, Fullerton CS, Norwood AE. Psychiatric dimensions of disaster: Patient care, community consultation, and preventive medicine. *Harv Rev Psychiatry.* 1995 Nov-Dec;3(4):196-209.

6. Solnit R. The Uses of Disaster: Notes on Bad Weather and Good Government. *Harper's Magazine.* 2005 Oct;311(1865):33.

7. Solnit R. The Uses of Disaster: Notes on Bad Weather and Good Government. *Harper's Magazine.* 2005 Oct;311(1865):33.

8. Vlahov D, Galea S, Resnick H, Ahern J, Boscarino JA, Bucuvalas M, *et al.* Increased use of cigarettes, alcohol, and marijuana among Manhattan, New York, residents after the September 11th terrorist attacks. *Am J Epidemiol.* 2002;1 55(1 1):988-96.

9. Shalev AY, Freedman S. PTSD Following Terrorist Attacks: A Prospective Evaluation. *Am J Psychiatry.* 2005 Jun;1 62:1188-91.

10. Schuster MA, Stein BD, Jaycox L, Collins RL, Marshall GN, Elliot MN, *et al.* A national survey of stress reactions after the September 11, 2001, terrorist attacks. *N Eng J Med.* 2001 Nov 1 5;345(20):1 507-12.

11. Yehuda R, McFarlane AC, Shalev AY. Predicting the development of posttraumatic stress disorder from the acute response to a traumatic event. *Biol Psychiatry.* 1998 Dec 15;44(12):1305-13.

12. Stein MB, Jang KL, Taylor S, Vernon PA, Livesley WJ. Genetic and environmental influences on trauma exposure and posttraumatic stress disorder symptoms: a twin study. *Am J Psychiatry.* 2002 Oct;159:1675-81.

13. Fullerton CS, Ursano RJ. Psychological and Psychopathological Consequences of Disasters. In: Lopez-Ibor JJ, Christodoulou G, Maj M, Sartorius N, Okasha A, editors. Disasters and Mental Health. Chichester, West Sussex; Hoboken, NJ: John Wiley & Sons; 2005. p. 13-37.

14. Glass TA, Schoch-Spana M . Bioterrorism and the people: How to vaccinate a city against panic. *Clin Infect Dis.* 2002;34:217-23.

15. Holloway HC, Norwood AE, Fullerton CS, Engel CC, Ursano RJ. The threat of biological weapons: prophylaxis and mitigation of psychological and social consequences. *JAMA.* 1997 Aug 6;278(5):425-7.

16. Pastel R. Outbreaks of medically unexplained physical symptoms after military action, terrorist threat, or technological disaster. *Mil Med.* 2001;166(Suppl 2):44- 6.

17. McLeod WR. Merphos poisoning or mass panic? *Aust N Z J Psychiatry.* 1975 Dec;9 (4):225-9.

18. Lacy TJ, Benedek DM. Terrorism and weapons of mass destruction: Managing the behavioral reaction in primary care. *South Med J.* 2003 Apr;96(4):394-9.

19. Gamino LA, Elkins GR, Hackney KU. Emergency management of mass psychogenic illness. *Psychosomatics.* 1989 Fall;30(4):446-9.

20. DiGiovanni C Jr. Domestic terrorism with chemical or biological agents: Psychiatric aspects. *Am J Psychiatry.* 1999 Oct;156:1500-5.

21. Ritchie EC. Psychological problems associated with mission oriented protective gear. *Mil Med.* 2001 Dec;166(12 Suppl):83-4.

22. Stecklov G, Goldstein JR. Terror attacks influence driving behavior in Israel. *PNAS.* 2004 Oct 5;101(40):14551-6.

23. Marks A. US crime rate up, ending decade of decline: Violent crime spike renews debate over strategy: better technology or more police? *Christian Science Monitor.* 2002 Jun 25;Sect. USA:2.

24. Daniei Y, Brom D, Sills J, editors. The Trauma of Terrorism: Sharing Knowledge and Shared Care—An International Handbook. Binghamton, NY: Haworth Maltreatment & Trauma Press; 2005.

Psychological Sequelae of the September 11 Terrorist Attacks In New York City

Sandro Galea, M.D., M.P.H., Jennifer Ahern, M.P.H., Heidi Resnick, Ph.D.,
Dean Kilpatrick, Ph.D., Michael Bucuvalas, Ph.D.,
Joel Gold, M.D., David Vlahov, Ph.D.

ABSTRACT: *Background*. The scope of the terrorist attacks of September 11, 2001, was unprecedented in the United States. We assessed the prevalence and correlates of acute post-traumatic stress disorder (PTSD) and depression among residents of Manhattan five to eight weeks after the attacks. ***Methods***. We used random-digit dialing to contact a representative sample of adults living south of 110th Street in Manhattan. Participants were asked about demographic characteristics, exposure to the events of September 11, and psychological symptoms after the attacks. ***Results***. Among 1,008 adults interviewed, 7.5 percent reported symptoms consistent with a diagnosis of current PTSD related to the attacks, and 9.7 percent reported symptoms consistent with current depression (with "current" defined as occurring within the previous 30 days). Among respondents who lived south of Canal Street (i.e., near the World Trade Center), the prevalence of PTSD was 20.0 percent. Predictors of PTSD in a multivariate model were Hispanic ethnicity, two or more prior stressors, a panic attack during or shortly after the events, residence south of Canal Street, and loss of possessions due to the events. Predictors of depression were Hispanic ethnicity, two or more prior stressors, a panic attack, a low level of social support, the death of a friend or relative during the attacks, and loss of a job due to the attacks. ***Conclusions***. There was a substantial burden of acute PTSD and depression in Manhattan after the September 11 attacks. Experiences involving exposure to the attacks were predictors of current PTSD, and losses as a result of the events were predictors of current depression. In the aftermath of terrorist attacks, there may be substantial psychological morbidity in the population.

The attacks of September 11, 2001, represented the largest act of terrorism in U.S. history. Approximately 3,000 people were killed in New York City alone.[1] Severe lasting psychological effects are generally seen after disasters causing extensive loss of life, property damage, and widespread financial strain and after disasters that are intentionally caused.[2] These elements were all present in the September 11 attacks, suggesting that the psychological sequelae in New York City are substantial and will be long-lasting.

We conducted a study to determine the prevalence of psychopathologic disorders in Manhattan after September 11 and to identify predictors of these conditions. We focused on post-traumatic stress disorder

(PTSD) and depression, the two most commonly studied psychological sequelae of trauma and disasters.[3,5]

Methods

Data Collection and Sample

Data were collected through telephone interviews with a random sample of Manhattan residents between October 16 and November 15, 2001. The institutional review board of the New York Academy of Medicine approved the study, and oral informed consent was obtained from the study subjects.

The sampling frame consisted of adults living in households with telephones in Manhattan. We restricted the sample to households south of 110th Street, a demographically homogeneous area and the part of Manhattan that is closest to the World Trade Center. Using random-digit dialing, we screened households for geographic eligibility, and an adult in each household was randomly selected to be interviewed (whoever had the most recent birthday was selected). We made up to 10 attempts to contact an adult at each number. The overall cooperation rate for the survey was 64.3 percent.

Study Instruments

Respondents were asked questions from a structured questionnaire in English or Spanish. We asked questions about demographic characteristics, where the respondent was living before September 11, and the respondent's location during the attacks. For the analyses, total social support was categorized as low, medium, or high. We asked about three aspects of social support—emotional (i.e., "someone to love you and make you feel wanted"), instrumental (i.e., "someone to help you if you were confined to bed"), and appraisal (i.e., "someone to give you good advice in a crisis")—in the six months before September 11.[6] We also asked whether the respondent had experienced any of eight stressful events (e.g., the death of a spouse) in the previous year.

Respondents were asked whether they had directly witnessed the attacks, had feared they would die during the attacks, had friends or relatives who were killed during the attacks, had been displaced from home, had been involved in the rescue effort, or had lost a job or possessions because of the attacks. Documentation of a panic attack was based on a modified version of the National Institute of Mental Health Diagnostic Interview Schedule; the diagnosis required the development of at least four characteristic symptoms during or soon after the attacks.

PTSD was assessed with the use of the PTSD questionnaire from the National Women's Study, which is a modified version of the Diagnostic Interview Schedule for PTSD. For the diagnosis of current PTSD, this instrument has a coefficient of 0.71 for agreement with clinician-administered structured clinical interviews, and it uses a non–event-specific approach to the assessment of PTSD symptoms.[5] Current PTSD was defined as the presence of at least one recurrent symptom (e.g., intrusive memories or distressing dreams), three avoidance symptoms (e.g., efforts to avoid thoughts associated with the trauma or loss of interest in activities associated with it), and two symptoms of hyperarousal (e.g., difficulty falling asleep or concentrating). All symptoms must have persisted for 2 weeks or longer and must have been present within the previous 30 days to qualify as symptoms of current PTSD. In addition, for symptoms that involved specific content (e.g., memories or thoughts), we asked about the content; these symptoms had to be related to the September 11 attacks to qualify as symptoms of current PTSD. We used a modified, validated version of the Structured Clinical Interview in the Diagnostic and Statistical Manual of Mental Disorders, fourth edition, for a major depressive episode to determine the presence of depression within the previous 30 days.[7]

Statistical Analysis

We calculated both the overall prevalences of current PTSD and depression and the prevalences according to covariates of interest. Two-tailed chi-square tests were used to identify associations between covariates and either PTSD or depression. Multiple logistic regression was used to examine predictors separately for PTSD and depression. Covariates were considered in a multivariate regression model in which bivariate chi-square P values were less than 0.1. Differences in log likelihood (P<0.05) were used to determine whether variables would be retained in subsequent models. We tested for interactions between key predictor variables in the final models. Analyses were weighted to compensate for potential bias due to the number of adults in a household and the number of telephones. We used SUDAAN software to adjust all analyses for weighting.[8]

Results

Sample

Of the 1008 adults surveyed, 20 were excluded from the analysis because of missing weight variables (i.e., the number of adults or the number of telephones in the household). Overall, 52.0 percent of the respondents were women, and 71.6 percent were white; the mean (±SD) age was 42±15 years. Age, sex, race or ethnic group, and residence distributions in our sample were similar to estimates obtained from the 2000 U.S. Census for our sampling frame.[9] On September 11, 5.2 percent of the respondents lived south of Canal Street.

Prevalence of PTSD and Depression

The prevalence of PTSD was 7.5 percent (95 percent confidence interval, 5.7 to 9.3 percent), and the prevalence of depression was 9.7 percent (95 percent confidence interval, 7.3 to 11.3 percent). Overall, 13.6 percent of the respondents reported symptoms that met the criteria for either PTSD or depression, and 3.7 percent reported symptoms that met the criteria for both disorders.

Bivariate Analyses

Table 1 shows the results of bivariate analyses. The covariates associated with whether the respondent had PTSD were sex (P=0.005), residence before the attacks (P=0.04), level of social support (P=0.01), number of stressors in the 12 months before September 11 (P<0.001), whether the respondent witnessed the events (P=0.01), whether the respondent had a panic attack during or soon after the events (P<0.001), whether possessions were lost (P=0.01), whether the respondent was involved in the rescue effort (P=0.03), and whether the respondent lost a job because of the attacks (P=0.005).

Covariates associated with whether the respondent had depression were sex (P=0.03), race or ethnic group (P=0.03), yearly household income (P=0.006), level of education (P=0.007), level of social support (P<0.001), number of stressors in the 12 months before September 11 (P<0.001), whether the respondent had a panic attack during or soon after the events (P<0.001), whether a friend or relative died during the attacks (P=0.04), and whether the respondent lost a job because of the attacks (P=0.006).

Table 1. Bivariate Associations Between Characteristics of the Respondents and Current Post-Traumatic Stress Disorder (PTSD) or Depression

Variable	No. of Respondents†	PTSD	P Value‡	Depression	P Value‡
		%		%	
Total	988	7.5		9.7	
Sex			0.005		0.03
Male	469	4.8		7.3	
Female	519	9.9		12.0	
Race or ethnic group			0.07		0.03
White	702	6.5		7.4	
Black	49	9.3		11.9	
Asian	67	3.2		5.8	
Hispanic	114	13.8		20.4	
Other	17	19.1		19.1	
Annual household income			0.10		0.006
⩾$100,000	308	4.9		5.9	
$75,000–$99,999	96	10.2		9.1	
$40,000–$74,999	178	10.0		15.3	
$20,000–$39,999	135	12.5		16.5	
<$20,000	93	8.5		14.4	
Education			0.33		0.007
Graduate work	313	5.6		7.2	
College degree	441	8.2		7.5	
<College degree	229	8.5		16.8	
Residence before September 11			0.04		0.26
Between 110th St. and Canal St.	938	6.8		9.3	
South of Canal St.	50	20.0		16.8	
Social support in previous 6 mo			0.01		<0.001
High	313	4.4		5.6	
Medium	267	8.7		7.3	
Low	358	10.2		15.5	
No. of stressors in previous 12 mo			<0.001		<0.001
0	554	4.2		5.7	
1	251	7.3		8.8	
⩾2	183	18.5		24.1	
Directly witnessed the events			0.01		0.46
No	611	5.5		9.2	
Yes	370	10.4		10.8	
Symptoms of a panic attack during or soon after the events			<0.001		<0.001
No	864	4.0		7.6	
Yes	124	31.5		24.6	
Friend or relative killed			0.18		0.04
No	880	7.0		8.7	
Yes	108	11.3		17.8	
Lost possessions			0.01		0.70
No	949	6.6		9.6	
Yes	36	28.4		11.9	
Involved in rescue effort			0.03		0.25
No	877	6.4		9.2	
Yes	111	16.2		14.1	
Lost job because of attacks			0.005		0.006
No	924	6.2		8.5	
Yes	64	25.9		28.6	

*Current PTSD or depression was defined as symptoms consistent with the diagnosis within 30 days before the interview. The sample was weighted to account for the number of adults and number of telephones in the household.

†Numbers may not add up to 988 because not all the respondents answered all the questions.

‡The chi-square test was used for comparisons; P values are two-tailed.

Multivariate Analyses

In a multivariate logistic-regression model (Table 2), significant predictors of PTSD were Hispanic ethnicity as compared with white race (odds ratio, 2.6), two or more stressors in the 12 months before September 11 as compared with none (odds ratio, 5.5), a panic attack (odds ratio, 7.6), residence south of Canal Street before the attacks (odds ratio, 2.9), and loss of possessions due to the attacks (odds ratio, 5.6). The significant predictors of depression were Hispanic ethnicity (odds ratio, 3.2), two or more stressors in the 12 months before September 11 (odds ratio, 3.4), a panic attack (odds ratio, 2.6), a low as compared with a high level of social support (odds ratio, 2.4), the death of a friend or relative in the attacks (odds ratio, 2.3), and loss of a job because of the attacks (odds ratio, 2.8).

Discussion

In our survey of a representative sample of adults living south of 110th Street in Manhattan, conducted five to eight weeks after the September 11 attacks, 7.5 percent of the respondents reported symptoms consistent with the diagnosis of current PTSD, and 9.7 percent reported symptoms consistent with the diagnosis of current depression. These prevalences suggest that in the area below 110th Street approximately 67,000 persons had PTSD and approximately 87,000 had depression during the time of the study.[9] Although the estimated prevalences of current psychopathology vary according to the population studied, in a benchmark national study, the prevalence of PTSD within the previous year was 3.6 percent,[10] and the prevalence of depression within the previous 30 days was 4.9 percent,[11] suggesting that the prevalences in our survey were approximately twice the base-line values.

The prevalence of psychological sequelae of disasters has been documented in only a few community-based samples, and comparison of the findings is limited by differences in sampling frames and the interval between the event and the assessment. Using outcome measures that were similar to ours, Hanson et al. reported that the overall prevalence of PTSD was 4.1 percent six months after the 1992 civil disturbances in Los Angeles County.[12] The prevalence of depression in our study is similar to that reported after floods (9.5 percent).[13]

Table 2. Multivariate Associations Between Characteristics of the Respondents and Current Post-Traumatic Stress Disorder (PTSD) Or Depression.*

VARIABLE	ODDS RATIO (95% CI)†			
	PTSD		DEPRESSION	
Race or ethnic group				
White	1.0		1.0	
Black	0.9	(0.3–2.5)	1.4	(0.6–3.2)
Asian	0.6	(0.2–2.1)	0.9	(0.3–3.4)
Hispanic	2.6	(1.3–5.5)	3.2	(1.7–6.3)
Other	3.3	(0.6–17.9)	1.4	(0.2–10.5)
No. of stressors in previous 12 mo				
0	1.0		1.0	
1	2.2	(1.0–4.7)	2.1	(1.1–3.9)
2 or more	5.5	(2.6–11.6)	3.4	(1.8–6.6)
Symptoms of a panic attack during or soon after the events				
No	1.0		1.0	
Yes	7.6	(4.2–13.7)	2.6	(1.3–4.9)
Residence before September 11				
Between 110th St. and Canal St.	1.0			
South of Canal Street	2.9	(1.3–6.8)		
Lost possessions				
No	1.0			
Yes	5.6	(2.5–12.4)		
Social support in previous 6 mo				
High			1.0	
Medium			1.3	(0.6–2.7)
Low			2.4	(1.2–4.8)
Friend or relative killed				
No			1.0	
Yes			2.3	(1.1–4.6)
Lost job because of attacks				
No			1.0	
Yes			2.8	(1.2–6.3)

*Current PTSD or depression was defined as symptoms consistent with the diagnosis within 30 days before the interview.
† CI denotes confidence interval.

Persons directly affected by disasters have higher rates of post-event psychiatric disorders than persons indirectly affected.[14,15] Our survey showed that the prevalence of PTSD was higher among the persons who were most directly exposed to the attacks or their consequences (e.g., those living south of Canal Street, the area closest to the attacks, and those who lost possessions) than among persons with less direct exposure. Factors associated with grief (e.g., loss of a family member) increased the likelihood of depression, a finding that is consistent with the results of previous studies.[16,17]

We found bivariate associations between female sex and both PTSD and depression, a finding that is consistent with the results of most studies.[3,16,18] However, our adjusted models suggested that other factors may have been important mediators of the association between sex and psychopathology after this disaster. For example, the level of social support may have influenced the association between sex and depression.

Hispanic ethnicity was associated with both PTSD and depression, and the association was independent of other covariates. Although the relation between membership in a minority group and psychopathology after a disaster has been suggested in previous studies,[19] few have specifically examined the role of Hispanic ethnicity.[20] Research with veterans of the Vietnam War has shown that Hispanics may have a higher prevalence of PTSD than persons of other racial or ethnic backgrounds.[21] Sociocultural influences have been proposed as mediators of this relation.[22]

We also found a relation between a low level of social support and both PTSD and depression in bivariate analyses and between a low level of social support and depression in adjusted analyses. Social ties have a positive role in mental health.[23] After a disaster, a low level of social support has been shown to be related to PTSD and depressive symptoms.[24,25]

Our study provides strong evidence of an association between initial panic symptoms and subsequent psychopathology. Although the prognostic role of panic symptoms in determining the risk of PTSD or depression cannot be determined from a cross-sectional survey, this finding is consistent with previous research documenting associations between initial emotional responses to trauma and the development of PTSD.[26,27] These findings suggest that interventions addressing such initial reactions to a disaster may help prevent the development of long-lasting psychological sequelae.[28]

Prospective evaluations of PTSD in trauma victims and in the general population suggest that the symptoms of PTSD decrease substantially within three months after a traumatic experience[29] but that up to a third of cases of PTSD may not fully remit.[3,30] How long the psychological sequelae of the September 11 attacks will last remains to be seen, and it is possible that the prevalence of symptoms in our study reflects transient stress reactions to some degree. However, the ongoing threat of terrorist attacks may affect both the severity and the duration of these psychological symptoms.[31] More than 100,000 persons in New York City may lose their jobs as a result of the September 11 attacks,[32] and the cleanup efforts and disruption of services throughout the city will continue for a long time. In this context, the high prevalence of psychopathology that we documented among the residents of Manhattan is not surprising. Future research in New York City should determine the prognostic role of the factors that were associated with PTSD and depression in our study.

Supported by grants from the United Way of New York City, the New York Community Trust, and the National Institute on Drug Abuse (R01 DA14219-01S1).

We are indebted to Mr. Mark Morgan for invaluable contributions to the conduct of this study; to Dr. Joseph Boscarino for ongoing feedback; to Dr. Donald Hoover for statistical assistance; to Dr. Neal Cohen, Commissioner of Health for the New York City Department of Health, and Mr. Len McNally of the New York Community Trust, for their encouragement; to the interviewers at Schulman, Ronca, and Bucuvalas; and to all the persons who participated in the study during a difficult time for New Yorkers.

References

1. Dead and missing. New York Times. December 26, 2001:B2.

2. Rubonis AV, Bickman L. Psychological impairment in the wake of disaster: the disaster-psychopathology relationship. Psychol Bull 1991;109: 384-99.

3. Kessler RC, Sonnega A, Bromet E, Hughes M, Nelson CB. Posttraumatic stress disorder in the National Comorbidity Survey. Arch Gen Psychiatry 1995;52:1048-60.

4. Kilpatrick DG, Saunders BE, Veronen LJ, Best CL, Von JM. Criminal victimization: lifetime prevalence, reporting to police, and psychological impact. Crime Delinquency 1987;33:479-89.

5. Resnick HS, Kilpatrick DG, Dansky BS, Saunders BE, Best CL. Prevalence of civilian trauma and posttraumatic stress disorder in a representative national survey of women. J Consult Clin Psychol 1993;61:984-91.

6. Sherbourne CD, Stewart AL. The MOS social support survey. Soc Sci Med 1991;32:705-14.

7. Diagnostic and statistical manual of mental disorders, 4th ed.: DSM-IV. Washington, D.C.: American Psychiatric Association, 1994.

8. Shah B, Barnwell B, Bieler G. SUDAAN user's manual, release 7.5. Research Triangle Park, N.C.: Research Triangle Institute, 1997.

9. Bureau of the Census. Census summary tape, file 3A (STF3A). Washington, D.C.: Department of Commerce, 2000 (data file).

10. Department of Health and Human Services. Mental health: a report of the Surgeon General. Rockville, Md.: Substance Abuse and Mental Health Services

Administration, Center for Mental Health Services, National Institute of Mental Health, 1999. (Also available at http://www.surgeongeneral.gov/Library/MentalHealth/pdfs/front.pdf.)

11. Blazer DG, Kessler RC, McGonagle KA, Swartz MS. The prevalence and distribution of major depression in a national community sample: the National Comorbidity Survey. Am J Psychiatry 1994;151:979-86.

12. Hanson RF, Kilpatrick DG, Freedy JR, Saunders BE. Los Angeles County after the 1992 civil disturbances: degree of exposure and impact on mental health. J Consult Clin Psychol 1995;63:987-96.

13. Ginexi EM, Weihs K, Simmens SJ, Hoyt DR. Natural disaster and depression: a prospective investigation of reactions to the 1993 Midwest floods. Am J Community Psychol 2000;28:495-518.

14. North CS, Nixon SJ, Shariat S, et al. Psychiatric disorders among survivors of the Oklahoma City bombing. JAMA 1999;282:755-62.

15. Green B, Grace M, Lindy J, Gleser GC, Leonard AC, Kramer TL. Buffalo Creek survivors in the second decade: comparison with unexposed and nonlitigant groups. J Appl Soc Psychol 1990;20:1033-50.

16. Goenjian AK, Molina L, Steinberg AM, et al. Posttraumatic stress and depressive reactions among Nicaraguan adolescents after hurricane Mitch. Am J Psychiatry 2001;158:788-94.

17. Mazure CM, Bruce ML, Maciejewski PK, Jacobs SC. Adverse life events and cognitive-personality characteristics in the prediction of major depression and antidepressant response. Am J Psychiatry 2000;157:896- 903.

18. Shore JH, Vollmer WM, Tatum EL. Community patterns of posttraumatic stress disorders. J Nerv Ment Dis 1989;177:681-5.

19. Pole N, Best SR, Weiss DS, et al. Effects of gender and ethnicity on duty-related posttraumatic stress symptoms among urban police officers. J Nerv Ment Dis 2001;189:442-8.

20. Fothergill A, Maestas EGM, Darlington JD. Race, ethnicity and disasters in the United States: a review of the literature. Disasters 1999;23: 156-73.

21. Ortega AN, Rosenheck R. Posttraumatic stress disorder among Hispanic Vietnam veterans. Am J Psychiatry 2000;157:615-9.

22. Ruef AM, Litz BT, Schlenger WE. Hispanic ethnicity and risk for combat-related posttraumatic stress disorder. Cultur Divers Ethni Minor Psychol 2000;6:235-51.

23. Kawachi I, Berkman LF. Social ties and mental health. J Urban Health 2001;78:458-67.

24. Madakasira S, O'Brien KF. Acute posttraumatic stress disorder in victims of a natural disaster. J Nerv Ment Dis 1987;175:286-90.

25. Fullerton CS, Ursano RJ, Kao TC, Bharitya VR. Disaster-related bereavement: acute symptoms and subsequent depression. Aviat Space Environ Med 1999;70:902-9.

26. Harvey AG, Bryant RA. The relationship between acute stress disorder and posttraumatic stress disorder: a 2-year prospective evaluation. J Consult Clin Psychol 1999;67:985-8.

27. Tucker P, Pfefferbaum B, Nixon SJ, Dickson W. Predictors of post-traumatic stress symptoms in Oklahoma City: exposure, social support, peri-traumatic responses. J Behav Health Serv Res 2000;27:406-16.

28. Resnick H, Acierno R, Holmes M, Kilpatrick DG, Jager N. Prevention of post-rape psychopathology: preliminary findings of a controlled acute rape treatment study. J Anxiety Disord 1999;13:359-70.

29. Shalev AY, Freedman S, Peri T, et al. Prospective study of posttraumatic stress disorder and depression following trauma. Am J Psychiatry 1998; 15 5:630-7.

30. Rothbaum BO, Foa EB, Riggs DS, Murdock T, Walsh W. A prospective examination of posttraumatic stress disorder in rape victims. J Traumatic Stress 1992;5:455-75.

31. Shalev AY. Measuring outcome in posttraumatic stress disorder. J Clin Psychiatry 2000;61:Suppl 5:33-9.

32. Eaton L. Loss of 79,000 jobs adds to city's economic woes. New York Times. November 16, 2001:A1.

A National Survey of Stress Reactions After The September 11, 2001, Terrorist Attacks

Mark A. Schuster, M.D., Ph.D., Bradley D. Stein, M.D., M.P.H.,
Lisa H. Jaycox, Ph.D., Rebecca L. Collins, Ph.D., Grant N. Marshall, Ph.D.,
Marc N. Elliott, Ph.D., Annie J. Zhou, M.S., David E. Kanouse, Ph.D.,
Janina L. Morrison, A.B., Sandra H. Berry, M.A.

ABSTRACT: *Background* People who are not present at a traumatic event may experience stress reactions. We assessed the immediate mental health effects of the terrorist attacks on September 11, 2001. *Methods* Using random-digit dialing three to five days after September 11, we interviewed a nationally representative sample of 560 U.S. adults about their reactions to the terrorist attacks and their perceptions of their children's reactions. *Results* Forty-four percent of the adults reported one or more substantial symptoms of stress; 90 percent had one or more symptoms to at least some degree. Respondents throughout the country reported stress symptoms. They coped by talking with others (98 percent), turning to religion (90 percent), participating in group activities (60 percent), and making donations (36 percent). Eighty-four percent of parents reported that they or other adults in the household had talked to their children about the attacks for an hour or more; 34 percent restricted their children's television viewing. Thirty-five percent of children had one or more stress symptoms, and 47 percent were worried about their own safety or the safety of loved ones. *Conclusions* After the September 11 terrorist attacks, Americans across the country, including children, had substantial symptoms of stress. Even clinicians who practice in regions that are far from the recent attacks should be prepared to assist people with trauma-related symptoms of stress.

The terrorist attacks against the United States on September 11, 2001, shook the nation. Television coverage was immediate, graphic, and pervasive.[1,3] Newscasts included remarkable video footage showing two airplanes crashing into the World Trade Center and the aftermath of four airplane crashes.[2,3] People who are present at a traumatic event often have symptoms of stress, but there is evidence that adults and children need not be present to have stress symptoms,[4,6] especially if they consider themselves similar to the victims.[4] The events on September 11 were widely described as attacks on America, and most or all Americans may have identified with the victims or perceived the attacks as directed at themselves as well.

The immediate mental health effects of a national catastrophe experienced from afar—especially one that carries the threat of further attacks—have rarely been examined. We surveyed a nationally representative U.S. sample to determine the immediate reactions of adults to the attacks and their perceptions of their children's reactions.

Methods

Data Collection

We used random-digit dialing within the United States. The interview period was three to five days after the attack—from Friday evening, September 14, at the end of the national day of mourning declared by President George W. Bush, through Sunday evening, September 16, just before the start of the workweek, when the president encouraged Americans to return to their normal activities.[7] Trained interviewers conducted computer-assisted telephone interviews in English; the median duration of the interviews was 28 minutes. RAND's institutional review board approved the study procedures.

Sample

Adults (persons 19 years of age or older) who were at home when we called were eligible for the study; if two or more adults were at home, we randomly selected one to interview. We spoke with a total of 768 selected adults. Of these persons, 73 percent (560) were interviewed, 24 percent refused to be interviewed, and 3 percent agreed to be interviewed later in the weekend but the interview did not take place. Because of the extremely short time for this survey, we could not establish how many of the 3,505 telephone numbers we called might eventually have yielded an eligible person or been established as ineligible. At the end of the interview period, 683 telephone numbers were determined to be nonworking or business numbers; 182 were cell phones, pagers, fax machines, or other such ineligible numbers; 495 were unanswered after several attempts.

As compared with the U.S. population represented in the March 2001 Current Population Survey,[8] our sample slightly overrepresented women, non-Hispanic whites, and persons with higher levels of education and household income, which is typical of samples selected by means of random-digit dialing.[9,10] As a sensitivity analysis, we repeated all analyses after weighting the sample to resemble the population estimates from the Current Population Survey, which neither reduced the total sampling error nor substantially altered the results.

Respondents living with a child 5 to 18 years old were asked questions about the child (or about a randomly selected child if there were two or more children at home); information was obtained for a total of 170 children. Although we did not ask whether the respondent was the child's parent, we use the term "parent" because data from the Current Population Survey suggest that most adults in households with children are their parents.

Instrument and Key Measures

To assess reactions to the September 11 attacks, we selected and developed questionnaire items on the basis of prior research and current media reports. Except as otherwise noted, the questions specified a time frame of "since Tuesday"; questions about television viewing specified "on Tuesday."

To assess exposure to the attacks through television viewing, we asked respondents the amount of time (in hours, or in minutes if less than one hour) on September 11 that they and their children watched television coverage of the attacks. To assess stress in adults, we modified 5 questions about symptoms from the 17-question Posttraumatic Stress Disorder Checklist[11] (Table 1). The symptoms were selected from those reported by 50 percent or more of the survivors of the Oklahoma City bombing.[12] For the analysis, we defined a substantial stress symptom as one of the two highest of the five response options[13] ("quite a bit" or "extremely"). A substantial stress reaction was defined as one or more substantial stress symptoms. For children, we modified five items from the Diagnostic Interview Schedule for Children, Version IV (parent's version)[14] (Table 1). A stress reaction was defined as an affirmative response to at least one of the items.

To determine the distance of the respondents from all three crash sites, as well as from the takeoff and destination sites of the flights, we performed a geographic information system analysis, coding the location as the longitude and latitude for the center of the ZIP Code area (or of the telephone-exchange area for the 8 percent of respondents who provided no ZIP Code). We assessed the relation between stress in adults and the distances from individual sites, as well as the relation between stress and the distance from the nearest crash site and from the nearest of any of the sites. The strongest association was with the distance from the World Trade Center. Therefore, that is the association we report in this article. We also examined population density, a characteristic of location that we believed might be associated with differences in the perceived risk of terrorism and with reported stress.

TABLE 1. ADULTS WITH SUBSTANTIAL STRESS SYMPTOMS AND CHILDREN WITH STRESS SYMPTOMS AND WORRIES

Question	No. of Respondents	Substantial Stress (%)*
Adults		
Since Tuesday, have you been bothered by:		
Feeling very upset when something reminds you of what happened?	554	30
Repeated, disturbing memories, thoughts, or dreams about what happened?	557	16
Having difficulty concentrating?	558	14
Trouble falling or staying asleep?	555	11
Feeling irritable or having angry outbursts?	558	9
At least one of the above†	560	44
Children		
Since Tuesday, has your child been:		
Avoiding talking or hearing about what happened?	167	18
Having trouble keeping his or her mind on things and concentrating?	167	12
Having trouble falling asleep or staying asleep?	167	10
Losing his or her temper or being irritable?	167	10
Having nightmares?	167	6
At least one of the above	167	35
Since Tuesday, has your child been worrying about his or her safety or the safety of loved ones?	167	47

*For adults, substantial stress was defined as an answer of "quite a bit" or "extremely" on a five-point scale ("not at all," "a little bit," "moderately," "quite a bit," and "extremely"). For children, stress was defined as an answer of "yes" on a two-point scale ("yes," "no").

†Respondents who answered some but not all of the questions about stress are included.

Statistical Analysis

We report the results of univariate analyses (means and percentages) and bivariate analyses (Pearson's and Spearman's tests of correlation, t-tests, and chi-square tests of homogeneity). Where applicable, transformations of variables were used to satisfy the assumptions of these tests. Data have been weighted to account for multiple telephone lines in a household; our question about the number of telephone lines did not exclude inactive and data-transfer lines, so the results of significance tests may be conservative. We used the linearization method to estimate standard errors and to correct statistical tests for weights.[15] The 95 percent sampling error for reported percentages was no more than 4.3 percentage points for adults and no more than 7.7 percentage points for children. No imputation of missing values was performed.

Results

Adults

Forty-four percent of the U.S. adults we surveyed reported at least one of five substantial stress symptoms since September 11, 2001 (Table 1); 68 percent experienced at least one symptom "moderately" and 90 percent experienced at least one symptom "a little bit." Stress reactions varied significantly according to sex, race or ethnic group, presence or absence of prior emotional or mental health problems, distance from the World Trade Center, and region of the country (Table 2).

On September 11, adult respondents watched television coverage of the attacks for a mean of 8.1 hours; 2 percent of respondents watched for less than 1 hour, 15 percent for 1 to 3 hours, 34 percent for 4 to 7 hours, 31 percent for 8 to 12 hours, and 18 percent for 13 hours or more. Extensive television viewing was associated with a substantial stress reaction (Table 2).

Adults responded to the attacks in various ways (Table 3). People with a substantial stress reaction were more likely than others to have talked at least "a medium amount" about their feelings (91 percent vs. 83 percent, P=0.008), turned to religion (84 percent vs. 69 percent, P<0.001), made donations (42 percent vs. 31 percent, P=0.01), and checked on the safety of family members and friends (83 percent vs. 69 percent, P<0.001).

Thirty-six percent of adults thought that terrorism was a "very serious" or "somewhat serious" problem in the area where they live and work. Forty-four percent thought terrorism would increase over the next five years, and 21 percent thought it would remain at the current level.

Children

Thirty-five percent of parents reported that their children had at least one of five stress symptoms; 47 percent reported that their children had been worrying about their own safety or the safety of loved ones (Table 1). Parents with a substantial stress reaction were more likely than others to report that their children had symptoms of stress (50 percent vs. 22 percent, $P < 0.001$).

TABLE 2. STRESS REACTIONS ACCORDING TO THE CHARACTERISTICS OF THE RESPONDENTS.*

CHARACTERISTIC OF RESPONDENT	ADULTS			CHILDREN		
	NO. OF RESPONDENTS	SUBSTANTIAL STRESS REACTION	P VALUE†	NO. OF RESPONDENTS	STRESS REACTION	P VALUE
		%			%	
Total	560	44		167	35	
Sex			0.006			0.05
Female	298	50		96	41	
Male	226	37		64	25	
Race or ethnic group			<0.001			0.41
White (non-Hispanic)	413	41		125	33	
Nonwhite	106	62		35	41	
Prior emotional or mental health problems‡			0.05			0.10
Yes	66	56		16	53	
No	489	42		150	32	
Distance from World Trade Center			<0.001			0.23
≤100 mi	44	61		13	52	
101–1000 mi	274	48		93	26	
≥1001 mi	242	36		61	44	
Region§			0.05			0.17
Northeast	93	55		30	43	
South	169	46		54	30	
Midwest	154	42		48	25	
West	144	36		35	47	
Population density			0.17			0.21
≤100 persons/mi²	122	39		35	26	
101–300 persons/mi²	107	48		30	38	
301–1000 persons/mi²	144	38		43	33	
1001–2000 persons/mi²	105	47		30	34	
≥2001 persons/mi²	82	52		29	46	
Hours of television viewing on September 11 about the attacks¶			0.001			
0–3 hr	94	37		—		
4–7 hr	185	39		—		
8–12 hr	175	46		—		
≥13 hr	102	58		—		

*For adults, substantial stress was defined as an answer of "quite a bit" or "extremely" to one or more of five questions about stress on a five-point scale ("not at all," "a little bit," "moderately," "quite a bit," and "extremely"). For children, stress was defined as an answer of "yes" to one or more of five questions about stress. P values were calculated with the use of Spearman's tests of correlation for ordered categories (population density, miles from World Trade Center, and hours of television viewing) and chi-square tests of homogeneity for unordered categories. Variables not included in the table were not significant at the $P<0.05$ level (respondent's age, respondent's level of education, number of children 5 to 18 years old, household income, sex of child, child's age, and number of hours of television viewing by child on September 11 about the attacks). To convert miles to kilometers, multiply by 1.609344; to convert square miles to square kilometers, multiply by 2.589988.

†In a multivariate model that included all characteristics with significant bivariate associations ($P<0.10$), all variables other than region and prior emotional or mental health problems were significantly associated with adult stress ($P<0.05$).

‡Respondents were asked whether they had needed help for emotional or mental health problems, such as feeling sad, blue, anxious, or nervous, during the 12 months before the attacks.[16]

§Regions were defined according to U.S. Census regions.

¶The percentages were almost identical when adults who avoided television and other reminders of the attack were omitted from the analysis ($P=0.003$).

Children watched television coverage of the attacks for a mean of 3.0 hours on September 11; 8 percent did not watch any of the coverage, 33 percent watched for 1 hour or less, 36 percent watched for 2 to 4 hours, and 23 percent watched for 5 hours or more. Older children watched more (Pearson's $r = 0.52$, $P < 0.001$); for example, 73 percent of children who were 5 to 8 years old watched for one hour or less, whereas 51 percent of those who were 17 or 18 years old watched for five hours or more. Thirty-four percent of parents tried to restrict (limit or prevent) their children's viewing of the televised coverage of the attacks; in this subgroup, the children watched an average of 2.3 hours of coverage, as compared with 3.4 hours for other children ($P = 0.005$). Parents were more likely to try to limit television viewing by younger children than by older children (Spearman's $r = 0.39$, $P < 0.001$).

Parents who reported that their children were stressed were more likely than others to restrict their children's television viewing (45 percent vs. 29 percent, $P = 0.05$); among children whose parents did not try to restrict television viewing, there was an association between the number of hours of television viewing and the number of reported stress symptoms (Pearson's $r = 0.27$, $P = 0.02$). The response to the question about whether the child worried about his or her safety or the safety of others was not significantly associated with whether parents tried to restrict television viewing or with the number of hours of television viewing by children whose parents did not try to restrict viewing.

One percent of parents reported that they (or other adults in the household) did not speak with their children about the attacks; 15 percent discussed the attacks for less than one hour, 48 percent for one to three hours, 22 percent for four to eight hours, and 14 percent for nine hours or more. The number of hours of discussion was higher for older children than for younger children (Pearson's $r = 0.27$, $P = 0.001$) and was associated with the number of hours of television viewing (Pearson's $r = 0.40$, $P < 0.001$). There was no significant association between the extent of communication and the degree of stress symptoms on the part of parents or children.

Discussion

A few days after the September 11 terrorist attacks, 44 percent of a nationally representative sample of adults reported that they had had at least one of five substantial stress symptoms since the attacks, and 90 percent reported at least low levels of stress symptoms. Children also experienced stress: 35 percent had at least one of five stress symptoms after the attacks. Although the rates of stress reactions were highest among subgroups previously found to have relatively high rates of trauma-related stress symptoms after disasters (e.g., women, nonwhites, and people with preexisting psychological problems[17,18]), we found high rates of substantial stress reactions in all subgroups.

TABLE 3. Coping Behavior And Other Reactions By Adults *

Question	Total No. of Respondents	Response			
		NOT AT ALL	A LITTLE BIT	A MEDIUM AMOUNT	A LOT
		percent			
How much have you talked with someone about your thoughts and feelings about what happened?	556	2	12	30	57
How much have you turned to prayer, religion, or spiritual feelings?	556	10	15	31	44
How much have you participated in a public or group activity in recognition of what happened?	559	40	26	23	11
How much have you avoided activities such as watching TV because they reminded you of what happened?	555	61	20	14	5
		YES			
		percent			
Have you donated blood or money or done any volunteer work?	559	36			
Have you gotten any extra food, gas, cash or other supplies you might need?	557	18			
Have you checked the safety of immediate family and friends?	556	75			
Have you checked on someone you thought was hurt / missing?	556	32			

*Each question referred to the interval between September 11 and the date of the interview (September 14, 15, or 16). Because of rounding, not all percentages total 100.

There are few data with which to compare our findings. Although the prevalence of trauma-related psychiatric disorders has been examined in community-based samples,[19,24] few studies have reported the prevalence of trauma-related symptoms of stress in people who do not necessarily meet criteria for a psychiatric disorder. One such study described a representative sample of adults in St. Louis in which 16 percent of respondents reported a lifetime history of at least 1 of 14 symptoms of stress related to a frightening event.[24,25] Although methodologic differences complicate the comparison, this rate is much lower than the rate of event-related stress in our study.

Catastrophes can have a pronounced effect on adults who are not physically present.[4] The effect may be greatest when a loved one or acquaintance is harmed, but others who may personalize the event and think of themselves as potential victims can also have stress symptoms.[4] Children exposed to a catastrophe largely through television coverage can also be affected, as after the Challenger explosion,[5] the Gulf War,[6] and the Oklahoma City bombing,[26,27] with symptoms of trauma-related stress persisting for as long as two years.[26] The potential for personalizing the September 11 attacks was large, even for those who were thousands of miles away at the time. Although the people we surveyed who were closest to New York had the highest rate of substantial stress reactions, others throughout the country, in large and small communities, also reported substantial stress reactions.

The level of stress was associated with the extent of television viewing. There are several possible explanations for this finding. The meaning and magnitude of the events were uncertain, and television provided information about what to do and whether the situation posed a personal threat; it may therefore have served as a method of coping for some people, an interpretation that is consistent with threat-appraisal models of coping and stress.[28,29] For others, particularly children,[30,31] watching television may have exacerbated or caused stress, especially with repeated viewing of terrifying images. Some unmeasured characteristics of the respondents (e.g., weak social support) may also have resulted in both increased television viewing and increased stress reactions. Our survey indicates that Americans responded to the attacks in various ways. Most turned to religion, and also to one another for social support. They checked on the safety of those they cared about, talked about their thoughts and feelings, and participated in activities such as vigils, which can provide a sense of community. They also made donations. Efforts to help people far away, which have been reported after other tragedies,[32] may have been means of coping in the aftermath of the attacks—trying to take constructive action in a time of uncertainty and helplessness. Some people avoided activities, such as watching television, that reminded them of the attacks. Although it has been postulated that avoidance interferes with the emotional processing necessary to recover fully from trauma,[33] the unusual circumstances and continuous coverage of the September 11 attacks may have made avoidance in the short term a healthy response.

Professional organizations recommend that parents restrict their children's television viewing during a crisis and discuss the event with them.[34,35,36] We found that parents did try to limit their children's television viewing, particularly in the case of younger children and those who were stressed, and parents also talked with their children, often at length, about the attacks. Although stress symptoms in parents are associated with stress symptoms in their children, we cannot determine from our data whether parental stress causes stress in children or whether children develop their parents' styles of reacting to a crisis. Parents who are experiencing stress may perceive stress in their children, whether or not it is present. However, many of the parents in our survey who reported stress reactions did not report such reactions in their children, suggesting that the parents did not assume that their children reacted as they did. Indeed, underreporting of children's stress seems more likely than overreporting. We selected symptoms we thought parents would know about, but prior research has shown that parents underestimate the stress that media images cause in their children.[37]

Our study has important implications for health. Although studies of prior disasters suggest that stress reactions diminish over time in the vast majority of people who have had indirect exposure, the September 11 attacks, the shocking televised images, and the profound ramifications are unprecedented. It remains to be seen whether stress reactions in people throughout the country will indeed diminish, especially with recurrent triggers from ongoing threats and further attacks. By intervening as soon as symptoms appear, physicians, psychologists, and other clinicians may be able to help people identify normal stress reactions and take steps to cope effectively. Clinicians can also tell parents what signs to look for in their children and how to respond to their needs. The psychological effects of the recent terrorism are unlikely to disappear soon. Many of the respondents in our survey said that they anticipated further attacks and that they thought the attacks could be local. Concern about future attacks could heighten anxiety. Ongoing media coverage may serve as a traumatic reminder, resulting in persistent symptoms. When people are anticipating disaster, their fears can worsen existing symptoms and cause new ones.[38,39] The events of September 11 made Americans realize that the United States is vulnerable to attack on a scale that few had thought possible. If there are further attacks, clinicians should anticipate that even people far from the attacks will have trauma-related symptoms of stress.

Supported in part by RAND and by grants from the Centers for Disease Control and Prevention (U48/CCU915773) and the National Institute of Mental Health (K12/MH00990).

We are indebted to M. Audrey Burnam, Rosalie Corona, and Bruce R. Hoffman for advice on the design of the study instruments; to Scot C. Hickey, David J. Klein, Adrian Overton, and Michela M. Zonta for assistance with programming; to Daniel F. McCaffrey and Matthias Schonlau for statistical consultation; to Donna M. Lopez and Alaida M. Rodriguez for assistance with the preparation of the manuscript; to M. Audrey Burnam, Michael A. Stoto, and Mary E. Vaiana for comments on the manuscript; to the staff of the RAND Survey Research Group for the extraordinary effort of conceiving and implementing this survey, especially Julie A. Brown, Christopher R. Corey, and Laural A. Hill; and to the study participants, who generously shared their experiences with us.

References

1. Kakutani M. Critic's notebook: rituals for grieving extend past tradition into public displays. New York Times. September 18, 2001:B11.

2. Barringer F, Fabrikant G. As an attack unfolds, a struggle to provide vivid images to homes. New York Times. September 12, 2001:A25.

3. Shales T. On television, the unimaginable story unfolds. The Washington Post. September 12, 2001:C1.

4. Dixon P, Rehling G, Shiwach R. Peripheral victims of the Herald of Free Enterprise disaster. Br J Med Psychol 1993;66:193-202.

5. Terr LC, Bloch DA, Michel BA, Shi H, Reinhardt JA, Metayer SA. Children's symptoms in the wake of Challenger: a field study of distant-traumatic effects and an outline of related conditions. Am J Psychiatry 1999;156:1536-44.

6. Cantor J, Mares ML, Oliver MB. Parents' and children's emotional reactions to TV coverage of the Gulf War. In: Greenberg BS, Gantz W, eds. Desert Storm and the mass media. Cresskill, N.J.: Hampton Press, 1993: 325-40.

7. Editorial Desk. In for the long haul. New York Times. September 16, 2001:10.

8. Current population survey: annual demographic file, 2001 (computer file). Washington, D.C.: Department of Commerce, Bureau of the Census.

9. Goff DC Jr, Sellers DE, McGovern PG, et al. Knowledge of heart attack symptoms in a population survey in the United States. Arch Intern Med 1998;158:2329-38.

10. Bell RA, Kravitz RL, Wilkes MS. Direct-to-consumer prescription drug advertising and the public. J Gen Intern Med 1999;14:651-7.

11. Asmundson GJG, Frombach I, McQuaid J, Pedrelli P, Lenox R, Stein MB. Dimensionality of posttraumatic stress symptoms: a confirmatory factor analysis of DSM-IV symptom clusters and other symptom models. Behav Res Ther 2000;38:203-14.

12. North CS, Nixon SJ, Shariat S, et al. Psychiatric disorders among survivors of the Oklahoma City bombing. JAMA 1999;282:755-62.

13. Schwarz ED, Kowalski JM. Malignant memories: PTSD in children and adults after a school shooting. J Am Acad Child Adolesc Psychiatry 1991;30:936-44.

14. Shaffer D, Fisher P, Lucas CP, Dulcan MK, Schwab-Stone ME. NIMH Diagnostic Interview Schedule for Children Version IV (NIMH DISC-IV): description, differences from previous versions, and reliability of some common diagnoses. J Am Acad Child Adolesc Psychiatry 2000;39:28-38.

15. StataCorp. Stata statistical software: release 7.0. College Station, Tex.: Stata Corporation, 2001.

16. Sturm R, Sherbourne CD. Are barriers to mental health and substance abuse care still rising? J Behav Health Serv Res 2001;28:81-8.

17. Freedy JR, Saladin ME, Kilpatrick DG, Resnick HS, Saunders BE. Understanding acute psychological distress following natural disaster. J Trauma Stress 1994;7:257-73.

18. Shore JH, Tatum EL, Vollmer WM. Psychiatric reactions to disaster: the Mount St. Helens experience. Am J Psychiatry 1986;143:590-5.

19. Stein MB, Walker JR, Hazen AL, Forde DR. Full and partial posttraumatic stress disorder: findings from a community survey. Am J Psychiatry 1997;154:1114-9.

20. Kessler RC, Sonnega A, Bromet E, Hughes M, Nelson CB. Posttraumatic stress disorder in the national comorbidity survey. Arch Gen Psychiatry 1995;52:1048-60.

21. Breslau N, Davis GC, Andreski P, Peterson E. Traumatic events and post-traumatic stress disorder in an urban population of young adults. Arch Gen Psychiatry 1991;48:216-22.

22. Breslau N, Kessler RC, Chilcoat HD, Schultz LR, Davis GC, Andreski P. Trauma and posttraumatic stress disorder in the community: the 1996 Detroit Area Survey of Trauma. Arch Gen Psychiatry 1998;55:626-32.

23. Davidson JR, Hughes D, Blazer DG, George LK. Post-traumatic stress disorder in the community: an epidemiological study. Psychol Med 1991;21:713-21.

24. Helzer JE, Robins LN, McEvoy L. Post-traumatic stress disorder in the general population: findings of the Epidemiologic Catchment Area Survey. N Engl J Med 1987;317:1630-4.

25. USDHHS, PHS, ADMHA, NIMH, Epidemiologic Catchment Area Program. Los Angeles ECA survey, Wave II. Los Angeles: University of California, Los Angeles, 1983.

26. Pfefferbaum B, Seale TW, McDonald NB, et al. Posttraumatic stress two years after the Oklahoma City bombing in youths geographically distant from the explosion. Psychiatry 2000;63:358-70.

27. Pfefferbaum B, Nixon SJ, Krug RS, et al. Clinical needs assessment of middle and high school students following the 1995 Oklahoma City bombing. Am J Psychiatry 1999;156:1069-74.

28. Lazarus RS, Folkman S. Stress, appraisal, and coping. New York: Springer Publishing, 1984.

29. Lazarus RS. Emotion and adaptation. New York: Oxford University Press, 1991.

30. Cantor J. Media violence. J Adolesc Health 2000;27:Suppl 2:30-4.

31. Pfefferbaum B, Nixon SJ, Tivis RD, et al. Television exposure in children after a terrorist attack. Psychiatry (in press).

32. Yacoubian VV, Hacker FJ. Reactions to disaster at a distance: the first week after the earthquake in Soviet Armenia. Bull Menninger Clin 1989; 53:331-9.

33. Foa EB, Jaycox LH. Cognitive-behavioral theory and treatment of posttraumatic stress disorder. In: Spiegel D, ed. Efficacy and cost-effectiveness of psychotherapy. Washington, D.C.: American Psychiatric Press, 1999:23-61.

34. How to talk to children and parents after a disaster. Washington, D.C.: American Academy of Child and Adolescent Psychiatry, 1999. (Accessed Octo-

ber 25, 2001, at http://www.aacap.org/publications/DisasterResponse/cp_disas.htm.)

35. AAP offers advice on communicating with children about disasters. Washington, D.C.: American Academy of Pediatrics, 2001. (Accessed October 25, 2001, at http://www.aap.org/advocacy/releases/disastercomm.htm.)

36. Helping young children cope with trauma. Washington, D.C.: American Red Cross, 2001. (Accessed October 25, 2001, at http://www.red-cross.org/services/disaster/keepsafe/childtrauma.html.)

37. Cantor J, Reilly S. Adolescents' fright reactions to television and films. J Commun 1982;32:87-99.

38. Kiser L, Heston J, Hickerson S, Millsap P, Nunn W, Pruitt D. Anticipatory stress in children and adolescents. Am J Psychiatry 1993;150:87-92.

39. Turner RH, Nigg JM, Paz DH. Waiting for disaster: earthquake watch in California. Berkeley: University of California Press, 1986.

Posttraumatic Stress Disorder in Survivors Of the Brooklyn Bridge Shooting

Brian Trappler, M.D. and Steven Friedman, Ph.D.

ABSTRACT: *Objective*: The authors documented the frequency of posttraumatic stress disorder (PTSD) in civilian victims of urban terrorism. *Method*: A recent shooting attack on a van of Hasidic students provided a unique opportunity to document responses of survivors in this targeted group. Eleven of 14 survivors were compared with age-matched subjects on a variety of questionnaires and clinical evaluations. *Results*: Of the 11 survivors, four were diagnosed with PTSD (all of whom also had concurrent major depressive disorder), one with major depressive disorder, and two with adjustment disorder. *Conclusions*: Findings are interpreted in the context of unique factors contributing to the heightened vulnerability of this group.

Although posttraumatic stress disorder (PTSD) has been extensively studied among war veterans (1), there is less information available about PTSD in civilian populations exposed to combat-types of experiences. In this article we report the effects of a shooting incident in which a gunman specifically targeted a Hasidic Orthodox group of male adolescents. We believe this to be the first report on survivors of a politically motivated terrorist attack in the United States.

Several previous studies have addressed rates of PTSD (ranging from 19% to 80%) in civilians following multiple shooting incidents (2-5). In one study (4) the authors found a high rate of comorbid diagnoses, primarily major depression (50% of women and 25% of men). The targeting of a specific group by the gunman appeared to increase the frequency of PTSD within that targeted group. It has also been shown, in a 14-month follow-up (5), that the degree of exposure—whether or not children were in the playground where the attack occurred—predicted the intensity of posttraumatic stress symptoms. In that study, knowing the child who was killed was associated with a greater number of symptoms, although this was true only for the less exposed children.

In 1994 there were several acts of terrorism that affected Jewish civilian populations around the globe, including the attack on a van carrying 15 yeshiva (religious school) students in Brooklyn in March 1994, the bombing of a Jewish community center in Buenos Aires in June 1994, an attack on a cafeteria in Jerusalem, and an explosion of a bus in downtown Tel Aviv. Lubavitcher Hasidim who live in Crown Heights (Brooklyn) are a highly conspicuous and visible population (6). Their vulnerability is heightened because of their degree of involvement in community outreach and outspoken position in Middle East politics.

This Crown Heights community had also been exposed to violence 2½ years before the attack on the van, during 72 hours of rioting in which a rabbinical student was knifed to death. More recently, individuals in this community experienced the stress of the catastrophic stroke and prolonged illness of their charismatic leader, the rebbe, who had led the group for the past 43 years.

On March 1, 1994, the Lubavitcher rebbe underwent surgery in Manhattan. The hospital van in which he was traveling from the hospital back to his headquarters in Brooklyn was escorted by numerous cars traveling in an informal convoy. Fifteen yeshiva students, ranging in age from 16 to 22 years, were in one van. While the van was on an entrance ramp to the Brooklyn Bridge, a gunman began firing at it. One student was killed instantly, and another was critically injured with a bullet wound to his head. Approximately 30 shots were fired. In the chaos occurring in the van itself, one student attempted to control the profuse bleeding from the head wound of the student next to him. Others lay on the seats or the floor of the van. The driver of the van was fired on numerous times at close range by the gunman, who drove his car alongside the van and used two semiautomatic pistols. Two additional students were wounded in the ensuing chase, one receiving a serious wound to the abdomen.

Method

Of the 15 boys in the van, 11 were available for evaluation (in addition to the boys who were killed or critically wounded, two left the country immediately after the shooting and were lost to follow-up). For comparison purposes we screened, with questionnaires, an age-matched group of adolescent boys from the same yeshiva.

The first author was in contact with the students within 24 hours, during which informal debriefings were begun. In addition, the entire group of survivors was also seen for one formal debriefing session within 7 days of the shooting. This debriefing consisted of education regarding the possible effects of a severely traumatic event and an opportunity for the group members to freely relate their experience. Formal evaluations, and brief group treatment of the survivors, began 8 weeks after the incident. As a comparison group, we evaluated 11 yeshiva students who were classmates of the van group. Informed written consent was obtained from all subjects.

Eight weeks after the shooting, the study group of 11 young men and the comparison group were evaluated with a battery of questionnaires. The study group completed the questionnaires before the beginning of a short-term (five-session), behaviorally oriented group treatment. Questionnaires included the Post-traumatic Stress Disorder Symptom Scale (unpublished scale of R. Yehuda), Beck Depression Inventory (7), Beck Anxiety Inventory (8), and Revised Impact of Event Scale (9, 10). The PTSD symptom scale quantifies the presence and frequency of all symptoms listed in DSM-IV as criteria for PTSD and is similar to a section of the Anxiety Disorders Interview Schedule-Revised (11) on PTSD.

Each member of the traumatized group was individually seen by the first author for a clinical evaluation and an explanation of the purpose of the study and the treatment. Subjects completed all questionnaires before the first group meeting. At the first group meeting all subjects were encouraged to talk about any, and all, psychological symptoms experienced over the past several weeks. After several group meetings, we arrived at a consensual DSM-IV diagnosis for each subject through use of all the gathered clinical information and results from the questionnaires.

Results

Of the 11 participants, four were diagnosed with PTSD (all four also had concurrent major depressive disorder), one with major depressive disorder, and two with adjustment disorder (one with mixed anxiety and depressed mood and one with anxiety). Four subjects did not fulfill criteria for an axis I disorder. Table I presents the data from the questionnaires. As seen in table 1, there were highly significant differences between the survivors and the comparison group. All measures indicated that the survivors were suffering from moderate depression, severe anxiety, and moderate to severe posttraumatic symptoms.

TABLE 1. Psychometric Scale Scores for Male Hasidic Students Who Survived a Shooting Attack and for Comparison Subjects

Scale and Item	Survivor Group (N=11)		Comparison Group (N=11)		Analyses	
	Mean	SD	Mean	SD	t (df=20)	P
Beck Depression Inventory (rated 0-63)	18.8	5.3	4.8	3.0	7.6	0.001
Beck Anxiety Inventory (rated 0-63)	29.4	8.0	6.7	2.2	9.1	0.001
Revised Impact of Event Scale						
Intrusive subscale (rated 7-28)	23.0	2.5	12.5	2.3	10.2	0.001
Avoidance subscale (rated 8-32)	22.0	2.5	14.9	3.9	5.1	0.001
Post-traumatic Stress Disorder Symptom Scale[a]						
Intrusive recollections	3.0	0.0				
Recurrent nightmares	2.2	0.8				
Feelings of reoccurrence	2.2	0.8				
Intense distress at reminders	2.3	0.7				
Physiological reactivity	2.0	0.9				
Avoidance of thoughts and feelings	2.3	0.7				
Avoidance of activities and situations	2.3	0.7				
Psychogenic amnesia	2.1	0.8				
Diminished interest	2.1	0.9				
Detachment	2.0	0.9				
Restricted affect	2.0	0.9				
Sense of foreshortened future	2.0	0.9				
Sleep disturbance	2.0	0.9				
Irritability or anger	2.0	0.9				
Difficulty concentrating	2.0	0.9				
Hypervigilance	2.1	0.9				
Exaggerated startle	2.1	0.9				

[a]Symptom list is from DSM-IV. Symptoms are rated on a scale of 0-3 (0=not at all, 1=once a week or less, 2=two to four times a week/somewhat, 3=five or more times per week/very much).

Informal reevaluation of the group 10 months after the incident and with the same instruments indicated that the index patients with depression, anxiety, and adjustment symptoms appeared to be spontaneously recovering and reintegrating socially, while the four subjects with PTSD were showing continued symptoms and functional impairment. For these four subjects residual symptoms persisted despite interventions described in this article and additional individual psychological treatment; this suggests that intense PTSD reactions may have a chronic course.

Discussion

The frequency of PTSD syndrome in this group appears somewhat higher (28%) then that described in two other studies of civilian shooting incidents (2, 3); however, the rate is similar to that in the study by North et al. (4) in which a gunman specifically targeted women. Although the present study is limited by the absence of a comprehensive structured clinical interview, the PTSD symptom scale (unpublished scale of R. Yehuda) reflects a limited structured clinical interview that quantifies the frequency of PTSD symptoms defined by DSM-IV.

There are several unique factors in this group that may have heightened their vulnerability (12, 13) to PTSD. Because the group was so closely cohesive (14), it was associated with an extremely intense experience of grief and loss as a result of the one fatality and the critical injury of another colleague. This may have led to comorbid anxiety and depression in the four subjects suffering with PTSD and significantly elevated scores on the Beck anxiety and depression scales for the entire group.

The death of one of the shooting victims and the critical injury of a second could have further implications in terms of depression (survivor guilt) both for survivors and members of the Orthodox Crown Heights community at large (5). This was suggested by our finding a somewhat elevated score on the Revised Impact of Event Scale (9, 10) for the comparison group. Since this shooting incident followed two other stressful events for the community, the 1991 Crown Heights riots and the illness of the group leader, the Lubavitcher rebbe, these results lend support to the clinical observation that PTSD is more likely to occur in victims with multiple previous negative life events (12).

Given the range of continued conflict throughout the globe and the use of indiscriminate violence and terrorism against civilians, clinicians are well advised to assess their patients for exposure to trauma. Further evaluation and follow-up are clearly warranted for individuals exposed to violence of this type.

Supported in part by NIMH grant MH-42545 and by funds from the Department of Psychiatry's practice plan.

References

1. Solomon Z, Neria Y, Ohry A, Waysman M, Ginzburg K: PTSD among Israeli former prisoners of war and soldiers with combat stress reaction: a longitudinal study. Am J Psychiatry 1994; 151: 554-559.

2. North S, Smith EM, McCool RE, Shea JM: Short-term psychopathology in eyewitnesses to mass murder. Hosp Community Psychiatry 1989; 12:1293-1295

3. Schwarz ED, Kowalski JM: Posttraumatic stress disorder after a school shooting: effects of symptom threshold selection and diagnosis by DSM-III, DSM-III-R, or proposed DSM-IV. Am J Psychiatry 1991; 148:592-597

4. North CS, Smith EM, Spitznagel EL: Posttraumatic stress disorder in survivors of a mass shooting. Am J Psychiatry 1994; 151: 82-88

5. Nader K, Pynoos R, Fairbanks L, Frederick C: Children's PTSD reactions one year after a sniper attack at their school. Am J Psychiatry 1990; 147:1526-1530

6. Trappler B, Greenberg S, Friedman S: Treatment of Hasidic Jewish patients in a general hospital medical-psychiatric unit. Psychiatric Services 1995; 46:833-835

7. Beck AT, Steer IZA: Beck Depression Inventory. San Antonio, Tex, Psychological Corp, 1993

8. Beck AT, Steer RA: Beck Anxiety Inventory. San Antonio, Tex, Psychological Corp, 1993

9. Horowitz MJ, Wilner N, Alvarez W: Impact of Event Scale: a measure of subjective stress. Psvchosom Med 1979; 41:209-218

10. Zilherg N, Weiss DS, Horowitz. MJ: Impact of Event Scale: a cross validation study and some empirical evidence. J Consult Clin Psychol 1982; 50:407-414

11. DiNardo PA, Barlow DH: Anxietv Disorders Interview Schedule–Revised (ADIS-R). Albany, NY, Graywind Publications, 1988

12. Jones JC, Barlow D: The etiology of posttraumatic stress disorder. Clin Psychol Rev 1990; 10:299-328

13. Kilpatrick DG, Resnick HS: Posttraumatic stress disorder associated with exposure to criminal victimization in clinical and community populations, in Posttraumatic Stress Disorder: DSM IV and Beyond. Edited by Davidson RT, Foa EB. Washington, DC, American Psychiatric Press, 1993, pp 113-143

14. Goenjian AK, Najarian LM, Pynoos RS, Steinberg AM, Manoukian G, Tavosian A, Fairbanks LA: Posttraumatic stress disorder in elderly and younger adults after the 1988 earthquake in Armenia. Am J Psychiatry 1994; 151:895-901

Psychological and Behavioural Reactions to The Bombings in London on 7 July 2005: Cross Sectional Survey of a Representative Sample of Londoners

G. James Rubin, Chris R. Brewin, Neil Greenberg,
John Simpson, Simon Wessely

ABSTRACT: *Objectives* To assess the impact of the bombings in London on 7 July on stress levels and travel intentions in London's population. *Design* A cross sectional telephone survey using random digit dialling was conducted to contact a representative sample of adults. Respondents were asked to participate in an interview enquiring about current levels of stress and travel intentions. *Setting* Interviews took place between 18 and 20 July. *Participants* 1010 participants (10% of the eligible people we contacted) completed the interviews. *Main outcome measures* Main outcomes were presence of substantial stress, measured by using an identical tool to that used to assess the emotional impact of 11 September 2001 in the US population, and intention to travel less on tubes, trains, and buses, or into central London, once the transport network had returned to normal. *Results* 31% of Londoners reported substantial stress and 32% reported an intention to travel less. Among other things, having difficulty contacting friends or family by mobile phone (odds ratio 1.7, 95% confidence interval 1.1 to 2.7), having thought you could have been injured or killed (3.8, 2.4 to 6.2), and being Muslim (4.0, 2.5 to 6.6) were associated with a greater presence of substantial stress, whereas being white (0.3, 0.2 to 0.4) and having previous experience of terrorism (0.6, 0.5 to 0.9) were associated with reduced stress. Only 12 participants (1%) felt they needed professional help to deal with their emotional response to the attacks. *Conclusions* Although the psychological needs of those intimately caught up in the attacks will require further assessment, we found no evidence of a widespread desire for professional counselling. The attacks have inflicted disproportionately high levels of distress among non-white and Muslim Londoners.

Introduction

The terrorist attacks on central London's transport network on 7 July 2005 caused 52 fatalities and some 700 injuries. The psychological effects of the attacks remain unknown. Shortly after the attacks in the United States on 11 September 2001, about 90% of the residents of New York City and Washington DC reported symptoms of stress, with 44% reporting substantial symptoms.[1] High levels of distress have also been seen among school students after the 1995 bombing of the Murrah Building in Oklahoma City[2] and in the Israeli population as a consequence of the ongoing intifada.[3] Not surprisingly, those most exposed to an attack show the highest levels of distress, but after 11 September emotional reactions were noted across the US and as far away as Italy.[4][5]

Emotional reactions to terrorist incidents vary. Some people develop well recognised psychiatric disorders such as depression or post-traumatic stress disorder. Others, while not meeting the criteria for a formal psychiatric diagnosis, still report higher levels of general anxiety or stress related symptoms. Still others report no psychiatric symptoms but show considerable changes in their behaviour[6] or their feelings about the future.[3]

After the attacks on 7 July, many commentators said that terrorism would have a reduced emotional impact on Londoners because of the city's history of dealing with IRA terrorism and the Blitz.[7] It has also been argued that Londoners were not unprepared for these attacks: British politicians and security officials have warned on many occasions that acts of terrorism in London were probable, if not inevitable, and British preparations for terrorism have extended to sending a leaflet to every household in the country in August 2004, providing advice about what to do in the event of a major incident.[8] Whether these experiences and preparations served to minimise the short term psychological effects of the recent attacks remains to be seen.

We surveyed a representative sample of Londoners to assess levels of distress and altered travel intentions after the terrorist attacks on 7 July. This survey will also serve as a baseline for a planned follow-up of this sample in six months. We also investigated several potential correlates of distress, including demographic variables, level of exposure, previous experience of terrorism, and uncertainty about the safety of others.

Methods

Market and Opinion Research International (MORI) conducted a telephone survey using a random digit dialling method for all London telephone numbers. The survey used proportional quota sampling, a standard method for opinion polls that entails setting quotas for participants on a range of demographic factors and ensures that the sample interviewed is representative of the population of interest. In this survey, we set quotas with regard to sex, age, working status, residential location, housing tenure, and ethnicity to make our sample representative of the demographic distribution of London in the most recent census data.

We invited people aged 18 or over and who spoke English to participate in an interview about "issues facing Londoners." The 20 minute interviews took place in the evenings from Monday 18 July to Wednesday 20 July 2005 and were completed before a second failed attack on London's transport network on Thursday 21 July.

A power calculation showed that a sample size of 1000 would provide us with a 95% confidence interval of -3% to 3% for our data.

Primary Outcomes

We measured two primary outcomes. Firstly, we assessed whether "as a result of the London bombings," participants experienced substantial stress, defined as responding "quite a bit" or "extremely" to one or more of five symptoms (see table 1 for wording). Other possible responses were "not at all," "a little bit," and "moderately." This measure was identical to that used in a study of the impact of the 11 September attacks on the adult US population.[1] Secondly, we assessed whether, once the transport system returned to normal, the participant intended to travel "more often," "less often," or "no difference" with regard to tubes, trains, buses, or travelling into central London. We excluded people who did not normally travel by these means for the relevant items. For comparison, we asked about travel intentions concerning cars and travel elsewhere in the UK.

Secondary Outcomes

Secondary outcomes included sense of safety for self and friends or relatives, which we measured by using items identical to those used in a survey of reactions to terrorism in Israel,[3] perceived likelihood of another attack on London in "the near future," current sense of safety on a four point scale from "very safe" to "very unsafe" when travelling by tube, train, bus, car, into central London, or elsewhere in the UK, and self efficacy for coping with terrorism.[3] Participants were also asked whether they had talked to someone about their thoughts and feelings regarding the bombings on a four point scale from "a great deal" to "not at all," whether they had spoken to any mental health specialist since the bombings, whether they felt they needed to speak to a mental health specialist, and whether they had spoken to a religious leader or adviser.

Respondents with children in a London school on 7 July were asked whether they had attempted to check on their children's safety and whether they went to the school earlier than usual to see or collect their children. All participants were asked whether they had attempted to check the safety of immediate friends and family on the day.

Predictor Measures

Demographic predictor variables consisted of all variables used to define the sampling quotas, together with having children under 18, religion, household income, and social class.[9] A single item measured whether the participant was in central London when he or she first heard about the explosions. We also measured exposure by using four items assessing whether the participant felt he or she might have been injured or killed, a friend or relative might have been injured or killed, they saw someone who was injured or killed, or a close friend or family member was injured or killed. These categories were not mutually exclusive.

Two items, which we combined for the analyses, inquired whether participants had previously been involved in a real terrorist incident or a false alarm about terrorism. We also asked if the participant had received and read the government leaflet concerning emergency preparedness.

We asked "how sure or unsure were you about the safety or whereabouts of any close friends or relatives who might have been in central London" to assess uncertainty over the safety of others on a four point scale from "very sure" to "very unsure." We also asked participants whether they had attempted to contact anybody by mobile phone and, if they had attempted to contact two or more people, how easy that had been on a four point scale from "very difficult" to "very easy."

Analysis

Because quota sampling rarely achieves a sample that is exactly representative of the target population, we first weighted our data in order to improve its representativeness. We calculated weights on the basis of the disparity between the demographic distribution achieved and the known demographic distribution of London and applied these to individual participants according to their demographic profile. In practice, because our quota sampling worked well, the effects of this weighting were small. Weighted and unweighted data are available from the authors on request.

We calculated univariate odds ratios to assess the association between each predictor variable and substantial stress or reduced travel intentions. We used logistic regressions to calculate a second set of odds ratios controlling for the role of age, sex, and social class—common confounders for psychological distress. We also calculated odds ratios to assess the association of reduced sense of safety while travelling and presence of substantial stress with travel intentions. We calculated all odds ratios separately for each variable. As such they are not independent of each other.

Table 1 Prevalence of stress among a representative sample of Londoners after the bombings on 7 July 2005. Values are numbers (percentages) of respondents unless otherwise indicated

As a result of the London bombings, to what extent have you been bothered by	Not at all	A little bit	Moderately	Quite a bit	Extremely	Substantial stress*	Results for 11 September study†
Feeling upset when something reminds you of what happened	316 (31)	270 (27)	166 (16)	156 (15)	100 (10)	256/1010 (25)	30
Repeated disturbing memories, thoughts, or dreams about what happened	764 (76)	108 (11)	54 (5)	48 (5)	29 (3)	77/1010 (8)	16
Having difficulty concentrating	827 (82)	91 (9)	44 (4)	26 (3)	17 (2)	43/1010 (4)	14
Trouble falling or staying asleep	856 (85)	72 (7)	35 (4)	28 (3)	13 (1)	41/1010 (4)	11
Feeling irritable or having angry outbursts	756 (75)	109 (11)	47 (5)	47 (5)	45 (5)	92/1010 (9)	9
Substantial stress on at least one item	—	—	—	—	—	311/1010 (31)	44

Numbers may not sum to 1010 owing to a small number (≤1%) of "don't know" responses. *Response of "quite a bit" or "extremely" taken as substantial stress.
†Response in US population to identical items immediately after 11 September 2001.[1]

Results

We contacted 11072 people, of whom 1059 were ineligible or over quota with regard to their demographics. Of the 10013 eligible respondents, 1207 agreed to participate and 1010 completed the interview (10.1%). This response rate is not unusually low for a telephone survey using quota sampling. Furthermore, given that response rates are not as valid an indication of non-participation in quota surveys as they are in random probability surveys, this figure should be taken as indicative only. We did not record reasons for non-participation. However, of the 197 people who started an interview but withdrew before completion, 21 were unhappy discussing the bombings, 8 did not believe the survey was relevant, 64 did not have time to continue, 36 refused to supply a reason, and 68 were dropped for technical or other reasons.

Responses to the primary outcomes are given in tables 1 and 2. Thirty one per cent of the sample reported substantial stress, and 32% reported that once the London transport system had returned to normal they intended to travel less by at least one of the methods asked about. Tables 3 and 4 show data for the secondary outcomes.

Table 2 Alterations in travel intentions after the bombings on 7 July among a representative sample of Londoners.* Values are numbers (percentages) of respondents

Response	No difference	More often	Less often
By tube	526/781 (67)	15/781 (2)	231/781 (30)
On an overground train	608/744 (82)	32/744 (4)	96/744 (13)
By bus	639/797 (80)	41/797 (5)	114/797 (14)
By car	712/838 (85)	92/838 (11)	27/838 (3)
Going into central London	719/920 (78)	17/920 (11)	181/920 (20)
Going elsewhere in the UK	853/920 (93)	28/920 (3)	37/920 (4)
Intending to travel less often by one or more of tube, train, bus or into Central London	—	—	318/1010 (32)

Numbers may not sum to the denominator owing to a small number (≤1%) of "don't know" responses. *The question was "Once the London transport system is back to normal, do you think you will travel more often or less often in the following ways, or will the London bombings make no difference to how often you travel in the following ways?"

When we controlled for age, sex, and social class where applicable, the following were significant correlates of substantial stress (see table 5 for comparison groups): being female; being from social class D or E; not owning your own home; being nonwhite, Muslim, or from another faith; having a household income of less than £30 000; believing that you or a close friend or relative might have been injured or killed; having a close friend or relative who was injured or killed; having no previous experience of terrorism; being unsure about the safety of others; and having had difficulty reaching people by mobile phone. In addition, Muslims reported significantly more stress than people of other faiths.

Similarly, the following showed significant associations with reduced intention to travel by either tube, train, bus or into central London (see table 6 for comparison groups): being female, being younger, being non-white, being religious, having a household income of less than £30 000, believing that you or a close friend or relative might have been injured or killed, having a close friend or relative who was injured or killed, not having read the government advice leaflet, having been unsure about the safety of others, having substantial stress, and feeling unsafe while travelling.

Table 3 Immediate responses to the 7 July bombings among a representative sample of Londoners

Question	No of positive responses (%)	
Did you, your partner, or another member of your family attempt to contact your children or the school to check their safety?*	42/174	(24)
Did you, your partner, or another member of your family go to school earlier than usual to collect or to see your children?*	45/174	(26)
Did you try to check the safety of any immediate family members or friends?	771/1010	(76)

*Only asked of respondents with children in a London school on the day of the bombings.

Discussion

Eleven to 13 days after the London attacks, 31% of respondents reported substantial stress levels. Although no equivalent measure was taken before the attack, as participants were asked about stress related symptoms experienced "as a result of the London bombings," it seems reasonable to ascribe most of this stress to the effects of terrorism. Direct exposure to the bombings was limited, with 8% of the sample having thought they might be injured or killed and 3% having seen someone injured or killed. In terms of indirect exposure, 60% were concerned that a friend or relative might have been injured or killed, and 4% reported knowing someone who was injured or killed. Unsurprisingly, levels of distress were highest among these participants. Overall, the prevalence of distress was less than that reported in the general adult

US population after 11 September 2001.[1] Several reasons may explain this difference, including the greater loss of life, dramatic imagery, and live television coverage of the New York attacks. The longer delay between the London attacks and our survey (11-13 days) compared with that between 11 September and the US survey (3-5 days), may also be important. An additional factor implied by our results may be previous experience of IRA terrorism in London, with significantly reduced short term emotional responses being observed among Londoners who had previously been exposed to terrorism or a terrorist false alarm. We also found some evidence consistent with the idea that preparation for terrorism can reduce its impact, with respondents who had read the government's advisory leaflet being less likely to have altered their travel intentions than those who had not read it. However, the correlational nature of our data makes it possible that some third variable such as personality may account for this latter association.

Table 4 Perceived sense of safety, self efficacy, and need to talk to someone about emotions among a representative sample of Londoners after the bombings on 7 July 2005

Question	No of positive responses (%)	% of responses in Israel terrorism study*
Do you feel your life is in danger from terrorism?	560/1010 (55)	60.4
Do you feel the lives of your close family members or those dear to you are in danger from terrorism?	588/1010 (58)	67.9
Do you think another attack on London is likely in the near future?	870/1010 (86)	—
Do you feel unsafe when travelling by tube?	361/781 (46)	—
Do you feel unsafe when travelling by overground train?	174/744 (23)	—
Do you feel unsafe when travelling by bus?	200/797 (25)	—
Do you feel unsafe when travelling by car?	30/838 (4)	—
Do you feel unsafe when going into central London?	300/710 (33)	—
Do you feel unsafe when going elsewhere in the UK?	91/966 (9)	—
Before the bombings, did you believe you would know what best to do if you were caught in a terrorist attack?	544/1010 (54)	—
How much have you talked with someone else about your thoughts and feelings about what happened?†	721/1010 (71)	—
As a result of the bombings, have you spoken to a psychiatrist, psychologist, counsellor, or other mental health specialist?	8/1010 (1%)	—
As a result of the bombings, do you think you need to speak to a psychiatrist, psychologist, counsellor, or other mental health specialist?	12/1010 (1)	—
As a result of the bombings, have you spoken to a religious adviser or leader?	43/1010 (4)	—

*Response in Israeli population to identical items during the ongoing intifada.[3]
†Responses of "a great deal" or "a fair amount" were classified as positive responses.

Given that the attacks disrupted London's transport network, we could not measure the psychological effects of the bombings in terms of actual alterations in travel behaviour. Instead, we assessed travel intentions. Most Londoners reported that the bombings would have no impact on their travel plans. However, a substantial minority (32%) reported that they would now reduce the amount they used the tube, trains, buses, or go into central London. Several factors probably mediate the impact of terrorism on such behaviours. In the case of London, whether the respondent uses public transport for leisure or is compelled to use it for work is probably important. As shown by our results, so too are perceptions of safety. Forty six percent of Londoners reported not feeling safe travelling by tube, and 33% did not feel safe in central London. Concerns about safety in general were also high at the time of the survey, with 55% believing their lives were in danger and 58% believing the same of their close family and friends. These are similar levels of concern to those expressed by the Israeli population in response to the current intifada.[3]

People Need to Be Able to Communicate

Seventy six per cent of respondents attempted to contact others in the immediate period after the bombings, a situation similar to that in New York after 11 September 2001.[1] Israelis also frequently check on the whereabouts of family and friends after attacks, with 83% of those who do so finding it to be a helpful coping strategy.[3] The importance of reassuring oneself about friends and relatives is shown by the significant association we found between being unsure about the safety of others and the presence of substantial stress, although the correlational nature of the data makes it difficult to identify the direction of causality. On 7 July, uncertainty about others was fuelled by the inability of the mobile phone networks to cope with demand. Seventy eight per cent of our sample reported that using their mobile was fairly or very difficult on the day. Again, those who experienced difficulty contacting others on their mobile were also significantly more likely to experience substantial stress. Although there is no doubt that priority should be given to emergency service use of the mobile network in the event of a major incident, these results imply that allowing ordinary people to communicate with each other is also an important function.[10]

Table 5 Predictors of the presence of substantial distress after the bombings in London on 7 July 2005

Variable	No (%)	No (%) with substantial stress	Unadjusted odds ratio (95% CI)	Adjusted odds ratio (95% CI)*
Sex:				
Female	529 (52)	195 (37)	1.9 (1.4 to 2.4)	—
Male	481 (48)	115 (24)	Ref†	—
Age:				
18 to 24	126 (13)	43 (34)	1.1 (0.7 to 1.9)	—
25 to 44	476 (47)	144 (30)	0.9 (0.6 to 1.4)	—
45 to 64	259 (26)	76 (29)	0.9 (0.6 to 1.4)	—
≥65	149 (15)	47 (32)	Ref	—
Social class‡:				
A/B	281	66 (23)	0.4 (0.3 to 0.6)	—
C1/C2	483 (50)	145 (30)	0.6 (0.4 to 0.9)	—
D/E	208 (21)	86 (41)	Ref	—
Working status:				
Working full-time	463 (46)	116 (25)	0.6 (0.5 to 0.8)	0.8 (0.6 to 1.1)
Not full time	547 (54)	195 (36)	Ref	Ref
Residential location:				
Inner London	394 (39)	120 (30)	1.0 (0.7 to 1.3)	1.0 (0.7 to 1.3)
Outer London	616 (61)	191 (31)	Ref	Ref
Housing tenure:				
House owner	562 (56)	145 (26)	0.6 (0.5 to 0.8)	0.6 (0.5 to 0.8)
Rents or other	448 (44)	166 (37)	Ref	Ref
Ethnicity:				
White	718 (71)	170 (24)	0.3 (0.3 to 0.5)	0.3
Other	292 (29)	141 (48)	Ref	Ref
Religion†:				
Muslim	86 (9)	53 (62)	3.5 (2.2 to 5.5)	4.0 (2.5 to 6.6)
None	218 (22)	37 (17)	0.4 (0.3 to 0.7)	0.5 (0.3 to 0.7)
Other faith	704 (70)	221 (31)	Ref	Ref
Income†:				
<£30 000	508 (57)	183 (36)	2.5 (1.9 to 3.5)	2.3 (1.6 to 3.4)
>£30 000	376 (43)	68 (18)	Ref	Ref
Parental status:				
Children under 18	313 (31)	100 (32)	1.1 (0.8 to 1.4)	1.0 (0.7 to 1.3)
No children	697 (69)	211 (30)	Ref	Ref
Location at time†:				
Central London	218 (22)	72 (33)	1.2 (0.8 to 1.6)	1.4 (1.0 to 2.0)
Elsewhere	783 (78)	234 (30)	Ref	Ref
I felt I might be injured or killed:				
Yes	80 (8)	48 (60)	3.7 (2.3 to 6.0)	3.8 (2.4 to 6.2)
No	930 (92)	263 (28)	Ref	Ref
I felt that a family member or close friend might be injured or killed:				
Yes	606 (60)	218 (36)	1.9 (1.4 to 2.5)	1.8 (1.4 to 2.5)
No	404 (40)	93 (23)	Ref	Ref
I saw someone who was injured or killed:				
Yes	27 (3)	12 (44)	1.8 (0.9 to 3.9)	1.8 (0.8 to 3.9)
No	983 (97)	299 (30)	Ref	Ref
A family member or close friend was injured or killed:				
Yes	35 (4)	19 (54)	2.7 (1.3 to 5.3)	2.7 (1.3 to 5.4)

Variable	No (%)	No (%) with substantial stress	Unadjusted odds ratio (95% CI)	Adjusted odds ratio (95% CI)*
No	975 (97)	292 (30)	Ref	Ref
Prior terror experience:				
Yes	299 (30)	70 (23)	0.6 (0.4 to 0.8)	0.6 (0.5 to 0.9)
No	711	241 (34)	Ref	Ref
Read government leaflet:				
Yes	375 (37)	101 (27)	0.8 (0.6 to 1.0)	0.8 (0.6 to 1.0)
No	635 (63)	210 (33)	Ref	Ref
Certainty about others†:				
Very or fairly sure	425 (47)	107 (25)	0.6 (0.4 to 0.8)	0.6 (0.5 to 0.8)
Very or fairly unsure	482 (53)	175 (36)	Ref	Ref
Difficulty in using a mobile†:				
Very or fairly difficult	449 (78)	156 (35)	1.6 (1.0 to 2.4)	1.7
Very or fairly easy	124 (23)	32 (26)	Ref	Ref

*Controlling for sex, age, and social class by using logistic regression.
†Ref=reference value.
‡Baseline value for analysis is not 1010 because of missing data, "don't know" responses, or previous screening questions.

Demographic Predictors of Stress

Interestingly, although belonging to any religious grouping was associated with significantly higher levels of stress than belonging to none, Muslim respondents reported the highest levels of stress compared with participants from other religions, with 62% reporting substantial stress. As in previous terrorist attacks,[1] respondents from ethnic minorities also experienced significantly worse emotional effects than white respondents. This increased prevalence of distress is not readily explainable by any pre-existing vulnerability among these groups as there is little evidence that ethnic minorities in the UK have consistently higher rates of minor mental disorder.[11][12] Whether these results partly reflect a response bias, with Muslim respondents attempting to maintain a distinction between themselves and the bombers, is unknown. Many of the other demographic predictors of stress that we identified have been reported previously, with women,[3][13][14] those on lower incomes[3] and younger adults[14] all reporting greater stress.

Limitations of the Study

Our study has some limitations. In particular, although the quota sampling and weighting ensured that our sample was demographically representative of London, the low response rate means that some bias may have affected our data. For example, individuals who were unaffected by the attacks may have been less interested in participating, as too may individuals with high levels of distress. These effects could potentially result in either underestimation or overestimation of the true prevalence of distress. To mitigate against this, interviewers were instructed to introduce the survey as concerning "issues facing Londoners," the bombings not mentioned until part way through the interview. The fact that relatively few of those who withdrew from the study after the interview had begun stated that the survey was not relevant to them or that they were too upset to talk about the attacks provides some reassurance that these biases were limited.

Table 6 Predictors of altered travel intentions after the bombings in London on 7 July 2005

Variable	No (%)	No (%) intending to travel less	Unadjusted odds ratio (95% CI)	Adjusted odds ratio (95% CI)*
Sex:				
Female	529 (52)	203 (38)	2.1 (1.6 to 2.8)	—
Male	481 (48)	108 (22)	Ref†	—
Age:				
18 to 24	126 (13)	53 (42)	3.7 (2.1 to 6.5)	—
25 to 44	476 (47)	172 (36)	2.9 (1.8 to 4.7)	—
45 to 64	259 (26)	63 (24)	1.7 (1.0 to 2.8)	—
≥65	149 (15)	24 (16)	Ref	
Social class‡:				
A/B	281	83 (30)	0.8 (0.6 to 1.2)	—
C1/C2	483 (50)	148 (31)	0.9 (0.6 to 1.2)	—
D/E	208 (21)	70 (34)	Ref	—
Working status:				
Working fulltime	463 (46)	130 (28)	0.8 (0.6 to 1.0)	0.7 (0.5 to 1.0)
Not full time	547 (54)	181	Ref	Ref
Residential				
Inner London	394 (39)	125 (32)	1.1 (0.8 to 1.4)	0.9 (0.7 to 1.3)
Outer London	616 (61)	186 (30)	Ref	Ref
Housing tenure:				
House owner	562 (56)	156 (28)	0.7 (0.6 to 1.0)	0.9 (0.7 to 1.2)
Rents or other	448 (44)	155 (35)	Ref	Ref
Ethnicity:				
White	718 (71)	187 (26)	0.5 (0.4 to 0.6)	0.6 (0.4 to 0.8)
Other	292 (29)	124 (42)	Ref	Ref
Religion†:				
Muslim	86 (9)	36 (42)	1.5 (1.0 to 2.4)	1.3 (0.8 to 2.2)
None	218 (22)	49 (23)	0.6 (0.4 to 0.9)	0.6 (0.4 to 0.9)
Other faith	704 (70)	226 (32)	Ref	Ref
Income†:				
<£30 000	508 (57)	169 (33)	1.4 (1.1 to 1.9)	1.6 (1.1 to 2.2)
>£30 000	376 (43)	99 (26)	Ref	Ref
Parental status:				
Children under 18	313 (31)	122 (39)	1.7 (1.3 to 2.3)	1.3 (0.9 to 1.8)
No children	697 (69)	190 (27)	Ref	Ref
Location at time†:				
Central London	218 (22)	71	1.1 (0.8 to 1.5)	1.0 (0.7 to 1.4)
Elsewhere	783 (78)	238 (30)	Ref	Ref
I felt I might be injured or killed:				
Yes	80 (8)	40 (50)	2.4 (1.5 to 3.8)	2.2 (1.4 to 3.6)
No	930 (92)	271	Ref	Ref

Variable	No (%)	No (%) intending to travel less	Unadjusted odds ratio (95% CI)	Adjusted odds ratio (95% CI)*
I felt that a family member or close friend might be injured or killed:				
Yes	606 (60)	220 (36)	2.0 (1.5 to 2.6)	1.7 (1.3 to 2.4)
No	404 (40)	91	Ref	Ref
I saw someone who was injured or killed:				
Yes	27 (3)	11	1.6 (0.7 to 3.5)	1.42 (0.6 to 3.2)
No	983 (97)	300 (31)	Ref	Ref
A family member or close friend was injured or killed:				
Yes	35 (4)	19 (56)	2.9 (1.5 to 5.8)	2.2 (1.1 to 4.7)
No	975 (97)	292 (30)	Ref	Ref
Prior terror experience:				
Yes	299 (30)	77 (26)	0.7 (0.5 to 1.0)	0.8 (0.6 to 1.1)
No	711	234 (33)	Ref	Ref
Read government leaflet:				
Yes	375 (37)	86 (23)	0.5 (0.4 to 0.7)	0.5 (0.4 to 0.7)
No	635 (63)	226 (36)	Ref	Ref
Certainty about others†:				
Very or fairly sure	425 (47)	108 (25)	0.6 (0.4 to 0.8)	0.7 (0.5 to 0.9)
Very or fairly unsure	482 (53)	181	Ref	Ref
Difficulty in using a mobile‡:				
Very or fairly difficult	449 (78)	165 (37)	1.1 (0.7 to 1.4)	1.0 (0.7 to 1.6)
Very or fairly easy	124 (23)	43 (35)	Ref	Ref
Has substantial stress:				
Yes	311	143 (46)	2.7 (2.0 to 3.6)	2.7 (2.0 to 3.6)
No	699 (69)	168 (24)	Ref	Ref
Feels "very unsafe on transport				
Yes	277 (23)	172 (76)	14.4 (10.1 to 20.5)	14.3 (9.8 to 20.9)
No	783 (78)	140 (18)	Ref	Ref

*Controlling for sex, age, and social class by using logistic regression.
†Ref=reference value.;
‡Base for analysis is not 1010 because of missing data, "don't know" responses, or previous screening questions.

Therapeutic Implications

What, if any, are the therapeutic implications of our results? Firstly, the psychological needs of people who were intimately caught up in the bombings through direct exposure or bereavement will need to be assessed after a reasonable time has passed. An appropriate response of this sort is being coordinated by the four mental health trusts covering the main hospitals who dealt with the injured. But what about the rest of us? Less than 1% of respondents had sought professional help for their negative emotions, and only 12 respondents felt they needed such help. On the other hand, 71% had spoken to friends or relatives about the attacks "a great deal" or "a fair amount." Our results therefore confirm those of previous studies that show that most people are able to turn to lay support networks after traumatic events.[15] Given that psychological debriefing in the immediate aftermath of a major incident is at best ineffective and at worst counter-productive,[16] these results are reassuring. We do not believe that it will be necessary to conduct large scale population based psychological interventions such as those used in New York after 11 September 2001.

Contributors: SW had the original idea for the study and developed the study design and interview questions with GJR, CRB, NG, and JS. We are also grateful to Avi Bleich, Mark Gelkopf, Mark Gill, Ron Kessler, Claire Lambert, and Robert Ursano for making additional suggestions at this stage. Interviewers working for MORI collected the data. GJR performed the statistical analyses and wrote the first draft of the paper. All authors contributed to further drafts. SW is the guarantor.
Funding: This study was funded by King's College London in advance of a grant application made to the Home Office. Competing interests: None declared. Ethical approval: South London and Maudsley NHS Trust Research Ethics Committee.

References

1 Schuster MA, Stein BD, Jaycox LH, Collins RL, Marshall GN, Elliott MN, et al. A national survey of stress reactions after the September 11, 2001,terrorist attacks. *N Engl J Med* 2001;345:1507-12.

2 Pfefferbaum B, Nixon SJ, Krug RS, Tivis RD, Moore VL, Brown JM, et al. Clinical needs assessment of middle and high school students following the 1995 Oklahoma City bombing. *Am J Psychiatry* 1999;156:1069-74.

3 Bleich A, Gelkopf M, Solomon Z. Exposure to terrorism, stress-related mental health symptoms, and coping behaviors among a nationally representative sample in Israel. *JAMA* 2003;2003:612-20.

4 Silver RC, Holman EA, McIntosh DN, Poulin M, Gil-Rivas V. Nationwide longitudinal study of psychological responses to September 11 *JAMA* 2002; 288:1235-44.

5 Apolone G, Mosconi P, La Vecchia C. Post-traumatic stress disorder. *N Engl J Med* 2002;346:1495-8.

6 Grieger TA, Fullerton CS, Ursano RJ, Reeves JJ. Acute stress disorder, alcohol use, and perception of safety among hospital staff after the sniper attacks. *Psychiatr Serv* 2003;54:1383-7.

7 London under attack. *Economüt* 2005July 9;9.

8 HM Government. *Preparing for emergencies. What you need to know.* www. preparingforemergencies.gov.uk (accessed 19 Aug 2005).

9 Market and Opinion Research International (MORI). How to use surveys in management decision. www.mori.com/pubinfo/pfh/how-to-use-surveys-in-managementdecision.shtml (accessed 22 Aug 2005).

10 Wessely S. Don't panic! Short and longterm psychological reactions to the new terrorism: the role of information and the authorities. *J Mental Health* 2005;1-6.

11 Meltzer H, Gill B, Petticrew M, Hinds K. *The prevalence of psychiatric morbidity among adults living in private households.* London: HMSO, 1995.

12 Weich S, Nazroo J, Sproston K, McManus S, Blanchard M, Erens B, et al. Common mental disorders and ethnicity in England: the EMPIRIC study. *Psychol Med* 2004;34: 1543-51.

13 North CS, Nixon SJ, Shariat W, Mallonee S, McMillen JC, Spitznagel EL, et al. Psychiatric disorders among survivors of the Oklahoma City bombing. *JAMA* 1999;282:755-62.

14 Schlenger WE, Caddell JM, Ebert L, Jordan BK, Rourke KM, Wilson D, et al. Psychological reactions to terrorist attacks. Findings from the national study of Americans' reactions to September 1 1.*JAMA* 2002;288:581-8.

15 Greenberg N, Thomas S, Iversen A, et al, Wessely S. Do military peacekeepers want to talk about their experiences? Perceived psychological support of UK military peacekeepers on return from deployment. *J Mental Health* 2003; 12:565-73.

16 Rose S, Bisson J, Wessely S. A systematic review of single-session psychological interventions following trauma. *Psychother Psychosom* 2003;72:176-84.

King's College London, Institute of Psychiatry, Department of Psychological Medicine, Weston Education Centre (PO62), London SE5 9RJ
G James Rubin *research fellow* Neil Greenberg *senior lecturer*
Simon Wessely *professor of epidemiological and liaison psychiatry*
University College London, Subdepartment of Clinical Health Psychology, London WC1E 6BT
Chris R Brewin *professor of clinical psychology*
Health Protection Agency, Centre for Emergency Preparedness and Response, Porton Down, Salisbury, Wiltshire SP4 0JG
John Simpson *head of emergency preparedness.*

Post-Traumatic Stress Reactions Following The March 11, 2004 Terrorist Attacks in a Madrid Community Sample: A Cautionary Note about the Measurement of Psychological Trauma

Carmelo Vázquez[1], Pau Pérez-Sales[2], and Georg Matt[3]
[1]Universidad Complutense de Madrid
[2]Hospital La Paz (Madrid) and Grupo de Acción Comunitaria (GAC), Madrid
[3]San Diego State University, USA

ABSTRACT: Posttraumatic stress reactions related to the Madrid March 11, 2004, terrorist attacks were examined in a sample of Madrid residents ($N = 503$) 18-25 days after the attacks, using multiple diagnostic criteria and different cut-off scores. Based on the symptoms covered by the Posttraumatic Stress Disorder Checklist-Civilian (PCL-C; Weathers, Litz, Herman, Huska, & Keane, 1993), rates of probable posttraumatic stress disorder (PTSD) ranged from 3.4% to 13.3%. Taking into account additional criteria from the *Diagnostic and Statistical Manual of Mental Disorders* (American Psychiatric Association, 2000, i.e., the impact of initial reaction and problems in daily functioning as a consequence of the traumatic event), only 1.9% of respondents reported probable PTSD. These results suggest that inferences about the impact of traumatic events on the general population are influenced by the definition of traumatic response. Our findings also revealed that the magnitude of posttraumatic reactions is associated with several risk factors, including living close to the attacked locations, physical proximity to the attacks when they occurred, perception of one's life being at risk, intensity of initial emotional reactions, and being a daily user of the attacked train lines. The use of different cut-off scores did not affect the pattern of risk to develop traumatic stress. The implications of these results for public health policies related to terrorist attacks are discussed.

Until the terrorist attacks of September 11, 2001 (S11), on American soil, there was scarce information on the psychological reactions of the general population, not necessarily affected in a direct manner by the events, subjected to massive attacks. For instance, in former similar events, such as the brutal bombing of a governmental building in Oklahoma City (USA) on April 19, 1995, in which 168 people died, the largest amount of the collected data was focused on the *direct* victims or on the people directly exposed to trauma (North, Nixon, Shariat et al., 1999). Nevertheless, there was little knowledge about the immediate reactions of the general population, the larger part of which was not directly exposed to the traumatic event. Despite the difficulties to conduct methodologically sound studies on the general population under these circumstances (see North & Pfefferbaum, 2002), the S11 events opened a new way of research by addressing the immediate reactions to trauma in the general population.

The earliest studies on the immediate effects of the S11 attacks were conducted within 2-3 days after the incident (Murphy, Wismar, & Freeman, 2003; Schuster et al., 2001), followed by a second wave of studies 1-2 months later (Blanchard et al., 2004; Galea et al., 2002; Schlenger et al., 2002; Silver, Holman, McIntosh, Poulin, & Gil-Rivas, 2002). A same line of research was also followed after the Madrid March 11, 2004 (M11), attacks (Conejero, de Rivera, Páez, & Jiménez, 2004; Miguel-Tobal, Cano-Vindel, Iruarrizaga, González, & Galea, 2004; Muñoz, Crespo, Pérez-Santos & Vázquez, 2004) and, more recently, on the London attacks on July 7, 2005 (Rubin, Brewin, Greenberg, Simpson, & Wessely, 2005). Although some of these studies have focused on the most extreme responses, such as the development of a full posttraumatic stress response as measured by categories like the Post Traumatic Stress Disorder (PTSD)—for example, Galea et al., 2002; Miguel-Tobal et al., 2004—the majority has used a dimensional approach by including symptom scales that reflect different degrees of stress reactions (e.g., Blanchard et al.; Muñoz et al.; Murphy et al.; Rubin, Brewin, Greenberg, Simpson, & Wessely, 2005; Schlenger et al.; Schuster et al.; Silver et al.). All these studies are making substantial contributions to our understanding of the short-term responses in the general populations directly or indirectly affected by terrorist attacks[1]. In addition, these studies are also adding to the literature on stress responses in populations not residing in the attacked areas but exposed through the intensive media coverage provided by TV, radio, and newspapers (Blanchard et al.; Murphy et al.; Schlenger et al.).

However, depending on the definition and measurement strategies of the psychological reactions, the results of these studies are quite disparate (see Table 1). This variability may be attributed to the specific characteristics of each event, the strategies of sample selection, and, perhaps more important, the use of different assessment strategies, which typically range from rather simple self-report symptom scales to clinical interviews following diagnostic criteria (Bryant & Harvey, 2000; Norris, Byrne, Diaz, & Kaniasty, 2001).

In regard to measurement strategies, researchers have typically used three different ways to assess the impact of these events on the general population. The first strategy, and probably the most frequently used, has been to use instruments that basically cover a number of symptoms related to traumatic stress reaction. One interesting example of this approach was carried out by scientists of the RAND Corporation by measuring between 3 to 5 days after the attack on the World Trade Center the psychological reactions in a representative sample of the nation (see Table 1). This paper was published on November, 15, 2001, in *The New England Journal of Medicine,* one of the publications with a larger impact factor in Medicine (Schuster et al., 2001). The study reported that 90% of the interviewed subjects experienced at least moderate levels of stress symptoms and 44% of the total sample reported having experienced at least one symptom of "substantial stress." In a second part of the same study, conducted 2 months after the attack, the authors found that 16% of those who had a substantial stress level in September 2001 still had that reaction in November of the same year (Stein et al., 2004). The initial conclusions of these studies were very alarming and suggested, according to these authors, the need for early psychological interventions, given that "by intervening as soon as symptoms appear, physicians, psychologists, and other clinicians may be able to help people to identify normal reactions and take steps to cope effectively" (Schuster et al., p. 1511). Likewise, they predicted that "the psychological effects of the recent terrorism are unlikely to disappear soon." However, a critical analysis of these studies may lead to different conclusions (see Vázquez, 2005). In fact, what the authors defined as "substantial stress" was simply to obtain a score of 4 ("quite a bit") or 5 ("extremely") in any of 5 selected items related to PTSD symptoms.[2]

In a study that addressed the initial stress reactions 9-23 days after the S11 attacks, Silver et al. (2002) found that 12.4% of their national representative sample at wave 1 showed high levels of symptoms, suggesting a probable acute stress disorder[3]. In a study conducted 2-3 weeks after the event, Muñoz et al. (2004) found that, in a Madrid representative sample of the general population, 47% of the subjects showed "significant symptoms of acute stress" (confusion, emotional estrangement, nightmares, avoidance of situations or places that remind one of the event, irritableness, nervousness). Nevertheless, both studies based their results on self-reported questionnaires that do not strictly follow the *Diagnostic and Statistical Manual of Mental Disorders* (4th edition; American Psychiatric

Table 1
Studies on the Psychopathological Impact on Stress-Related Responses (ASD & PTSD) in the General Population after the Attacks of September 11, 2001 (USA) and March 11, 2004 (Madrid, Spain)

Study	Time of assessment	Sample	Assessment	Instrument	Measures	Results
Schuster et al. (2001), RAND	3-5 days after S11, (Wave 1)	Nationally representative (N = 560 adults)	Telephone interview	PCL (5 item selected after Norris et al., 1999)	Substantial Stress[a]	44% at least 1 substantial stress symptom 90% experienced at least one symptom "a little bit"
Stein et al. (2004), RAND	2-3 months after S11 (Wave 2)	Follow-up of Schuster et al. (2001) sample (N = 395 adults)	Telephone interview	PCL (5 item selected after Norris et al., 1999)	Substantial Stress[a]	21% still reported at least 1 substantial stress symptom
Rasinski et al. (2002), NORC	4-6 months after S11	National sample and NYC sample (N = 1101 adults)	Telephone interview	PCL (fulfillment of DSM-IV symptom criteria)		PTSD: 15% NYC; 8% rest of the country
Schlenger et al. (2002)	1-2 months after S11	Nationally representative (N = 273 adults, NY and Washington oversampled)	Telephone interview	PCL, framed to S11 events ≥ 50)	Probable PTSD (cut-off score ≥ 50) Nonspecific distress	Probable PTSD: 11.2% in NYC; 2.7% in Washington, DC; 3.6% major metropolitan areas; and 4.0% rest of the country More than 60% of NYC with children reported 1 or more children upset by attacks.
Silver et al. (2002)	9-23 days after S11 - Wave 1 (W1) 2 months after S11 (W2): 6 months after S11 (W3):	Web panel, nationally representative adults: (W1: N = 2729) (W2: N = 933, non-NY residents) (W3: N = 787)	Self-report	Stanford Acute Stress Reaction Questionnaire (SASRQ)-W1 Impact of Events Scale-R, framed to S11 events (W2 and W3)	ASD symptoms (W1) PTSD symptoms (W2 and W3)	ASD: 12.4% PTSD symptoms (W2): 17% PTSD symptoms (W3): 5.8%
Murphy et al. (2003)	2-3 days after S11	African-American undergraduates, St. Louis, NO (N = 219)	Self-report	PCL-C	Probable PTSD (cut-off score ≥ 50)	Probable PTSD: 5%

(Table 1. continued)

Study	Time of assessment	Sample	Assessment	Instrument	Measures	Results
Galea et al. (2002, 2003)	5-9 weeks after S11 (W1) 4-5 months after S11 (W2) 6-9 months after S11 (W3)	Telephoned Manhattan adult residents, oversampling those living south of 110th St: W1: N = 998 adults W2: N = 2,001 adults W3: N = 1,570 adults	Telephone interview	DIS, framed to S11 events	PTSD (DSM-IV criteria)	PTSD (W1): 7.5% (Manhattan); 20% if living south Canal St. (i.e., World Trade Center area) PTSD (W2): 1.7% PTSD (W3): 0.6%
Blanchard et al. (2004)	6-10 weeks after S11	Undergraduates (Albany, NY = 5 07; Augusta, GA = 336; Fargo, ND = 526)	Self-report	PTSD (PCL, S11-framed) Acute stress (ASD) in 2 weeks after S11	Probable PTSD (cut-off score > 40) Probable ASD	Probable PTSD: 11.3% in Albany, 7.4% in Augusta and 3.4% in Fargo Probable ASD: 28% in Albany, 19% in Augusta and 9.7% in Fargo.
Matt & Vázquez (2006)	6-10 weeks after S11	2000-2002 multiple cohorts of San Diego undergraduates (Total N = 2411)	Self-report	PCL-C	Substantial stress[a] Probable PTSD (cut-off score ≥ 50)	Substantial stress: 38% Probable PTSD: 8.4% (Spring 2000, N = 771), 9.8% (Spring 2002, N = 694)), 6.7% (Fall 2002, N = 946)
Muñoz et al. (2004)	2-3 weeks after M11, 2004	Madrid general population sample (N = 1179)	Self-report	Acute Stress Disorder Scale (ASDS)	ASD symptoms	47% symptoms related to ASD.
Miguel-Tobal et al. (2005)	4-15 weeks after M11, 2004	Telephoned Madrid adult residents, oversampling those living in the three affected areas (N = 1589)	Telephone interview	DIS, framed to M11 events	PTSD (DSM-IV criteria)	PTSD: 4% PTSD attributable to the M11 events: 2.3%
Rubin et al. (2005)	11-13 days after July 7, 2005	London general population sample (N = 1010)	Telephone interview	PCL (5 item selected after Norris et al., 1999)	Substantial stress[a]	Substantial stress: 31%
Present study	3-4 weeks after March11	Madrid general population sample (N = 503)	Self-report	PCL-C and item covering the PTSD DSM-IV criteria	Substantial stress[a] Probable PTSD by using multiple criteria: 1) PCL cut-off score > 44 2) PCL cut-off score ≥ 50 3) PCL and DSM-IV criteria	Substantial stress: 59.2% Probable PTSD: 1) 13.3 % cut-off score > 44 2) 3.4 % cut-off score ≥ 50 3) 1.9 % DSM-IV criteria

Note. ProNote. ASD = Acute Stress Disorder; DIS = Diagnostic Interview Schedule; PCL-C = Posttraumatic Stress Disorder Checklist-Civilian; PTSD = Posttraumatic Stress Disorder

[a] "Substantial stress" is defined when respondents endorse a degree of severity of 4 ("quite a bit") or 5 ("extremely") to any of five selected items from the PCL-C (see text). Adapted From Vázquez, 2005.

Association, 1994) diagnostic criteria for acute stress disorder (ASD). As far as we know, only the study of Blanchard et al. (2004) has evaluated the presence of probable *DSM-IV* (1994) cases of ASD, although it was based only on scorings of a questionnaire (see Table 1). In this study, in which three subsamples of university students participated after S11 in different areas of the USA, the results showed the students of Albany (New York State) had a higher prevalence of probable ASD cases (28.0%) than the students who were more distant, such as those who lived in Fargo (North Dakota)–9.7%. Nevertheless, as we will discuss later, that one third of a university sample of students living in Albany (100 miles from Manhattan) might correspond to cases of a diagnosed mental disorder (i.e., ASD) seems to be a rather overestimated figure.

In our opinion, these data about "substantial stress" or "symptoms of acute stress," suggesting a widespread clinical disorder in the general population, might lead to overestimation of epidemiological needs unless a careful analysis of the data and measurement strategies is previously made. It does not seem these figures, even if significant, correspond to a need for psychological intervention or truly correspond with clinical significant conditions, especially in studies where low diagnostic thresholds are used, and which are based on self-report tools (Muñoz et al., 2004; North & Pfefferbaum, 2002), which may be vulnerable to social desirability biases. Being upset or having "substantial stress" does not mean having a clinical disorder (Wessely, 2004), but rather having a normal reaction to an abnormal situation. Therefore, studies trying to identify subthreshold levels of traumatic responses, such those of Schuster et al. (2001) or Stein et al. (2004) based on simple definitions of stress (e.g., "substantial stress"), may induce public alarm and confusion (Shalev, 2004; Southwick & Charney, 2004)[4].

A second measurement strategy has been the use of symptom questionnaires and cut-off scores to screen for the presence of a *probable* mental disorder. One of the most frequently used questionnaires has been the Posttraumatic Stress Disorder Checklist-Civilian (PCL-C; Weathers, Litz, Herman, Huska, & Keane, 1993), a self-report instrument covering the 17 symptoms included in the definition of PTSD as currently described in the *DSM-IV* (1994). In terms of probable PTSD diagnoses based on the PCL-C scores, Schlenger et al. (2002) found that among their nationally representative sample of 2,273 adults, interviewed 1-2 months after S11, the overall rates of probable PTSD using the cut-off score of 50 were 11.2% in New York City, 2.7% in Washington, DC,

3.6% in major metropolitan areas, and 4% in the rest of the country. However, using a cut-off score of 40 on the same instrument, Blanchard et al. (2004) have published that the prevalence of probable PTSD for their university samples from Albany, Augusta, and North Dakota were, respectively, 11.3, 7.4, and 3.4%. Unfortunately, there is no agreement on the best cut-off strategies and different results may be related to this important diagnostic decision.

Finally, a third measurement strategy is to use full diagnostic criteria to verify the presence of mental disorders (typically PTSD or ASD). In this case, a diagnosis of PTSD, for example, must include not only symptoms (Criteria B, C, and D according to the *DSM-IV* [1994] criteria –see Table 2) but also other requirements (e.g., Criterion F: social impairment in daily activities). The studies of the groups of Galea, et al. (2002) in the US and Miguel-Tobal et al. (2004) in Spain are good examples of this diagnostic approach. By using structured telephone interviews related to *DSM-IV* (1994) criteria, in a sample of Manhattan citizens, it was found that in the 5-9 weeks after S11, only 7.5% of those who had experienced direct exposure presented a probable PTSD condition, and among those who were not directly exposed, only 4.2% presented PTSD. In any case, the prevalence rate of PTSD in New York, as a whole, was of 7.5%, a figure that, although it is twice as high as the one found in the American population *before* S11 (i.e., 3.6%; Kessler, Sonnega, Bromet, Hughes, & Nelson, 1995), it does not seem extraordinarily high, given the magnitude of the event.

In view of the disparities of results of different studies which have used different instruments and/or measurement strategies (see Table 1), we designed this study to test to what extent use of different cut-off scores in the PCL-C, all of them published in the literature (see Ruggiero et al., 2003), might significantly affect estimates of probable cases within a sample of the general population of Madrid assessed 2-3 weeks after the terrorist attacks. A second goal of our study was to explore the impact of assessing diagnostic criteria in addition to trauma-related symptoms, to estimate probable cases of PTSD. In fact, one of the main diagnostic limitations of the studies based on symptom checklists is that they typically do not cover other *required* criteria to diagnose PTSD (see North & Pfefferbaum, 2002). These symptom-based instruments adequately cover Criteria B, C, and D of the *DSM-IV* (1994) definition of PTSD (i.e., symptoms), but not Criterion A2 (i.e., initial subjective response)[5] and, more important, Criterion F (i.e., significant problems in the *daily functioning*)—see Table 2. This latter criterion is extraordinarily important, as the inclusion of functioning difficulties may reduce epidemiological figures of mental disorders in the general population up to one half (Narrow et al., 2002). Thus, we designed the study to include assessment of Criteria A and F in addition to the PTSD symptoms, which are well covered by the PCL-C. Our overall hypothesis was that the impact of the traumatic event in the general population, according to what was already known after the S11 US attacks, would be rather limited (see Vázquez, 2005) and, furthermore, that impact would depend largely on the criteria used to define "cases." Finally, we explored the role of exposure risk factors on both post-traumatic symptoms and probable PTSD by using different cut-off scores.

Table 2 Outline of the DSM-IV-TR (APA, 2000) Diagnostic Criteria for PTSD

Posttraumatic Stress Disorder (PTSD)

Criterion A1. Exposed to a traumatic event that involved physical threat and,

Criterion A2. Subjective reactions of fear, helplessness, or horror

Criterion B. Reexperiencing the event (1 out of 5 symptoms):

    1. Intrusive recollections

    2. Recurrent, distressing dreams

    3. Acting or feeling as if the event were recurring

    4. Distress at exposure

    5. Physiological reactivity on exposure

Criterion C. Persistent avoidance (3 out of 7):

    1. Efforts to avoid thoughts, feelings, or conversations associated with trauma

    2. Efforts to avoid activities, places, or people that arouse recollections of trauma

    3. Inability to recall important aspects of the trauma

    4. Diminished interest to participate in significant activities

    5. Feelings of detachment from others

    6. Restricted range of affect

    7. Sense of foreshortened future Criterion

Criterion D. Hyperarousal (1 out of 5):

    1. Insomnia.

    2. Irritability or outbursts of anger

    3. Difficulty concentrating

    4. Hypervigilance.

Criterion F: Significant distress or social impairment

Method

Participants

One week after the M11, 2004, attack, a class of university psychology students in Madrid was asked to participate in a study on the effects of terrorist attacks. Students completed a questionnaire and recruited two other adult persons, aged 18 and older, who were in Madrid on March 11, 2004. The final total sample consisted of 503 respondents (67% female) whose average age was 31.4 years: 194 university students and 309 persons from the general population[6]. All participants returned the questionnaires 18-25 days after the terrorist event.

Measures

Initial reactions (Criterion A2, DSM-IV). To explore whether different initial reactions could affect the development of subsequent trauma-related symptoms, we used a 10-point rating scale, ranging from 0 (*not at all*) to 10 (*extreme intensity),* on which participants rated the intensity of "fear," "feelings of horror," and "helplessness" in the first hours after the trauma occurred. In addition to these three symptoms that make up *DSM-IV* (1994) and *DSM-IV-TR* (2000) Criterion A2 for PTSD, we also examined other initial reactions that may play an important role in the development of PTSD (e.g., fear that someone known to the person could have been affected, bodily symptoms such as sweating, trembling, feeling upset and angry—Bracha et al., 2004; Brewin, 2003). Participants also rated the duration in hours of these emotional reactions in the 24-hour period following the attacks.

Post-traumatic symptoms (Criteria B, C and D, DSM-IV). The Posttraumatic Stress Disorder Checklist-Civilian (PCL-C; Weathers et al., 1993) is a 17-item self-report measure of posttraumatic stress reactions that adequately covers the set of symptoms associated with PTSD as defined in the *DSM-IV* (1994) and *DSM-IV-TR* (2000)— Criteria B (Reexperiencing), C (Avoidance), and D (Hyperarousal). Items are scored on a scale anchored from 1 (*not at all*) to 5 (*extremely).* The possible range of scores is 17–85. Test-retest reliability at 2-3 days has been reported at .96 (Weathers et al., 1993), and the overall diagnostic efficiency has been found to be acceptably high at .90 (Blanchard, Jones-Alexander, Buckley, & Forneris, 1996). In our study, the scale was shown to be highly consistent (Cronbach's α = .89).

Similar to the majority of studies related to the S11 events (e.g., Blanchard et al., 2004), the PCL-C was *explicitly* framed with respect to the M11 terrorist attacks (i.e., whereas in the standard instructions, participants are asked to indicate how much they have been bothered by those symptoms in the last month, in our instructions, participants were asked to inform on their symptoms since the day of the attacks). The scores on the PCL-C were used in three different ways:

1.   PCL-C total scores. PCL total score and the three subscales which correspond to the *DSM-IV* (1994) Criteria B, C, and D respectively

2.   Substantial stress level (SL). To compare our data with those from previous studies (Matt & Vazquez, 2006; Rubin et al., 2005; Schuster et al., 2001; Stein et al., 2004), SL was defined as a response of 4 or 5 to one or more than five PCL-C items.

3. Probable PTSD diagnosis. To determine rates of psychological distress related to PTSD, three strategies differing in restrictiveness were compared:

3.1. *Low threshold criterion* (PCL total score > 44). This criterion, which minimizes the number of false negative cases, has been repeatedly used in epidemiological studies related to the S11 attacks (Blanchard et al., 2004).

3.2. *High threshold criterion* (PCL ≥ 50). A cut-off score of 50 or above has also been used in national studies on the effects of the S11 attacks (Schlenger et al., 2002). Yet, to reduce false positive cases (see Ruggiero et al., 2003), items were computed only when reaching a severity threshold (i.e., a score of 4 or 5: *quite a bit* or *extremely,* respectively)[7].

3.3. *Clinical criteria based on psychometric measures.* We established a *DSM-IV*-based strategy consisting of checking whether a given criterion was fulfilled. Criterion A2 was considered met when a participant responded with a score of 8 or above to any of the reactions described in *DSM-IV* (1994; i.e., horror, fear, or helplessness)[8]. Criterion B, C, and D were met whenever a participant met the number of symptoms required respectively for each criterion (one out of five reexperiencing symptoms, three out of seven avoidance symptoms, and two out of five hyperarousal symptoms). Presence of a symptom was defined by a score of 4 or 5 on each corresponding PCL-C item. Criterion F was met if a participant scored 8 or above on the Global functioning item[9].

Global functioning (Criterion F, DSM-IV). Problems in "global functioning" (Criterion F for PTSD, according to *DSM-IV,*1994, and *DSM-IV-TR,* 2000) assessed the extent to which the M11 events were still affecting participants' daily activities—at work, at home, or in interpersonal relations—on a scale of 1 (*not affected in daily activities*) to 10 (*extremely affected in daily activities*)

Exposure to the events. To explore the role of exposure in the reactions to the terrorist attacks, we included questions used by Galea et al. (2002), Schuster et al. (2001), and items recommended by the Office of Behavioral and Social Sciences Research of the National Institutes of Health (2002) to assess the impact of the S11 attack. The questionnaire asked respondents to report whether they had directly witnessed the attacks, lived close to the scenarios where the attacks happened, used to take the train lines that were attacked, or had friends or relatives who were wounded or killed during the attacks. We also included retrospective self-report measures of media exposure (newspapers, TV, radio or Internet) during the week of the attacks.

Results

Posttraumatic Stress Responses (PCL-Total Scores)

The mean PCL-C total score was 31.9 (SD = 12.9)—see Table 3. An analysis of sex differences showed that women had a more intense reaction than men as reflected in higher scores on the PCL-C total, $t(487)$ = 3.15, $p < .002$; symptoms of reexperiencing, $t(487) = 3.85, p < .001$; and hyperarousal, $t(487) = 2.97, p < .003$. Yet, there were no significant sex differences on avoidance total score, $t(487) = 1.16, p < .11$.

Substantial Stress

Overall, a high percentage of respondents (59.2%) manifested a "substantial stress level" as defined by Schuster et al. (2001). Women were more likely than men (61.7% vs. 52.0%) to report substantial stress levels, $\chi^2(1, N = 488) = 4.04, p < .04$ (Figure 1). The most prevalent symptom (for men and women) was "feeling very upset when something reminded you of what happened" (94% of the sample), and the least prevalent was "trouble remembering important parts of the event" (14.1%). An interesting result emerged from our study when the overall magnitude of the severity of the PCL-C items was analyzed (Figure 2). The mean magnitude of the PCL-C symptoms ($M = 1.88$) did not even reach the severity threshold of 2 (i.e., "a little bit"), which casts some doubts about catastrophic discourses on the implications of this disaster for general population. As can be seen in Figure 2, almost identical results have been found in different samples after the S11 attacks.

Table 3

Risk Factors, Levels of Exposure and Levels of Post-Traumatic Stress Symptoms and Probable PTSD (Based on PCL Scores)

Risk factors and levels of exposure	PCL scores M and (SD)				Probable PTSD (%)		
	Total Score	Reexperiencing	Avoidance	Hyperarousal	PCL > 44 (Including all items)	PCL > 50 (Only items scoring > 4)	$DSM\text{-}IV$ criteria (PCL and additional items)
Overall sample (N = 503)	31.9 (12.9)	10.9 (3.6)	10.9 (3.8)	10.1 (4.3)	13.3	3.4	1.9
Gender							
Female (N = 339)	32.8 (10.5)**	11.3 (3.7)**	11.1 (3.9)	10.5 (4.4)**	14.4	3.8	2.1
Male (N = 148)	29.6 (9.4)	9.9 (3.3)	9.9 (3.3)	9.2 (3.9)	11.3	2.0	1.4
Location of residence***							
Proximity 1 - (N = 54)	37.6 (12.9)	12.8 (4.1)	12.8 (4.8)	12.0 (5.3)	29.6	11.1	5.8
Proximity 2 - (N = 40)	32.6 (8.7)	11.3 (3.8)	10.6 (2.8)	10.0 (3.8)	12.5	0.0	0.0
Proximity 3 - (N = 246)	31.3 (9.3)	10.5 (3.2)	10.7 (3.5)	10.0 (3.9)	10.6	1.6	1.2
Proximity 4 - (N = 159)	30.9 (10.8)	10.8 (3.7)	10.6 (4.1)	9.5 (4.2)	12.6	4.4	2.5
Personally exposed							
Yes (N = 20)	41.1 (13.4)***	14.2 (4.2)***	13.5 (5.4)**	13.3 (4.9)***	30.0*	15.0**	5.0*
No (N = 483)	31.5 (9.9)	10.8 (3.5)	10.8 (3.8)	9.9 (4.2)	12.6	2.9	1.9
Perception of life at risk							
Yes (N = 147)	36.9 (11.6)***	12.4 (3.8)***	12.4 (4.5)***	12.1 (4.8)***	25.2***	7.5**	4.2*
No (N = 338)	30.0 (9.0)	10.4 (3.3)	10.3 (3.4)	9.4 (3.7)	8.9	1.8	1.2
Knowing someone directly affected							
Yes (N = 218)	33.8 (11.4)***	11.3 (3.8)*	11.4 (4.4)**	11.1 (4.7)***	17.9**	5.9**	3.7*
No (N = 285)	30.5 (9.1)	10.6 (3.4)	10.5 (3.4)	9.4 (3.8)	9.8	1.4	0.7
User of affected train lines							
Yes (N = 73)	35.8 (11.8)***	12.1 (4.0)*	11.9 (4.3) **	11.8 (4.8)***	24.7**	6.8	5.6*
No (N = 429)	31.2 (9.9)	10.7 (3.5)	10.7 (3.8)	9.8 (4.1)	11.4	2.8	1.4

Note. Proximity of residence to where the bombs exploded (1 = same neighborhood or very close; 2 = same area, not neighborhood; 3 = Madrid metropolitan area; 4 = Madrid, outside metropolitan area).
*p < .05. **p < .01. ***p < .001.

Probable PTSD Diagnosis

Table 4 shows the data on probable PTSD diagnosis based on PCL scores using different strategies. As can be seen in the table, rates of PTSD changed significantly depending on which criterion is used. For the entire sample, using the cut-off score > 44 proposed by Blanchard et al. (1996), 13.3% of the sample received a probable PTSD disorder, whereas the prevalence rate dropped to just 3.4% when the stricter criterion suggested by Ruggiero et al. (2003) was used instead. Thus, applying different criteria commonly used in studies with the PCL-C may result in a *fourfold* difference between probable diagnostic rates.

Finally, according to the approach modeled after *DSMIV* (1994) criteria, only 1.9% of the total sample received a probable diagnosis of PTSD—one seventh of the PCL> 44 strategy. Further investigation showed that sex differences were significant only for a subset of symptoms. More specifically, a significantly higher proportion of women than men showed

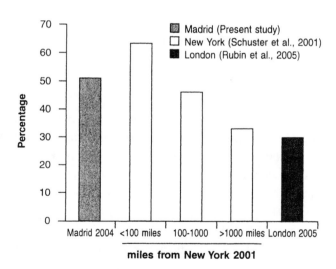

Figure 1. Prevalence of "Substantial Stress" Reactions (as Defined by Schuster et al., 2001) among Different Samples from the General Population in the US (Living at 3 Different Locations at Different Distances From Manhattan), Madrid, and London after their Respective Terrorist Attacks

a strong initial emotional reaction to the event (Criterion A), $\chi^2(1, N = 481)$ = 48.9, $p < .0001$; and more symptoms related to reexperiencing (Criterion B), $\chi^2(1, N = 486) = 4.43$, $p < .03$. Considering all criteria together, women and men showed similar levels (2.1% vs. 1.4%) of probable PTSD, $\chi^2(1, N = 485) = 0.27$, $p < .60$. Items that were related to avoidance behaviors (Criterion D) and global functioning (Criterion F)—see Table 4—were much less frequent than items related to reexperiencing and hyperarousal.

Initial Reactions and Posttraumatic Response

With the exception of bodily symptoms ($M = 3.2 \pm 3.2$), the average initial reaction was rather intense, ranging from $M = 6.0 \pm 3.1$ (fear) to $M = 7.5 \pm 2.6$ (helplessness). This included the three symptoms of the *DSM-IV* (1994) definition of Criterion A as well as other reactions (e.g., feelings of anger, "fear that someone I know could be affected," and feeling "upset" about what had happened). The average duration of the initial reaction was 1.9 ± 1.0 hours and, in general, the intensity of these emotional reactions was significantly correlated with all the PCL-C scores (correlations between emotional reactions and PCL-C total score ranged from $r = .54$, $p < .001$ for bodily symptoms to $r = .32$, $p < .001$ for anger).

Risk Factors and Stress Reactions

To investigate the effects of place of residence on posttraumatic stress-related symptoms, we conducted a series of univariate ANOVAs with proximity of residence to the places of the attacks as between-subject factor and PCL scores as response variables. The univariate tests revealed a statistically significant main effect on the total PCL-C, $F(3, 495) = 6.5$, $p < .001$, $\eta^2 = .04$; reexperiencing, $F(3, 494) = 6.1$, $p < .001$, $\eta^2 = .04$; avoidance, $F(3, 495) = 4.8$, $p < .001$, $\eta^2 = .03$; and hyperarousal, $F(3, 495) = 5.2$, $p < .001$, $\eta^2 = .03$. Post-hoc MSD tests revealed a similar pattern in all dependent variables (see Table 3), showing that people living "very close to or in the same neighborhood" where the bombs exploded had more symptoms than people living in other places.

A series of t-tests for independent samples was also conducted to explore other risk factors (see Figure 2). The results revealed higher significant total PCL-C scores in participants who were close to where the bombs exploded (i.e., "personally exposed"), $t(501) = 4.1$, $p < .001$; who perceived their life at risk, $t(483) = 7.1$, $p < .001$; were physically injured, $t(501) = 4.1, p < .001$; personally knew someone affected by the explosions, $t(501) = 3.6, p < .001$; or who were users of the train lines where the bombs exploded, $t(501) = 3.6, p < .001$. An identical pattern of results was found on the three subscales of the PCL-C (reexperiencing, avoidance, and hyperarousal)—see Figure 2. Yet, there was no significant difference for being a user of trains in general.

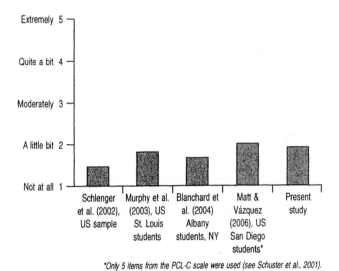

*Only 5 items from the PCL-C scale were used (see Schuster et al., 2001).

Figure 2. Mean Severity (From 1 = *Not At All* to 5 = *Extremely*) of the PTSD Symptoms Assessed by the PCL-C Scale in Different Samples of the General Population within the Days or Weeks Immediately after S11-2001 and M11-2004

The analysis of participants' global functioning revealed that, on a 0-10 scale, the average was not high ($M = 3.7\pm2.2$). Sex differences revealed that, compared to men, women had more difficulties in daily activities, $t(475) = 4.27, p < .001$ ($M = 3.84$ vs. 3.32) in relation to the M11 attacks.

As was also the case with raw PCL-C scores, further analyses revealed that risk factors were significantly associated with probable diagnoses of PTSD. In the case of the PCL> 44 criterion, living closer to the areas affected, $\chi^2(3, N = 499) = 14.05, p < .003$; having been directly exposed, $\chi^2(1, N = 503) = 5.02, p < .02$; having perceived life at risk,

$\chi^2(1, N = 485) = 22.84, p < .001$; having been physically injured, $\chi^2(1, N = 485) = 11.81, p < .001$; knowing someone directly affected, $\chi^2(1, N = 502) = 6.96, p < .008$; and being a user of the attacked train lines, $\chi^2(1, N = 502) = 9.49, p < .002$; were all significantly associated with the likelihood of having a PTSD disorder, as defined by these criteria. Similar results were obtained with the other two criteria.

Although PCL-C scores were significantly higher in women than in men, sex analyses of categorical diagnoses revealed no significant association between sex and probable PTSD, using either the PCL> 44—$\chi^2(1, N = 489) = 1.63, p < .20$—, the PCL > 50—$\chi^2(1, N = 489) = 1.04, p < .3\ 1$—, or the *DSM-IV-TR* (2000) criteria—$\chi^2(1, N = 485) = 0.27, p < .60$.

Table 4
Percentage of Participants Meeting Levels of Substantial Stress (SL) and Probably PTSD According to Different Diagnostic Strategies

	Total sample	Male	Female	PCL definition: *DSM-IV*-based definition ratio
Psychometric criteria (PCL scores)				
Substantial Stress (Selected PCL-C items scored 4 or 5)	59.2	52.0	61.7*	
PTSD using PCL > 44	13.3	11.3	14.4	7:1
PTSD using PCL > 50 *and* items scoring > 4	3.4	2.0	3.8	1.7:1
DSM-IV-based clinical criteria				
All *DSM-IV* criteria	1.9	1.4	2.1	1:1
Criterion A2 (Initial reaction to the event)	78.2	58.2	86.9**	
Criterion B (Reexperiencing: 1/5)	56.2	49.0	59.3*	
Criterion C (Avoidance: 3/7)	3.8	2.8	4.2	
Criterion D (Hyperarousal: 2/5)	19.1	15.8	20.5	
Criterion F (Functioning)	6.3	5.6	6.6	
Criteria B + C + D (cluster of symptoms)	3.2	2.0	3.6	
Criteria A2 + B + C + D (Initial reaction and symptoms)	2.0	1.4	2.1	

*$p < 0.05$. **$p < 0.01$.

Media Exposure

Media coverage of the M11 attacks was intense and extensive and attracted a large audience. Similar to S11 USA audiences, where Schuster et al. (2001) found that the average American adult watched approximately 8 hours of TV coverage on that day, participants in the Madrid study watched TV news for an average of 5.1 hours/day during the first three days. Furthermore, during the first week, they listened to radio news an average of 1.8 hours/day, read newspapers an average of 4.1 hours/day, and browsed Internet news an average of 1.4 hours/day.

More specifically, participants believed that their initial reactions (Criterion A) were highly affected by the impact of the TV images they watched within the first hours after the attacks (33.6% said that TV images affected them "very much," 39.0% "a lot," 22.5% "to some extent," and 4.2% "not at all"). Participants also acknowledged that exposure to news, in general, affected their mood negatively ("not at all" = 3.0%; "to some extent" = 31.8%; "quite a bit" = 37.8%; "quite a lot" = 16.9%; "very much" = 9.9%) although in similar proportion respondents also recognized that exposure to news helped them to better understand what happened ("not at all" = 7.2%; "to some extent" = 16.9%; "quite a bit" = 32.4%; "quite a lot" = 31.8%; "very much" = 11.3%). Zero-order correlations between the amount of media exposure and the total PCL - score were significant for the average daily TV watching during the first 3 days ($r = .14$, $p < .01$) and during the first week ($r = .14$, $p < .05$) as well as for the daily radio listening ($r = .15$, $p < .01$). Correlations between PCL symptoms and reading newspapers and watching Internet news did not reach statistical significance.

Discussion

The sample of citizens of Madrid experienced patterns and levels of emotional distress in the first days following the terrorist attacks of M11 that were similar to those reported in the general USA population after the S11 attacks. The level of "substantial stress" in our sample (59.2%) was very similar to that found by Schuster et al. (2001)—61%—in their subsample of US citizens living closer to the World Trade Center but higher than the percentage of Londoners affected by the July 2005 attacks (31%). Rubin et al. (2005) have argued that differences between the impact of the attacks on the US and London samples may be due, among other causes, to differences in the magnitude of the events, the limited TV coverage of the London attacks, and even the previous experience of the British people with IRA terrorist attacks. However, as we said before, although the concept of substantial stress may be clinically "unsubstantial," these differences among samples from different places still remain unexplained.

Based on the symptoms reported in a questionnaire, a preliminary study conducted by Muñoz et al. (2004) between 18-24 March 2004 showed that 47% of a Madrid general population sample ($N = 1,179$) had an acute stress reaction in relation to the M11 attacks, as measured by the Acute Stress Disorder Scale (ASDS; Bryant & Harvey, 2000). Yet, although initial psychological reactions to the M11 events were in some cases dramatic and, as our data showed, intense initial reactions (Criterion A2) were very common, there is also mounting evidence that these acute responses are limited in scope and quickly return to normal levels (Marshall, Spitzer, & Liebowitz, 1999; McNally, Bryant, & Ehlers, 2003; Muñoz et al., 2004). Silver et al. (2002) found that 17% of their nationwide sample of adults residing outside New York City reported posttraumatic stress symptoms 2 months after S11, but only 6% reported symptoms at 6 months. A similar pattern has been found for PTSD diagnoses in the general population. Galea et al. (2003) analyzed the prevalence of PTSD in the general population of New York City in three consecutive telephone surveys conducted one month, four months, and six months after S11, 2001 showing that prevalence rates declined from 7.5% to 0.6% six months after the incident. Therefore, the *transitory nature* of traumatic stress responses found in the majority of the general population suggests that acute emotional distress should not be mistaken for direct indicators of later PTSD. As McNally et al. (2003) and Silver et al. (2002) have argued, high initial emotional responses may be part of the natural recovery, improving without the assistance of professional help in the presence of supportive environments. Thus, a pattern of acute stress reactions after trauma in the hours, days, or even weeks after a traumatic event occurs should be cautiously interpreted (Kilpatrick et al., 1998; North & Pfefferbaum, 2002). In fact, there is a strong debate about the clinical and epidemiological significance of this type of findings. Studies attempting to identify subthreshold levels of traumatic responses (e.g., Muñoz et al., 2004; Stein et al., 2004) based on simple definitions of stress may induce public alarm and confusion (Shalev, 2004; Southwick & Charney, 2004). Immediately after the S11 attacks, health policymakers predicted a major mental health crisis among New York citizens (Herman, Felton, & Susser, 2002; Stephenson, 2001). A similar scenario was predicted in Madrid by governmental authorities (Sampedro, 2004). Yet, the epidemiological studies conducted in New York (Galea et al., 2002) and in other US cities (Schlenger et al., 2002) had already shown that prevalence rates of PTSD disorders in the general population were not disproportionate relative to pre-S11 attack rates and dropped significantly during the first few months after the tragedy. Consistent with these findings, the data from large managed behavioral health organizations had similarly shown a pattern of no significant increases in prescription of psychotropic medications between September 2001 and January 2002 (McCarter & Goldman, 2002) or in the incidence of PTSD or other mental disorders in the New York Veteran Hospitals network (Boscarino, Galea, Ahern, Resnick, & Vlahov, 2002; Rosenheck & Fontana, 2003). Furthermore, the overall magnitude of the general population's stress reaction is quite low. Both in our study, as in previous ones (see Figure 2), the overall mean intensity of the PTSD symptoms was never above 2 on a 1-5 scale.

In the present study, we used three different strategies to diagnose PTSD based on the PCL-C. Using two different scoring methods and a clinical approach, we observed the prevalence rate to drop from 13.3% to 1.9%. In fact, using structured interviews and following *DSM-IV-TR* (2000) criteria, Miguel-Tobal et al. (2004) estimated that only 4% of their Madrid sample fulfilled PTSD criteria, and 2.3% had a probable PTSD which was attributable to the M11 terrorist attacks.

Researchers and policy makers should pay attention to these variations in probable prevalence rates, which depend upon the use of different diagnostic and threshold criteria (North & Pfefferbaum, 2002), for an adequate and sensible planning of health services (Southwick & Charney, 2004). Unfortunately, there is no sound epidemiological study, as far as we know, that had been conducted in the Madrid general population on the prevalence of PTSD *before* March 11, 2004. Yet, it is interesting to note that, in an ongoing project on the prevalence of *DSM-IV-TR* (2000) mental disorders in six European countries (ESEMeD/MHEDEA, 2004)—Belgium, France, Germany, Italy, the Netherlands, and Spain (total N = 21,425)—PTSD 12-month and lifetime-prevalence rates are noticeably smaller (0.9%–1.9%, respectively) than those found in comparable US studies (e.g., Kessler et al., 1995). Future studies should pay attention to the possibilities of directly comparing the figures on psychological reactions to traumatic events in different countries and cultures.

Our findings are consistent with other studies showing that physical proximity to traumatic events is an important risk factor for developing traumatic responses (Cano-Vindel et al., 2004; North, Smith, & Spitznagel, 1994; Sprang, 1999). In the case of the S11 attacks, Schlenger et al. (2002) found that 1-2 months after S11, probable diagnosis of PTSD based on a PCL-C score of 50 or above, was much more common in the New York City metropolitan area (11.2%) than in the rest of country (4.0%), where the prevalence rates were within the range observed before S11 in the US general population. Using a structured telephone interview and *DSM-IV* (1994) criteria, Galea et al. (2002) found that 5-9 weeks after S11, the prevalence of PTSD was approximately twice as high among residents of Manhattan than the 12-month prevalence rates found in the general population—7.5% versus 3.6% (Kessler et al., 1995). Similarly, Blanchard et al. (2004) have reported that probable PTSD based on a PCL-C cut-off score affected 11.3% of their sample of undergraduates from the University of New York at Albany, whereas the same disorder was much less likely to affect students in more distant areas of the country.

Regarding the impact of mass media exposure, the Madrid sample had a similar exposure to that found in comparable studies. The impact of this exposure is significant but almost restricted to the TV watched in the first week. Furthermore, the effect size of this finding was relatively small. In any case, although there is a public debate about the role of mass media in the development of PTSD and other traumatic responses, Ahern et al. (2002) have shown that frequent television viewing of the S11 attacks had an impact on PTSD symptoms and depression only in individuals who had a direct event experience (e.g., direct witnessing or having a friend or relative killed) but not in those who had no direct experience.

Our findings portray a response to these traumatic events that is consistent with other research, showing a dramatic surge in some PTSD symptoms immediately following S11 with little, if any, implication for psychopathology in the general population (McNally et al., 2003), and a number of significant risk factors associated both with PCL scores and categorical PTSD diagnoses. However, the pattern of results on the magnitude of the response calls for the need to be cautious about the dangers of confounding normal emotional distress with clinically significant disorders, especially when using psychometric criteria as the main source of data. The dangers of this kind of decision, from an epidemiological and public health perspective of media and population impact in terms of fear and alarm, should be seriously considered (Southwick & Charney, 2004). Although the present study cannot be considered as a robust epidemiological research, mainly due to sampling limitations, it provides some critical hints on the limitations of methods that intend to screen for mental disorders in the population. In our opinion, epidemiological estimates of similar studies should be carefully examined, as variations in diagnostic cut-off scores and strategies may have dramatic effects on the resulting estimates. Researchers and policy makers should pay attention to these variations in probable prevalence rates, which depend upon the use of different diagnostic and threshold criteria (North & Pfefferbaum, 2002), for an adequate and sensible planning of health services (Southwick & Charney). It is likely that an appropriate way to provide more reliable estimates of the impact of terrorist attacks on the general population is to focus not only on symptoms (e.g., Blanchard et al., 2004; Schuster et al., 2001; Stein et al., 2004) but also on the impact on functioning (see North & Pfefferbaum, 2002), as this could be one of the most relevant criteria for seeking help in victims of trauma (Shalev, 2004). In fact, the results of our study support the idea that two components of the formal definition of PTSD (i.e., avoidance behaviors and a deficit in psychosocial functioning) are crucial to increase or to decrease the estimations of PTSD prevalence (see also Brewin, Andrews, & Rose, 2000). Data from simple self-report measures only covering symptoms should be viewed with caution unless the authors use cut-off scores that maximize specificity and include questions on effective psychosocial functioning. In brief, an adequate assessment should systematically include: (a) being directly physically or psychologically threatened by the event versus being only exposed to information about the event, (b) the presence of an initial emotional reaction of unbearable fear or horror, and (c) a sustained impact of the symptoms on daily functioning since the event.

The present study has also some limitations. As we have already mentioned, the snowball procedure used in our study is not an adequate method to arrive at reliable epidemiological figures of any disorder. Thus, our results should not be considered valid estimates of the prevalence of mental disorders in the Madrid population and, in fact, this was not our goal in designing the study. Furthermore, although the use of self-report measures is common in this type of studies, it would be preferable to use structured interviews to provide diagnoses of trauma-related psychological disorders. Finally, although our results clearly suggest that the assessment of psychosocial dysfunctions related to the trauma reduces the rates of diagnosed PTSD, such assessments should be conducted using more sophisticated measures in future studies.

As a final point, we would like to stress that, in the case of the Madrid attack, a number of unique political circumstances created a complex social scenario where positive and negative emotions were particularly mixed during the first days after the tragedy. In fact, the Spanish general elections took place just 3 days after these attacks and were marked by an intense emotional climate. One of the next steps of our group will be to analyze the role of these negative and positive emotions (Fredrickson, Tugade, Waugh, & Larkin, 2003; Pérez-Sales, Cervellón, Vázquez, Vidales, & Gaborit, 2005; Vázquez, Cervellón, Pérez Sales, Vidales, & Gaborit, 2005) in the development and/or maintenance of post-traumatic symptoms taking advantage of that extraordinary occasion.

This research was partially financed by a grant from the Pfizer Foundation (Spain). We want to thank Beatriz Armada for her continuous support of our project and Jesús Sanz, Sandro Galea, Chris Brewin, and Richard MacNally for their helpful comments on earlier versions of this manuscript. We are also indebted to María José Collado, Lourdes López and to many other students at the Facultad de Psicología (UCM) who volunteered to collaborate in gathering information for this research.

Endnotes

1. For a review of other selected subsamples of affected people after the M11 attacks in Madrid, see the papers by Iruarrizaga, Miguel-Tobal, Cano-Vindel, & González (2004) on the impact on victims and relatives, and González-Ordi, Miguel-Tobal, Cano-Vindel, & Iruarrizaga (2004) on the impact on emergency personnel.

2. The items chosen were those reported as present by 50% or more of the survivors of the bombing attack in Oklahoma City (North et al., 1999): 1) "Feeling very upset when something reminds you of what happened?"; 2) "Repeated, disturbing memories, thoughts, or dreams about what happened?"; 3) "Having difficulty concentrating?"; 4) "Trouble falling or staying asleep?"; 5) "Feeling irritable or having angry outbursts?".

3. The study of Silver et al. (2002) only assessed symptoms belonging to the ASD category of the DSM-IV but not the rest of the diagnostic criteria; therefore, it cannot be clearly stated whether or not they were probable ASD cases.

4. Similar variations in results have been found when researchers have studied initial psychological reactions with the controversial category of Acute Stress Disorder (ASD)—see Vázquez (2005). This new category was first introduced in the *DSM-IV* (APA, 1994)—see a systematic critical review by Marshall,

Spitzer and Liebowitz, 1999—to cover the measurement of psychological reactions to traumatic events within the first 30 days after a traumatic event.

5. Although initial response is restricted to Criterion A2, we assume that all participants met Criterion A1 as the nature of the M11 traumatic experience literally fits the definition of trauma described in the *DSM-IV* Criterion A1: "the person experienced, witnessed, or was confronted with an event or events that involved actual or threatened death or serious injury, or a threat to the physical integrity of self or others."

6. We conducted a series of analyses comparing PCL-C scores in both samples, finding no significant differences in any PCL scale. Thus, both samples were combined in this report.

7. A score of 3 or above is required for items 1, 2, 9, 10, 12, and 15, whereas a score of 4 or above is required for the rest of the items.

8. A score of 8 or above in a 1-10 scale would be equivalent to a score of 4 or above in the 1-5 scale of the PCL-C.

9. Criterion E (duration of symptom more than 1 month) was not directly assessed as this study was conducted between the third and fourth week after the attacks. Thus, the responses covered a 3-4 week period, as the PCL instructions asked subjects to rate the severity of symptoms *since* March 11

References

Ahern, J., Galea, S., Resnick, H., Kilpatrick, D., Bucuvalas, M., Gold, J., & Vlahov, D. (2002). Television images and psychological symptoms after the September 11 terrorist attacks. *Psychiatry, 65,* 289-300.

American Psychiatric Association (1994). *Diagnostic and statistical manual of mental disorders* (4th ed.). Washington, DC: Author.

American Psychiatric Association (2000). *Diagnostic and statistical manual of mental disorders* (4th ed., text revision). Washington, DC: Author.

Blanchard, E.B., Hickling, E.J., Barton, K.A., Taylor, A.E., Loos, W.R., & Jones-Alexander, J. (1996). One-year prospective follow-up of motor vehicle accident victims. *Behaviour Research and Therapy, 34,* 775-786.

Blanchard, E.B., Jones Alexander, J., Buckley, T.C., & Forneris, C.A. (1996). Psychometric properties of the PTSD Checklist (PCL). *Behaviour Research and Therapy, 34,* 669-673.

Blanchard, E.B., Kuhn, E., Rowell, D.L., Hickling, E.J., Wittrock, D., Rogers, R. L., Johnson M.R., & Steckler D.C. (2004). Studies of the vicarious traumatization of college students by the September 11th attacks: Effects of proximity, exposure and connectedness. *Behavior Research and Therapy, 42,* 19 1-205.

Boscarino, J.A., Galea, S., Ahern, J., Resnick, H., & Vlahov, D. (2002). Utilization of mental health services following the September 11th terrorist attacks in Manhattan, New York City. *International Journal of Emergency Mental Health, 4,* 143-155.

Bracha, H.S., Williams, A.E., Haynes, S.N., Kubany, E.S., Ralston, T.C, & Yamashita, J.M. (2004). The STRS (Shortness of Breath, Tremulousness, Racing Heart, and Sweating): A brief checklist for acute distress with panic-like sympathetic indicators; development and factor structure. *Annals of General Hospital Psychiatry, 3,* 8.

Brewin, C.R. (2003). *Posttraumatic stress disorder: Malady or myth?* New Haven, CT: Yale University Press.

Brewin, C.R., Andrews, B., & Rose, S. (2000). Fear, helplessness, and horror in posttraumatic stress disorder: Investigating *DSMIV* Criterion A2 in victims of violent crime. *Journal of Traumatic Stress, 13,* 499-509.

Bryant, R.A., & Harvey, A.G. (2000). *Acute stress disorder: A handbook of theory, assessment, and treatment.* Washington, DC: American Psychological Association.

Cano-Vindel, A., Miguel-Tobal, J. J., González-Ordi, H., & Iruarrizaga, I. (2004). Los atentados terroristas del 11-M en Madrid: la proximidad de la residencia a las áreas afectadas. *Ansiedad y Estrés, 10* (2-3), 18 1-194.

Conejero, S., de Rivera, J., Páez, D., & Jiménez, A. (2004). Alteración afectiva personal, atmósfera emocional y clima emocional tras los atentados del 11 de marzo. *Ansiedad y Estrés, 102-3,* 299-3 12

ESEMeD/MHEDEA (2004). Prevalence of mental disorders in Europe: Results from the European Study of the Epidemiology of Mental Disorders (ESEMeD) Project. *Acta Psychiatrica Scandinavica, 109,* 21-27.

Fredrickson, B.L., Tugade, M.M., Waugh, C.E., & Larkin, G.R. (2003). What good are positive emotions in crises? A prospective study of resilience and emotions following the terrorist attacks on the United States on September 11th, 2001. *Journal of Personality and Social Psychology, 84,* 365-376.

Galea, S., Ahern, J., Resnick, H., Kilpatrick, D., Bucuvalas, M., Gold, J., & Vlahov D. (2002). Psychological sequelae of the September 11 terrorist attacks in New York City. *New England Journal of Medicine, 346,* 982-987.

Galea, S., Vlahov, D., Resnick, H., Ahern, J., Susser, E., Gold, J., Bucuvalas, M., & Kilpatrick, D. (2003). Trends of probable post-traumatic stress disorder in New York City after the September 11 terrorist attacks. *American Journal of Epidemiology, 158,* 514-524.

González-Ordi, H., Miguel-Tobal, J.J., Cano-Vindel, A., & Iruarrizaga, I. (2004). Efectos de la exposición a eventos traumáticos en personal de emergencias: consecuencias psicopatológicas del atentado terrorista del 11-M en Madrid. *Ansiedad y Estrés, 10,* 207-217.

Herman, D., Felton, C., & Susser, E. (2002). Mental health needs in New York State following the September 11th attacks. *Journal of Urban Health, 79,* 322-33 1.

Iruarrizaga, I., Miguel-Tobal, J.J., Cano-Vindel, A., & González, H. (2004). Consecuencias psicopatológicas tras el atentado terrorista del 11-M en Madrid en víctimas, familiares y allegados. *Ansiedad y Estrés, 10,* 195-206.

Kessler, R.C., Sonnega, A., Bromet, E., Hughes, M., & Nelson, C.B. (1995). Posttraumatic stress disorder in the National Comorbidity Survey. *Archives of General Psychiatry, 52,* 1048-1060.

Kilpatrick, D.G., Resnick, H.S., Freedy, J.R., Pelcovitz, D., Resick, P., Roth, S., & van der Kolk, B. (1998). The posttraumatic stress disorder field trial: Evaluation of the PTSD construct - Criteria A through E. In T. Widiger, A. Frances, H. Pincus, R. Ross, M. First, W. Davis, & M. Kline (Eds.), *DSM-IV Sourcebook* (Vol. 4, pp. 803-844). Washington, DC: American Psychiatric Press.

Marshall, R.D., Spitzer, R., & Liebowitz, M.R. (1999). Review and critique of the new *DSM-IV* diagnosis of acute stress disorder. *American Journal of Psychiatry, 156,* 1677-1685.

Matt, G.E., & Vázquez, C. (2006). *Psychological distress and resilience among distant witnesses of the 9/11 terrorist attacks: A natural experiment using multiple baseline and follow-up cohorts.* Manuscript submitted for publication.

McCarter, L., & Goldman, W. (2002). Use of psychotropics in two employee groups directly affected by the events of September 11. *Psychiatric Services, 53,* 1366-1368.

McNally, R.J., Bryant, R., & Ehlers, A. (2003). Does early psychological intervention promote recovery from traumatic stress? *Psychological Science in the Public Interest, 4,* 45-79.

Miguel-Tobal, J.J., Cano-Vindel, A., Iruarrizaga, I., González, H., & Galea, S. (2004). Consecuencias psicológicas de los atentados del 11-M en Madrid. Planteamiento general de los estudios y resultados en la población general. *Ansiedad y Estrés, 10,* 163-179.

Muñoz, M., Crespo, M., Pérez-Santos, E., & Vázquez, J.J. (2004). Presencia de síntomas de estrés agudo en la población general de Madrid en la segunda semana tras el atentado terrorista del 11 de Marzo de 2004. *Ansiedad y Estrés, 10,* 147-161.

Murphy, R.T., Wismar, K., & Freeman, K. (2003). Stress symptoms among African-American college students after the September 11, 2001 terrorist attacks. *Journal of Nervous and Mental Disease, 191,* 108-114.

Narrow, W.E., Rae, D.S., Robin, L.N., & Regier, D.A. (2002). Revised prevalence estimates of mental disorders in the United States: Using a clinical significance criterion to reconcile 2 surveys' estimates. *Archives of General Psychiatry, 59,* 115- 123.

Norris, F., Byrne, C. Diaz, E., & Kaniasty, K. (2001). 50,000 disaster victims speak: An empirical review of the empirical literature, 198 1–2001. Report for the National Center for PTSD and Center for Mental Health Services.

North, C., Nixon S., Shariat, S., Mallonee, S., McMillen, J., Spitzanagel, E., & Smith, E. (1999). Psychiatric disorders among survivors of the Oklahoma City bombing. *Journal of the American Medical Association, 282,* 755-762.

North, C.S., & Pfefferbaum, B. (2002). Research on the mental health effects of terrorism. *JAMA, 288,* 633-636.

North, C., Smith, E. & Spitznagel, E. (1994). Posttraumatic stress disorder in survivors of a mass shooting. *American Journal of Psychiatry, 151,* 82-88.

Office of Behavioral and Social Sciences Research. *Assessing the effects of the attacks on America.* Retrieved on August 30, 2002 from the National Institutes of Health Website: http:iobssr.od.nih.gov/Activities/911/ attack.htm/

Pérez Sales, P., Cervellón, P.,Vázquez, C., Vidales, D., & Gaborit, M. (2005). Posttraumatic factors and resilience: The role of shelter management and survivors' attitudes after the earthquakes in El Salvador (2001). *Journal of Applied Social Psychology, 15,* 368-382.

Rosenheck, R., & Fontana, A. (2003). Use of mental health services by veterans with PTSD after the terrorist attacks of September 11. *American Journal of Psychiatry, 160,* 1684-1690.

Rubin, G.J., Brewin, C.R., Greenberg, N., Simpson, J., & Wessely, S. (2005). Psychological and behavioural reactions to the bombings in London on 7 July 2005: Cross-sectional survey of a representative sample of Londoners. *Psychological Medicine, 331,* 606. (BMJ, doi:10.1136/bmj.38583.728484. 3A, published 26 August 2005).

Ruggiero, K.J., Del Ben, K., Scotti, J.R., & Rabalais, A.E. (2003). Psychometric properties of the PTSD Checklist-Civilian Version. *Journal of Traumatic Stress, 16,* 495-502.

Sampedro, J. (2004, March 19). 150,000 madrileños sufrirán trastornos psicológicos leves. *El País*, p. 30.

Schlenger, W.E., Caddell, J.M., Ebert, L., Jordan, B.K., Rourke, K.M., Wilson, D., Thalji, L., Dennis, J.M., Fairbank, J.A., & Kulka, R A. (2002). Psychological reactions to terrorist attacks: Findings from the National Study of Americans' Reactions to September 11. *JAMA, 288*, 581-588.

Schuster, M.A., Stein, B.D., Jaycox, L., Collins, R.L., Marshall, G.N., Elliott, M.N., Zhou, A.J., Kanouse, D.E., Morrison, J.L., & Berry, S.H. (2001). A national survey of stress reactions after the September 11, 2001, terrorist attacks. *New England Journal of Medicine, 345*, 1507-1512.

Shalev, A.Y. (2004). Further lessons from 9/11: Does stress equal trauma? *Psychiatry, 67*, 174-177.

Silver, R.C., Holman, E.A., McIntosh, D.N., Poulin, M., & Gil-Rivas, V. (2002). Nationwide longitudinal study of psychological responses to September 11. *JAMA, 288*, 1235-1244.

Southwick, S.M., & Charney, D.S. (2004). Responses to trauma: Normal reactions or pathological symptoms. *Psychiatry, 67*, 170-173.

Sprang, G. (1999). Post-disaster stress following the Oklahoma City bombing: An examination of three community groups. *Journal of Interpersonal Violence, 14*, 169-183.

Stein, B.D., Elliott, M.N., Jaycox, L., Collins, R.L., Berry, S.H., Klein, D.J., & Schuster, M.A. (2004). A national longitudinal study of the psychological consequences of the September 11, 2001 terrorist attacks: Reactions, impairment, and help-seeking. *Psychiatry, 67*, 105-117.

Stephenson, J. (2001). Medical, mental health communities mobilize to cope with terror's psychological aftermath. *JAMA, 286*, 1823-1825.

Vázquez, C. (2005). Stress reactions of the general population after the terrorist attacks of S11 (USA) and M11 (Madrid, Spain): Myths and realities. *Annuary of Clinical and Health Psychology, 1*, 9-25. (http://www.us.es/apcs/vol1esp.htm).

Vázquez, C., Cervellón, P., Pérez Sales, P., Vidales, D., & Gaborit, M. (2005). Positive emotions in earthquake survivors in El Salvador (2001). *Journal of Anxiety Disorders, 19*, 313-328.

Weathers, F.W., Litz, B.T., Herman, D.S., Huska, J.A., & Keane, T.M. (1993, October). *The PTSD Checklist: Reliability, validity and diagnostic utility.* Paper presented at the annual meeting of the International Society for Traumatic Stress Studies, San Antonio, TX.

Wessely, S. (2004). When being upset is not a mental problem. *Psychiatry, 67*, 153-157.

Psychiatric Aspects of Terrorist Violence: Northern Ireland 1969-1987

Peter S. Curran

ABSTRACT: For 18 years, Northern Ireland has suffered a changing pattern of civil disorder. Early years were marked by widespread sectarian rioting, shootings, and bombings, which heightened community tension and caused much social and commercial disruption. However, in recent years, terrorist organisations have been more selective in their acts of violence. There are methodological difficulties in assessing the psychological impact of civil disorder and terrorism. But, as well as can be judged from community surveys, hospital admissions and referral data, psychotropic drug usage, suicide and attempted suicide rates, and from assessment of the actual victims of violence, society has not 'broken down' nor has the impact been judged considerable. Possible explanations are discussed.

For almost 20 years there has been a campaign of terrorist violence waged in Northern Ireland. However, the casual visitor or tourist rarely witnesses, much less is liable to be the victim of, any act of violence, as it has become so sporadic and the targets of the terrorist's gun or bomb so selective. Indeed, the population is now far more likely to be injured or killed in a road traffic accident than by a bomb or a bullet.

Ireland has a long and turbulent history, with peaks of civil violence and disorder going back over centuries. Northern Ireland was conceived in, and delivered through, the threat of violence, but in no time in its history has the island had such a prolonged spell of civil violence as since 1969. Prior to the mid-1960s, Northern Ireland had been a comparatively insular backwater, largely forgotten about by Dublin and London, each sovereign parliament content to leave government to a devolved, local (Stormont) parliament presiding over two opposing communities. It was a highly polarised society—indeed, with institutionalised polarisation, educationally, occupationally, and culturally. All of this was to change in the late 1960s and what began originally as legitimate political and civil protest and unrest soon gave way to widespread street rioting, especially in the cities of Belfast and Derry. Those early years were marked by tremendous social upheaval and population shifts as thousands scurried to the comparative and necessary safety of the ghetto, within which the respective paramilitary organisations formed or were reactivated. Those ghetto interfaces in Belfast have now become the battlegrounds of inter-necine strife. Thousands demonstrated and counter-demonstrated in open confrontation, and whole streets were burned down. The British Army entered the scene initially to be greeted as peacemakers, but prompted the reactivation of the dormant Republican movement, which then reac-tivated Loyalist paramilitary movements, and the violence ineluctably spiraled. The Irish Republican Army (IRA) launched a campaign of bombing targets throughout Northern Ireland and Great Britain. Para-military feuding and sectarianism reigned. In the early 1970s the popula-tion was terrified by the campaign of nowarning or late-warning indis-criminate bombings, and by sectarian murder gangs killing people simply labelled by their actual or supposed political or religious associations. One atrocity provoked another, equally inhumane and gruesome, and the 18-year history has been pock-marked by some particular incidents of quite indescribable cruelty. Local political machinations and initiatives were abandoned, and finally direct rule from Westminster was resignedly imposed and government policy for some 10 years now has been to con-tain the situation to what Reginald Maudling, a former Home Secretary, once described as "the acceptable level of violence." The frequency and type of violence has changed with the passage of time. The number of explosions and weight of explosive used has been dramatically reduced. The number of shooting incidents per annum has dropped from a peak in 1972 of more than 10,500 incidents. As the violence has changed in type and quality over time, so has the population in its perceptions, attitudes, and hopes. The targets for, and numbers of, shootings have changed now, with the current republican policy of having less mass bombings and more selected targets of policemen and soldiers. Internecine murder gangs are less prevalent now than 15 years ago, so fewer people are now affected or immediately touched by violence than in the early part of this troubled period. The number of injuries to and deaths of civilians has markedly reduced to the politically 'acceptable level'. In 1969, there were 13 deaths. In 1972, 468 civilians, policemen, and soldiers were killed. Between 1973 and 1976 the average was 252 per year, but for the past 10 years the death rate has dropped to an annual total of approxi-mately 80 per year.

However, Northern Ireland cannot be considered a natural labora-tory for the study of violence and its effect on psychiatric morbidity. The issues are complex and the area has other particular problems. It is true that at times the situation has approximated to war but it has not been like a war where a largely united population faces a common enemy. Indeed, in the early 1970s, it had elements of a civil war, when paramilitary guerilla groups killed each other and whoever else got in the way, as they fought for supremacy and traditional territorial boundaries. Within recent history, there has been civil disorder and riot at massive public gatherings such as prevailed in America in the 1960s, or more recently in Great Britain as in Brixton, Toxteth, Tottenham, or Southall. Then, regrettably, there has been a litany of terrorist atrocities as gruesome as any perpetrated by the diverse other international terrorist groups. Terrorism aims to achieve political gain by terrorising the population but, in seeking to assess the psychological effect on the indigenous population and the victims of violence, one cannot ignore the fact that in Northern Ireland there are other stressors and significant psychosocial variables of importance. Besides these acts of terrorist violence and widespread civil strife and disorder, there exist the chronic ongoing problems of cultural and sectarian alienation and misunderstanding, constitutional ambiguity, poor social conditions in some areas, and severe unemployment.

Measurement of Psychological Effects

There are methodological difficulties in seeking to measure the psychological effects of terrorist violence.

1. Who to Study?

The nature of the population studied will affect estimates of impairment. Does one study the victims of violence who have gone to hospitals or their general practitioners (GPs) or to the law seeking compensation—all self-selecting samples of victims? Who or what is a victim is rather hard to define. If a 1000 lb car bomb explodes in Belfast's city centre, perhaps several thousand people are affected. Many flee home, perhaps to report nothing. Some will go to the public house. Some will go to the law. Some will go to hospitals where they may or may not receive or need treatment. Some are casual visitors who never return. In fact, a vulnerable person at home 5 miles away, hearing the same explosion or even watching it on television news, might react more adversely psychologically than some 18-year-old male who thoroughly enjoys the excitement.

2. The Violent Act

The nature of the violent act/stressor/life event is important, but the problem is its ranking. Surviving an assassination attempt, being 'kneecapped', kidnapped, or held captive, being caught in a bomb explosion, or living in a street with endemic rioting, petrol bombing, and community tension, makes the items we consider important in existing reliable and valid life-event schedules pale into comparative insignificance.

3. When to Study Victims

We recognise there are phases to psychological reactions and exactly when a person is examined or studied will often determine the clinical findings and phenomenology.

4. How to Measure

Researchers in Ireland and throughout the world have all used different tools for measurement of psychological impairment—the General Health Questionnaire (Cairns & Wilson, 1985), various psychometric tests, the presence or absence of post-traumatic stress disorder, ICD-9 traditional diagnoses, admission and referral rates to hospitals, drug-prescribing habits, and GP attendance rates.

5. Who Is Measuring

The perceptions of the examiners and their levels of expertise in measuring the psychological impact of violent acts differ and this may explain the remarkable variation between authors. Following the Tower of London bomb explosion, orthopaedic surgeons (Tucker & Lettin, 1975) from St Bartholomew's Hospital found that 4 out of the 37 victims had psychological symptoms (11%). Following the Old Bailey bomb explosion, other surgeons (Caro & Irving, 1973) from the same hospital found 24 out of 160 victims emotionally shocked (15%). A group from the Royal Victoria Hospital (Hadden et al., 1978), reporting on 1,532 consecutive victims of terrorist bombings, found 50% to be psychologically disturbed. Shenouda et al. (1980), detailing the casualty overload following the 1979 Southall riots, found most of the casualties "as being in a state of commotional shock". Perhaps the implication is that, in the immediate aftermath of a bomb, psychological disturbance is common if looked for, but will go largely undetected if not. This must have important implications for disaster planning services as much as for psychiatric services.

Admission and Referral Rates

Again, there are logistical problems, since changes in psychiatric referral and admission rates do not necessarily mean real changes in psychiatric morbidity. Patients may not be referred to psychiatry by GPs until their own treatment efforts have failed, perhaps a year later. Psychiatrists do not see those victims successfully treated by the GPs or those patients whose reactions spontaneously repair. Delayed reactions are known to occur. The availability of beds and services may affect rates of recorded morbidity. Victims of intimidation, abuse, and violence may migrate from the area. However, examining the international literature across wars, different arenas of terrorism, and instances of disorder and riot, certain themes seem to emerge.

During and after the 1975-1976 Lebanese civil war (Nasr et al., 1983), admissions to psychiatric hospitals decreased. Out-patient consultations fell dramatically, far more than could be explained by difficulties in transport or communications during the war. But, after the cessation of hostilities, out-patient consultations rebounded to more than could be coped with.

In May 1969 there was a week of racial rioting in Kuala Lumpur which left 172 dead and 415 injured. Over the next 6 months, there was no increase in admission, but there was a rebound increase in outpatient referrals (Tam & Simons, 1973). In 1968, following the assassination of Martin Luther King, there were 4 days of rioting in Baltimore. There was a sharp drop in admissions, with no rebound effect afterwards (Klee & Gorwitz, 1970). During the Algerian civil war (Porot, 1957), the Spanish civil war (Mira, 1939), and during World War II in England (Hemphill, 1941; Lewis 1942; Dohan, 1966), the evidence is of no increased demand for psychiatric services or beds.

In 1971 in two separate articles, Lyons, a general adult psychiatrist, and Fraser, a child psychiatrist, separately analysed the incidence of referrals and admissions at the time of the initial 1969 Belfast riots. Lyons noted no increase over the usual level in admissions, while Fraser, in a close geographical analysis of the data, noted no change in the number of admissions either from areas directly affected by the riots, or areas of intermediate disturbance. Lyons also looked at general practices and noted no change, or sometimes a reduction, in patients attending GPs' surgeries over a 6-week period of riot.

This survey of the literature provides evidence against an increase in admissions and referrals and possibly morbidity during civil disorder or war, although the evidence regarding out-patient referrals is contradictory, some sources implying a rebound increase later.

Psychotropic Drug Usage

Little has been written about the relationship between civil disorder and terrorism and the use of psychotropic drugs, except that by a Northern Irish group (King et al., 1982), who reported data on psychotropic-drug prescribing in the province from 1966 until 1980. In a detailed analysis, this group drew tentative conclusions about the influence of civil violence. They noted that in 1975, one person in eight of the adult population received psychotropic drugs, but this was no higher than in England or Sweden at the same time. Remembering that the peak years of civil violence and disorder in Northern Ireland were in the years 1969-1972, the trends of drug prescriptions over time were examined. They noted an annual 20% increase in tranquilliser prescribing from 1966 until 1969. But, from 1970 until 1976, the increase was only 10%, and so it was held that the peak years of civil violence in the years 1969-1972 had "no direct relationship to tranquilliser prescribing in the province as a whole". But that study was of the whole province, whereas most violence was centred in Belfast. In 1971, Fraser had carried out a detailed analysis of drug-prescription rates in Belfast at the time of the widespread 1969 Belfast riots. While he was cautious in his interpretation of the data, there seems no doubt that there was a highly significant increase then in tranquilliser-prescribing rates within the specific area of riot. The increase in tranquilliser-prescription rates varied from 26% in one general practice to 135% in another.

So, in urban areas where civil violence is concentrated there is possibly an increase in tranquilliser consumption with the risk of long-term dependency. But it must not be forgotten that within those same urban riot-torn areas there do exist other important sociodemographic variables (unemployment, low per capita income, overcrowding etc.) that may contribute towards tranquilliser consumption.

Parasuicide

Carstairs (1984) reported a 30% decrease in parasuicide rates in Poland during the Solidarity crisis. The evidence from Northern Ireland is conflicting. O'Malley (1972, 1975) noted an increase in parasuicide and attributed this to the stress of civil violence. However, Lyons & Bindal (1977), in another Belfast general hospital, found no evidence of any such relationship. Practising psychiatrists in Belfast would probably now agree that there is no significant trend between acts of terrorist violence and parasuicide and the experience seems to be that people take overdoses and cut themselves for the same reasons as elsewhere in the world. Furthermore, from ordinary consultation practice, the impression is that civil disorder and violence have not replaced the usual sources of human unhappiness and stress that lead to referral.

Suicide

Durkheim (1951) commented on the widespread observation of reduced suicide rates in the mid-19th century, in European countries affected by civil violence. He declared that the reduced suicide rate was "due not to the crisis but to the struggles it occasions. As they force men to close ranks and confront the common danger, the individual thinks less of himself and more of the common cause". In more modern times, Mira (1939) reported no increase in suicide during the Spanish civil war.

My own group (Curran et al., in prep.) has compared Northern Irish suicide rates with England and Wales. Traditionally, the suicide rate in Ireland has always been reportedly lower than in England and Wales. Throughout the UK, the rates of suicide have increased over the past 15 years, but in Northern Ireland they have increased more rapidly than in England and Wales—indeed, in one year (1983) overtaking. In 1972, Lyons described how the suicide rate in Northern Ireland in 1970 was almost half of the annual rate of the 3 years prior to the onset of widespread civil disorder and terrorism. In explanation, he opted for the theory of an inverse relationship, claiming that the reduced incidence of depressive illness and suicide was because of the opportunity to externalise aggressive impulses. In the years 1970-1972, when the suicide rate dramatically dropped, the homicide rate rapidly increased. This was an immediately attractive theory which received much interest. However,

Heskin (1980), and other methodologists, have harshly criticised Lyons' data and his interpretations. While not denying that Lyons' conclusions might still be valid, regardless of the methods by which they were drawn, it might equally well be argued that the reason for such a dramatic fall in 1970 was because, for the 3 or 4 years prior to that, the suicide rate in Northern Ireland had, for other reasons, actually increased when, at the same time, the rate in England and Wales continued gradually and progressively to decline. It may be that, during the prodromal period of tension (1967-1969) and before the violence erupted, the suicide rate in Northern Ireland actually increased.

However, a certain common theme seems to have emerged. Judging from hospital referrals and admission data, suicide and attempted-suicide rates, the practices of psychoactive-drug prescriptions, and community-based studies, as have been described by Cairns & Wilson (1985), the campaign of terrorist violence does not seem to have resulted in any obvious increase in psychiatric morbidity.

Reasons for There Being No Marked Increase In Morbidity

Human beings are certainly resilient and adaptive, but possibly various explanations are required to explain the finding of no obvious general increase in psychiatric morbidity in the community.

1. Non-Reporting

Possibly, some people affected by feelings caused by the reality of civil disorder or an act of terrorism assume there is nothing that can be done for their feelings, and do not report to the caring agencies.

2. Migration

Perhaps the psychologically vulnerable and affected selectively migrate from the area of disturbance over a period of time and are lost to epidemiology.

3. Denial and Habituation

An individual may show a reaction of denial, whether as part of a phasic reaction as outlined by Horowitz (1976), or as a more fixed reaction as suggested by Cairns & Wilson (1985). Lyons (1979) considers habituation responsible for the apparently low levels of psychopathology.

4. Latency Period

Perhaps cases may not be detected because there exists a latency period of some months, as noted by Porot (1957) in Algeria. Belfast surgeons (Kennedy & Johnston, 1975) have remarked "we have seen the bilateral amputee remain calm and co-operative and stoical in the protective hospital environment, only to break down on discharge from hospital". However, in my experience, delayed reactions are comparatively rare, despite claims from the American literature that post-traumatic stress disorder can appear late in American Vietnam veterans.

5. Catharsis

Participation in violence may have a cathartic effect. Lyons (1972) noted the general decrease in recorded depression in Belfast during a troubled year and drew on previous observations (Freud, 1952; Abraham, 1953) that depressive illness can be caused by the inhibition of aggressive impulses and responses to frustration. Such a theory would explain depression being endemic in societies where overt aggression is culturally disapproved of. Lyons had claimed a reduction in male depression in Belfast, and particularly in the areas of most severe rioting, which compared with a sharp increase in male depression in the neighbouring peaceful county of Down.

6. The Already-ill May Improve Psychologically

It is a common observation in psychiatric practice that certain patients with neurotic symptoms seem to cope better when faced with external stress. Many writers have so commented. Mira (1939), reflecting upon the Spanish war, noted "I have the impression that many depressed mentally ill people were better when confronted with the actual demands and situations that arose during the war than when they were concerned only with their conflicts". It might be supposed that war and civil unrest and terrorist acts would cause psychological upset and insecurity as the population awaits hostility or feels helpless and at the mercy of coming events. It might be expected that a patient with a weak ego and unstable psychological equilibrium would peak with anxiety, but perhaps this is not so. Ierodiakonou (1970) reported on 14 existing patients under psychotherapy when the Cyprus civil war erupted. Only 4 of the 14 patients, two being phobic and two being obsessionally neurotic, felt more insecure and fearful. The other ten felt more calm, were without fear or anxiety, and actually reported increased self-confidence with a compensatory optimism, hoping the war would change them for the better. It may be that patients who develop affective symptoms based on some personal intrapsychic conflict will attribute them to the presence of external danger rather than the true source.

7. Cohesion

Currently, in Northern Ireland, the frequency of terrorist acts and civil disorder and riot is only a fraction of what pertained 10 or 15 years ago. It has to be recognised that it may be only a very small proportion of the total population who have ever actually been victims of terrorist acts. In my own research (Kee et al., 1987), we found that only half the victims had emotional reactions lasting longer than 3 months and amounting, in our opinion, to psychiatric-illness states. It has to be considered that the psychological ill effect on that small number of actual victims of terrorist acts might, incredible though it seems, be buffered by a state of rebound psychological well-being in the rest of the community. The evidence for this possibility lies in Greenley et al.'s (1975) report of the research opportunity afforded to his group, which had already been engaged in a community survey of mental health in New Haven, Connecticut. For the purposes of the original study, sex, race, and area of residence (urban/suburban) of 938 persons had been noted, and they had been psychologically appraised. Severe rioting with arson, looting, assault, and vandalism occurred in the following year, specifically in the inner urban, largely black, area with the surburban, largely white, area untouched.

Suburban male Whites felt significantly better psychologically both during and after the riot 2 years later. Suburban female Whites felt no different during the rioting, but significantly better psychologically after the rioting. Among the urban population, black and white, male and female, no group felt worse. In fact, the black women felt better psychologically during the rioting. While these results must be always interpreted within the political, social, and cultural forces pertaining in the USA around 1968, they do seem to suggest that riot can have beneficial psychological effect, possibly through collective processes, including group cohesion. It may very well be that there is a balance of effects, beneficial and adverse, within a population. A certain number of people develop psychological distress as might be expected of those who witness terrifying situations or tragedies or catastrophies, but remarkably, a larger number may actually improve psychologically.

This trend has been noted elsewhere. Fogelson (1970), reflecting upon the American 1960s riots, noted "the outpouring of fellow feeling, of mutual respect and common concern . . . camaraderie . . . carnival spirit . . . exhilaration so intense as to border on jubilation . . . a sense of pride, purpose and accomplishment . . . their common predicament revealed in the rioting, blacks looked again at one and other and saw only brothers". And so it may very well be and have been in Northern Ireland. During rioting and spells of sectarian disorder, following killings of the most horrific nature, certain subpopulations and communities may bind together in a sense of common purpose and common outrage, just as happened in World War II, in the London Blitz, or in the Spanish civil war, when people felt united against a common enemy. Maybe, in the Belfast ghettos, there is a feeling of a real or indeed a supposed common enemy, whether it be the British, the Irish, the Catholics, the Protestants, the Army, the police or whoever. Identification and feeling 'one of us' against 'them' may defend each population and its members against overt psychological disturbance in the face of chronic civil disorder and tension, sectarianism, and acts of terrorist violence.

References

ABRAHAM, K. (1953) *Selected Papers on Psychoanalysis*. New York: Basic Books.

CAIRNS, E. & WILSON, R. (1985) Psychiatric aspects of violence in Northern Ireland. *Stress Medicine, 1,* 193201.

CARO, D. & IRVING, M. (1973) The Old Bailey bomb explosion. *The Lancet, 1,* 1433-1435.

CARSTAIRS, G. M. (1984) Mental health and the environment in developing countries. In *Mental Health and the Environment* (.ed. H. L. Freeman). London: Churchill Livingstone.

DOHAN, F. C. (1966) Wartime changes in hospital admissions: schizophrenia. *Acta Psychiatrica Scandinavica,* 42, 1-23.

DURKHEIM, E. (1951) *Suicide.* Translated by l. A. Spaulding & G. Simpson. Glencoe, Illinois: Free Press (MacMillan).

FOGELSON, R. M. (1970) Violence and grievances: reflections on the 1960s riots. *Journal* of *Social Issues, 26*, 141-163.

FRASER, R. M. (1971) The cost of commotion: an analysis of the psychiatric sequelae of the 1969 Belfast riots. *British Journal* of *Psychiatry, 118,* 257-264.

FREUD, S. (1952) *Mourning and melancholia: collected papers* (ed. J. Strachey) vol. 4. London: Hogarth Press.

GREENLEY, J. R., GILLESPIE, D. P. & LINDENTHAL, J. J. (1975) A race riot's effects on psychological symptoms. *Archives of General Psychiatry,* 32, 1189-1195.

HADDEN, W. A., RUTHERFORD, W. H. & MERRETT, J. D. (1978) The injuries of terrorist bombing: a study of 1532 consecutive victims. *British Journal* of *Surgery, 65*, 525-531.

HEMPHILL, R. E. (1941) The influence of the war on mental disease: a psychiatric study. *Journal* of *Mental Science, 87,* 170-182.

HESKIN, K. (1980) Northern Ireland: a psychological analysis. Dublin: Gill and MacMillan.

HOROWITZ, M. J. (1976) Diagnosis and treatment of stress response syndromes: general principles. In *Emergency and Disaster Management* (eds H. J. Parad, H. L. Resnik & L. G. Parad). Bowie, Maryland: The Charles Press Publishers.

IERODIAKONOU, C. S. (1970) The effect of a threat of war on neurotic patients in psychotherapy. *American Journal of Psychotherapy, 24,* 643-651.

KEE, M., BELL, P., LODGHREY, G. C., RODDY, R. J. & CURRAN, P. S. (1987) Victims of violence: a demographic and clinical study. *Medicine, Science and the Law,* 27, 241-247.

KENNEDY, T. & JOHNSTON, G. W. (1975) Civilian bomb injuries. In *Surgery of Violence* (ed. Martin Ware). London: BMA publication.

KING, D. J., GRIFFTTHS, K., REILLY, P. M. & MERRETT, J. D. (1982) Psychotropic drug use in Northern Ireland, 1966-1980: prescribing trends, inter- and intra-regional comparisons and relationship to demographic and socioeconomic variables. *Psychological Medicine, 12*, 819-833.

KLEE, G. D. & GORWITZ, K. (1970) Effects of the Baltimore riots on psychiatric hospital admissions. *Mental Hygiene, 54*, 447-449.

LEWIS, A. (1942) Incidence of neurosis in England under war conditions. *The Lancet, ii,* 175-183.

LYONS, H. A. (1971) Psychiatric sequelae of the Belfast riots. *British Journal of Psychiatry, 118,* 265-273.

_____ (1972) Depressive illness and aggression in Belfast. *British Medical Journal, i,* 342-345.

_____ & BINDAL, K. K. (1977) Attempted suicide in Belfast. *Journal of the Irish Medical Association, 70,* 328-332.

_____ (1979) Civil violence—the psychological aspects. *Journal of Psychosomatic Research, 23,* 373-393.

MIRA, E. (1939) Psychiatric experience in the Spanish war. *British Medical Journal, i,* 1217-1220.

NASR, S., RACY, J. & FLAHERTY, J. A. (1983) Psychiatric effects of the civil war in Lebanon. *Psychiatric Journal* of *the University of Ottawa, 8,* 208-212.

O'MALLEY, P. P. (1972) Attempted suicide before and after the communal violence in Belfast, August 1969 - a preliminarv study. *Journal of the Irish Medical Association, 65,* 109- 113.

_____ (1975) Attempted suicide, suicide and communal violence. *Journal* of *the Irish Medical Association, 68,* 103-109.

POROT, M. (1957) *Les retentissements psychopathologiques des evenments d'Algerie. Press Medicale, 65,* 801-803.

SHENOUDA, N. A., GREIG, A. D. & DIGNAN, A. P. (1980) Casualty overload from the Southall riots. *British Medical Journal, 281,* 975.

TAN, ENG-SEONG & SIMONS, R. C. (1973) Psychiatric sequelae to a civil disturbance. *British Journal* of *Psychiatry, 122,* 57-63.

TUCKER, K. & LETTIN, A. (1975) The Tower of London explosion. *British Medical Journal, iii,* 287-289.

Peter S. Curran, MRCPsych, Consultant Psychiatrist, Mater Infirmorum Hospital, Crumlin Road, Belfast BT14 6AB, Northern Ireland

Section II: Continuous Trauma Paradigm

Multiple Traumatisation as a Risk Factor of Post-Traumatic Stress Disorder

Nadežda Savjak

Department of Psychology, University of Banja Luka

ABSTRACT: Paper presents a part of results obtained in 1998 within action study of the psychological effects of war traumatisation in Republika Srpska. Special attention is paid to the additional impact of multiple exposure to war sufferings regarding the degree of the traumatisation (the loss of loved ones, direct life threat, the participation in combats, and the testimony of the death of other people). 229 persons were assessed in 8 towns of Republika Srpska. The comparison of the results of refugees and domicile persons at the Reaction Index—Revised speaks in favour of their significantly higher vulnerability even three years after the end of war. Total degree of the traumatisation, as well as the symptoms of intrusion, avoidance, and hyper-arousal are significantly more frequent. In 42.5% of refugees (in relation to 26.7% of domicile persons) there is PTSD risk. The intensification of criteria proves that 17% of refugees are at high risk (in relation to 5.2% of the domiciled). It is obvious that refuge presents a traumatic event for many people, and not only a chronic burden. The results suggest that the effect of direct jeopardy, combat stress, and the testimony of somebody else's death fade in time, but that the culmination of tangible, social, and human losses in refuge is a serious risk factor for mental health.

Introduction

During the war in Bosnia and Hercegovina adults and children were often directly and indirectly exposed to a broad spectrum of traumatic or severely stressful events and circumstances. About one third of the population of the Republika Srpska (420,000) are refugees or internally displaced persons. The majority of men spent several years on the frontlines. About 12,000 persons were killed and several thousand people were declared "missing". After the loss of a nuclear family member or close persons, direct threat to life, wounding or witnessing violence, life goes on in a very unstable socio-economic environment.

Numerous researchers reported that levels of war-related exposure to trauma and extreme adversity are associated with an increased risk for posttraumatic stress disorder-PTSD (Kleber & Brom, 1992; Cheung, 1994; Malekzai et al., 1996; Joseph et al., 1997; Blair, 2000).

After direct and indirect exposure to high-magnitude trauma, the stressful and protracted post-war period came. We face the long lasting consequences of the traumatic war experiences, then chronic stresses which originate from the destroyed socio-economic and physical infrastructure, economic slump, unemployment, political instability, and from the uncertain future.

The existence within this area goes beyond the concepts of crisis and stress. One could say that it is *a crisis of life style.* As the time is passing, the consequences of cumulative exposure to traumatic events, unprocessed experiences and postwar adversities become more apparent (depression, suicides, complicated grief reactions, psychosomatic complaints, substance abuse, family violence).

Social support is a very significant protective factor in coping with war-related traumatic experiences (Kleber & Brom, 1992; Shalev et al., 1998). Unfortunately, except for family support, which is a powerful clue in our society, there are many reasons for the suspicion that the educational, social and health sectors were paid proper and sufficient attention to mental health promotion, prevention, treatment and rehabilitation of traumatised war victims. The system of the mental health care services had many shortcomings even before the war. All resources were directed toward the development of the mental health services on the secondary level of health care. The vast majority of the mental health professionals were attached to the psychiatric hospitals and to the psychiatric wards of general hospitals. Mental health services were functioning within the medical model of health care. There are no Centres for crisis intervention, clubs, group work, self-help groups, SOS line, etc. Concepts and practice community psychology and psychiatry had no solid grounds in the reality of the Republika Srpska.

Problem

Studies of PTSD among Vietnam veterans reported that 10-20 years after demobilisation a high percentage of them (15.2%–23.9%) met DSM criteria for this kind of disorder (Kulka & Schlenger, 1994; Kleber & Brom, 1992; Joseph et al., 1997).

Apparently, displacement as accumulated loss presents an even more powerful risk factor of PTSD occurrence and persistence. In a sample of Afghan and Cambodian refugees who live in the USA, the reported PTSD prevalence ranges from 45% to 86% (Carlson & Rosser-Hogan, 1993; Cheung, 1994; Malekzai et al., 1996; Blair, 2000). According to the results, accumulated traumas (especially the death of close persons) and stressors, and the adaptation of a new social environment, significantly increase vulnerability (Joseph et al., 1997).

There is not much data on PTSD prevalence in adults within the territory of former Yugoslavia. However, reported PTSD prevalence among refugees in collective centres was ranging from 26% to 35% (Harvard Program in Refugee Trauma, 1996; Powell et al., 2000), and among Croatian soldiers it ranged from 14% to 31% (Gustovic-Ercegovac & Komar, 1994). Posttraumatic stress is also present within the non-displaced population: three years after the war in Bosnia and Herzegovina, 10-18% of that population in Banja Luka and Sarajevo—i.e. those who were not displaced—suffer from PTSD (Powell et al., 2000). In the present contribution we are interested in the effect of displacement and accumulated war-related traumas on the persistence of PTSD symptoms in the postwar circumstances in the Republika Srpska.

Hypotheses

1. We expect the risk of chronic PTSD in *displaced persons* to be significantly higher than in those who were not displaced, and symptoms to be significantly more frequent.

2. *Displaced persons* who experienced (a) the loss of close persons or (b) direct life threat or (c) witnessed somebody's death or (d) had combat exposure would more frequently have PTSD symptoms than *non-displaced persons* who experienced similar traumatic events.

3. *Displaced persons* who experienced (a) the loss of close persons or (b) direct life threat or (c) witnessed somebody's death or (d) had combat exposure would more frequently have PTSD symptoms than *displaced persons* who had not experienced those traumatic events.

Method

In 1998, the Foundation for Training, Research and Public Works of the Republika Srpska supported by the World Bank, engaged a team of clinical psychologists for the project "Demobilisation and Reintegration". They conducted an actionable research of the traumatisation level in participants of the employment program, mainly refugees and veterans, and provided them with psycho-educational training and counseling. Out of the extensive research project, only the results relevant to the observation of the effect of displacement and other war related events on the persistence of PTSD are extracted here. The assessment was conducted in groups (20-30 subjects). Subjects were promised full anonymity. We advised them that the results of the study will not assist them in terms of finding employment and that the analysis of group results will be used in the creation of the psychological assistance program.

Sample

The selection of the sample of 299 unemployed subjects was performed by the Employment Bureaus. All subjects—180 males (78.6%) and 49 females (21.4%)—were assessed with the extensive psychodiagnostic battery. Less than a half of the sample—94 (41%)—were refugees and displaced persons (Mean age = 36.2; SD = 7.34). The average age of 135 non-displaced subjects is lower (Mean age = 32.9; SD = 5.36). About 45% of participants were soldiers. Most of the subjects have completed secondary school (78.2%). About a half of the sample (51.8%) were married.

Most of the participants were directly exposed to a broad spectrum of potentially traumatic or severely stressful war-related events and circumstances:

1. Death of loved one or close persons
- child - 2.6%
- spouse - 3.9%
- father - 13.5%
- mother - 5.7%
- sibling - 13.1%
- realtives - 40.2%
- close friend - 51.1%

2. Direct life threat during the war - 65.9%

3. Physical injury and wounding
- personal wounding - 23.6%
- serious personal wounding - 7.4%
- child - 3.1%
- father - 5.7%
- sibling - 13.1%
- relative(s) - 30.6%
- close friend - 46.3%

4. Witnessing violence
  − witnessing the wounding of other person(s) - 62.9%
  − witnessing the death of other persons - 53.7%
  − witnessing the death of soldier(s) in combat - 45.4%
  − witnessing the wounding of soldier(s) in combat - 47.2%
5. Killing enemy soldier in combat - 10.5 %
6. Captivity during war - 5.7%
7. Separation from family members due to war - 21.0%
8. Serious marital conflicts after war - 7.0%
9. Serious conflicts with friends - 5.2%
10. Divorce - 6.1%
11. Substance abuse of close family member after war - 7.9%
12. Inadequate living conditions - 24.0%
13. Job conflict with senior - 13.5%

About 40 percent of the participants and 52 percent of the refugees underwent accumulated losses of close family members.

Instruments

Inventory of life events includes 65 stressful traumatic war-related and post-war experiences, facilitating the identification of cumulative exposure (Pynoos et al., 1998).

The Reaction Index-Revised (Pynoos et al., 1998) is a 17-item self-report scale of posttraumatic stress symptoms experienced during the past month. The scale is an updated version of the widely used UCLA Reaction Index (Pynoos et al., 1987), and is consistent with DSM-IV PTSD criteria. Its 17 items assess the presence of symptoms in the last month, to be answered on a standard 5-point Likert-type rating scale (0=never, 1=rarely, 2=sometimes, 3=often, 4=almost always), keeping in mind the traumatic experience (Criterion A). The authors reported high internal consistency (Chronbach's Alpha = .92) and moderate to strong convergent validity (.37–.63). The correlation of this instrument with CAPS is reported as $r = 0.929$ and diagnostic validity was 0.9 (Blanchard et al., 1996). The authors identify a total scale score of 35 or above as falling within the clinically distressed range.

Results

The results reported that symptoms of intrusion, avoidance and hyper-arousal in the displaced group are significantly more frequent over the past three years after the war than in a population of non-displaced persons (Table 1). The first hypothesis is confirmed.

Table 1. Differences in the means of the total score of PTSD and partial scores in displaced and non-displaced groups

	Non-displaced (N=135)	Refugees Displaced (N=94)	T	Significance
	Means			
Total PTSD Score	18.88	29.83	6.55	p<0.01
Intrusion	4. 84	8.06	5.87	p<0.01
Avoidance	8.31	12.38	5.50	p<0.01
Hyper-arousal	5.37	9.40	6.29	p<0.01

Persons considered at risk for posttraumatic stress disorder were those who fulfilled the DSM IV criteria by answering the questions with "2," "3" or "4" as follows:
- Criterion B—symptoms of re-experiencing (on at least 1 out of 5 items)
- Criterion C—symptoms of avoidance (on at least 3 out of 7 items)
- Criterion D—symptoms of hyper-arousal (on at least 2 out of 5 items)

In assessing persons at *high risk* for PTSD, the same principle was used, although only the answers of level "3" and "4" were considered.

On the basis of the self-report, 42.5% of the displaced subjects (compared to 26.7% of non-displaced) were at risk for PTSD according to DSM IV criteria.

Approximately 17% of the displaced group, as opposed to 5.2% of non-displaced subjects, are at *high risk* of PTSD.

Table 2. Differences in the risk of PTSD in displaced and non-displaced groups

	Non-Displaced (N = 135)	Refugees Displaced (N = 94)	Chi^2	Significance
	Percent / N			
Subjects at Risk of PTSD	26.7%	42.5%		
YES	36	40	6.29	p<0.02
NO	99	54		
Subjects at High Risk of PTSD	5.2%	17.0%	7.34	p<0.01
YES	7	16		
NO	128	78		

Exclusive of displacement, subjects at risk for PTSD (N=76, i.e., 33.2% of all participants) had experienced multiple traumatisation (an average of 8.4 war events).

Approximately one half of this group reported more than 8 of potentially traumatic events (Table 3).

The analysis of statistically significant differences in terms of frequency of PTSD symptoms between refugees and non-displaced (Scheffe's test of multiple comparisons in Table 4) confirms hypothesis 2 on the whole. There are statistically significant differences in the level of the traumatisation between displaced subjects who experienced (a) the loss of the close persons or (b) combat exposure or (c) direct life threat or (d) witnessing death and non-displaced subjects who underwent the same war events.

Table 3. The exposure to potentially traumatic and stressful war and postwar experiences in the group of subjects at risk for PTSD

Number of Traumatic And Stress Events	F N = 78	Percent	Cumulative Percent
1	3	3.9	3.9
2	3	3.9	7.8
3	8	10.5	18.3
4	9	11.8	30.1
5	3	3.9	34.0
6	7	9.2	43.2
7	3	3.9	47.1
8	3	3.9	51.0
9	6	7.9	58.8
10	3	3.9	62.7
11	5	6.5	69.2
12	5	6.5	75.7
13	5	6.5	82.2
14	3	3.9	86.1
15	3	3.9	90.0
16	2	2.6	92.6
18	3	3.9	96.5
20	2	2.6	100.0

But our findings suggest that exposure to direct life threat, combat exposure and witnessing death in refugees and displaced persons (multiple traumatisation) does not lead to more frequent symptoms three years after war. We found the level of PTSD symptoms in refugees and displaced persons only in the case of the death of loved one (close persons).

There were no statistically significant differences in the level of PTSD symptoms between non-displaced subjects who were and were not exposed to the death of close persons or (b) a direct life threat or (c) combat exposure or (d) witnessing death. Accordingly, only hypothesis 3a is confirmed.

Table 4. Cumulative effects of war events during displacement: total PTSD scores

TRAUMATIC EVENT		NON – DISPLACED		REFUGEES DISPLACED	
		Exposure To Traumatic Events		Exposure To Traumatic Events	
		NO	YES	NO	YES
		Group 1	Group 2	Group 3	Group 4
Loss Close Persons	N	77	58	51	43
	M	18.37*	18.07*	25.94*	34.33
	SD	12.44	10.99	11.93	11.08
		F Ratio = 16.92, F Prob.000 df= 228			
Combat Exposure	N	73	62	45	49
	M	17.60*	19.05*	29.12	28.77
	SD	11.22	12.52	11.23	13.25
		F Ratio= 13.18, F Prob. 0000 df=228			
Direct Life Threat	N	50	85	28	66
	M	17.65*	18.57*	30.52	28.27
	SD	17.65	18.58	12.11	12.35
		F Ratio = 13.31, F Prob. 000 df= 228			
Witnessing Death	N	69	66	38	56
	M	17.08*	19.44*	27.38	30.91
	SD	10.68	12.82	12.29	12.13
		F Ratio = 14.19, F Prob. 000 df =228			

*means that are statistically different from the means reported in group 4

Discussion

Refugee experiences during the war are obviously a serious risk factor for PTSD occurrence and persistence. The symptoms of intrusion, avoidance and hyper-arousal in refugees are significantly more frequent three years after the war than in a population of non-displaced persons.

Displacement itself presents an accumulation of material, psychological and social losses. The loss of close persons, especially family members, obviously increases vulnerability, i. e., leads to more frequent PTSD symptoms, particularly in the refugees and displaced persons. The significant effect of this painful experience on the frequency of PTSD symptoms three years after the war can be explained by:

- The effect of frequent postwar stressors and secondary adversities that occurred after refuge and displacement, which became "triggers" in the process of reactivating the original traumatic experiences (Blair, 2000; Blanchard et al., 1996; Vlajković, 1988; Vlajković et al., 1997; Pynoos et al., 1998).

- Struggle to meet basic personal and family needs can act as a barrier to processing past experiences and aggravate normal mourning and coping with loss (Rando, 1993).

- Loss reminders, "empty situations" and secondary adversities after the death of close persons are probably more frequent than trauma reminders (reminders of immediate life threat, witnessing violence or combat experiences).

The present results show that additional exposure to direct life danger, combat experiences, and witnessing death in the displaced population does not, in most cases, increase vulnerability three years after the end of the war. The longlasting traumatogenic effects of the exposure to those events are not so obvious either within refugees, or within the non-displaced group. It seems that, except in the case of traumatic death of a loved one, the impact of certain war-related traumas fades as time goes on.

This somewhat contradicts the findings of other researchers on the impact of cumulative war experiences, particularly when they consider the effects of witnessing violence (Kleber & Brom, 1992; Joseph et al., 1997; Blair, 2000; Cheung, 1994).

It should not be forgotten that the non-existence of statistically significant differences in terms of the frequency of symptoms still does not show the non-existence of differences in terms of the severity of symptoms and their impact on the mental health. Symptoms that appear could rarely be very intensive and can seriously disturb psychosocial functioning.

Conclusion

Psychological consequences of war cannot be reduced only to PTSD. But these findings provide important indications of possible and practical interventions in war areas. In the creation of the programs of psychosocial support in community and clinical work, one should pay special attention to a very vulnerable group, i.e., displaced persons who have experienced the death of close persons. Unfortunately, we can say, with no doubt, that current resources and their networks are not capable—along with the number of mental health professionals, the quality of their training, or the diversity of established social and health services—to meet the post-war needs in the field of mental health of the traumatised population in the Republika Srpska. There is an ongoing, but quite slow, reconstruction of the organization of mental health and social services. Hopefully, Centres planned for mental health will be community-oriented and prevention-focused.

References

Blair, G.R. (2000). Risk factors associated with PTSD and major depression among Cambodian refugees in Utah. *Health & Social Work, 25* (1), 23-30.

Blanchard, E. B., Jones-Alexander, J., Buckley, T. C., Forneris, C. A. (1996). Psychometric properties of the PTSD Checklist (PCL). *Behaviour Research and Therapy, 34*(8), 669-673.

Cheung, P. (1994). Post traumatic stress among Cambodian refugees in New Zealand. *International Journal of Social Psychiatry, 40* (1), 17-26.

Dijagnostički i statisticki priručnik za duševne poremećaje DSM-IV. (1996). Jastrebarsko, Naklada Slap.

Gustovic-Ercegovac, A., Komar, Z. (1994). *Socijalna integracija hrvatskih vojnika sa problemima prilagodbe.* Zagreb, Institut za primijenjena drustvena istraživanja.

Harvard Program in Refugee Trauma, Harvard School of Public Health, Harvard Medical School and Ruke NGO. (1996). *Trauma and Disability: Long-term Recovery of Bosnian Refugees.* Zagreb.

Joseph S., Williams R., Yule W. (1997). *Understanding Post-traumatic Stress—A psychosocial Perspective on PTSD and Treatment.* London, John Wiley & Sons.

Kleber, R. J., Brom, D. (1992). *Coping with trauma: theory, prevention and treatment.* Amsterdam, Swets and Zeitlinger.

Kulka, A. R., Schlenger, W. (1994). Survey Research and Field Design for the Study of Post-Traumatic Stress Disorder. In *Trauma and Healing under War Conditions.* Zagreb, WHO.

McFarlane, A. (2000). Posttraumatic Stress Disorder: A model of the longitudinal course and the role of risk factors. *Journal of Clinical Psychiatry, 61* (51), 15-20.

Malekzai, A. S. B., Niazi, J. M., Paige, S. R., Hendricks, S. E. (1996). Modification of CAPS-1 for diagnosis of PTSD in Afghan refugees. *Journal of Traumatic Stress, 9*(4), 891-893.

Powell, S., Rosner, R., Butollo, W. (2000). Obrasci bijega. Izvještaj Uredu federalnog vladinog komesara za povratak izbjeglica, reintegraciju i povezanu rekonstrukciju u Bosni i Hercegovini. Sarajevo.

Pynoos, R., Layne, C. M., Saltzman, R., Sandler, I. (1998). Priručnik za rad sa adolescentima traumatizovanim u ratu. Banjaluka, UNICEF—Republički prosvjetno pedagoški zavod.

Pynoos, R. S., Rodriguez, N., Steinberg, A., M., Stuber, M., Fredericks, C. (1999). *Reaction-Index-Revised.* (Unpublished psychological test). Los Angeles, University of California.

Rando, T. A. (1993). *Treatment of complicated mourning.* Champaign, IL: Research Press.

Shalev, A.Y., Freedman, S., Peri, T., Brandes, D., Sahar, T., Orr, S., Pitman, R. (1998). Prospective study of posttraumatic stress disorder and depression following trauma. *American Journal of Psychiatry; 155*, 630-637.

Vlajkovié, J. (1998). *Životne krize i njihovo prevazilaženje.* Beograd, Plato.

Vlajkovié, J., Srna, J., Kondié, K., Popovié, M. (1997). *Psihologija izbeglištva.* Beograd, Nauka.

Mental Health and Resiliency Following 44 Months of Terrorism: A Survey of an Israeli National Representative Sample

Avi Bleich[†1,2], Marc Gelkopf[*†1,2], Yuval Melamed[1] and Zahava Solomon[3]

Address: [1]Lev Hasharon Mental Health Center, PO Box 90000, Netanya 42100, Israel (affiliated to the Sackler Faculty of Medicine, Tel-Aviv University, Israel), [2]NATAL: The Israel Trauma Center for Victims of Terror and War, Israel and [3]Shappel School of Social Work and Adler Research Center, Tel Aviv University, Israel

* Corresponding author †Equal contributors

ABSTRACT: *Background*: Israeli citizens have been exposed to intense and ongoing terrorism since September 2000. We previously studied the mental health impact of terrorism on the Israeli population (Bleich et al., 2002), however the long-term impact of ongoing terrorism has not yet been examined. The present study evaluated the psychological sequelae of 44 months of terrorism in Israel, and sought to identify factors that may contribute to vulnerability and resilience. *Methods*: This was a telephone survey using strata sampling of 828 households, which reached a representative sample of 702 adult Israeli residents (84.8% contact rate). In total, 501 people (60.5%) agreed to participate. The methodology was similar to that of our previous study. Exposure to terrorism and other traumatic events, number of traumatic stress-related symptoms (TSRS), percentage of respondents with symptom criteria for post-traumatic stress disorder (PTSD), traumatic stress (TS) resiliency and feelings of depression, anxiety, optimism, sense of safety, and help-seeking were the main outcome measures. *Results*: In total, 56 participants (11.2%) were directly exposed to a terrorist incident, and 101 (20.2%) had family members or friends exposed. Respondents reported a mean ± SD of 5.0 ± 4.5 TSRS; 45 (9%) met symptom criteria for PTSD; and 72 (14.4%) were TS-resilient. There were 147 participants (29.5%) who felt depressed, 50 (10.4%) felt anxious, and almost half (235; 47%) felt life-threatening danger; 48 (9.7%) felt the need for professional help. Women and people of Arab ethnicity had more TSRS, more PTSD, and less TS resiliency. Injury following a life-threatening experience, a major stressful life event, and a major loss of income were associated with PTSD. Immigrant status, lower education, low sense of safety, low sense of social support, high societal distress, and injury following life-threatening experiences were associated with TSRS. TSRS did not increase with exposure severity. This study revealed less depression and functional impairment, similar rates of PTSD, increased help-seeking and poorer TSRS and TS resiliency than our initial study, 2 years previously. *Discussion*: The response of people in Israel to 4 years of terrorism is heterogeneous. Vulnerability factors change over time; Arab ethnicity, immigrant status and less education, not found to be risk factors in our previous study, were found in the present study to contribute to trauma-related distress. Prior experience of highly stressful events increases vulnerability to adverse psychological effects of terror.

Background

Since late September 2000, when the Al-Aqsa Intifada (the second Palestinian uprising) erupted, Israel has experienced repeated deadly terror attacks, which have claimed large numbers of civilian casualties, disrupted daily life, and created an atmosphere of fear and insecurity. By May 2004, 1,030 people had been killed, and 5,788 injured in more than 13,000 terrorist attacks [1]. Approximately 0.1% of the population was injured or killed—an equivalent percentage in the USA would equate to some 295,000 people. The extensive, graphic, real-time, and repeated media coverage of the attacks has also contributed to the sense of a shared massive national crisis.

Given the recent rise in terror attacks worldwide, it is important to try to understand how people react to terror, the factors that foster vulnerability or promote resilience, and how society is affected over time.

Several studies have examined stress-related mental health symptoms and coping behaviors following terrorism. Studies of the impact of September 11 (the terrorist attacks in the USA in 2001) found that both people who experienced the attack directly [2] and those who experienced it indirectly, such as through the media [3,4], showed elevated levels of distress, lowered sense of security, and pathological reactions such as post-traumatic stress disorder (PTSD) and depression. Studies carried out in Spain [5], France [6,7], Ireland [8], Algeria [9], Sri Lanka [10], Australia [11], Guatemala [12], Japan [13], Britain [14] and Israel [15] similarly point to the psychological impact of exposure to terror.

On the whole, however, these studies do not address the impact of continuous terror on entire populations. The issues of whether responses to long-term, continuous terror differ from response to shorter episodes of terror and whether and how such terror affects vulnerability and resiliency have yet to be evaluated. Additional unresolved issues include whether there is a process of habituation that helps people learn to cope adaptively with terror or whether the continual stress of ongoing terrorism accumulates over time, and whether terror has different effects on different sectors of the population. In addition, the relation between ongoing terror and societal concerns has not yet been studied. Does the ongoing threat of continuous terror leave room for concern about other societal issues or does it so absorb people's thinking and emotional energy that it blocks out concern with such issues?

In the present study we also relate to the concept of resilience, defined by Bonano [16] (pp. 20–21) as 'the ability . . . to maintain a relatively stable, healthy level of psychological and physical functioning' in the face of highly disruptive events. This concept is particularly important in view of findings following a range of traumatic events, which show that large percentages of people (40–78.2%) exposed to such events are either entirely or almost symptom-free [3,17-20].

The present study attempts to fill in some of the gaps. Conducted in May 2004, after 44 months of ongoing terror attacks in Israel, this is a follow-up of our previous study on Israelis' responses to terror [15]. The original study examined the psychological impact of terrorism on a representative sample of Israelis 19 months after the outbreak of the Al-Aqsa Intifada in October 2000 [15]. The present study was a telephone survey of a different sample of Israelis, and assessed a range of psychological responses among various sectors of the population: men and women, Jews and Arabs, religious and non-religious, Israeli-born and immigrants. The analyses focused on the correlates of and contributors to vulnerability and resilience. In addition to examining the role of individual factors (e.g., exposure, psychological features, demographic features, and prior life experiences), it also examined the possible role played by distress concerning other societal problems, a factor not considered in previous studies.

Methods

Sampling

The sample was obtained by a within-strata random-sampling method from a large database maintained by the Dahaf Polling Institute (Tel-Aviv, Israel). The database, pooling method and strata criteria have been described in our previous study [15].

The target population consisted of all adult Israeli residents aged 18 years or older. Accordingly, 828 households were telephoned. In total, 702 people were randomly reached by telephone (84.8% contact rate); of these 501 agreed to participate in the study, yielding a final participation rate of 60.5%, and a representative sample of the Israeli population with a maximum sampling error of 4.5%.

The participants' demographic characteristics are shown in Table 1. The sample consisted of 242 men (43.3%) and 259 women (51.7%), aged from 18 to 91 years (mean ± SD 44.8 ± 17.1). There were 430 Jews (85.8%) and 71 Israeli Arabs (14.2%). In the sample, 252 participants (56.3%) had received a year or more of post-high school education, 220 (43.9%) had completed high school, and 29 (5.8%) had attended only elementary high school. Of the Jewish Israelis, 39 (9.2%) reported that they were religious, 122 (28.6%) that they were traditional, 25 (5.9%) that they were ultra-orthodox, and 240 (56.3%) that they were atheist. Most of the sample lived in urban areas. Of the 430 Jews, 237 (55.4%) were born in Israel and 191 (44.6%) were immigrants; all the Arab participants were born in Israel. There were 189 (40.5%) participants who reported a net family income below the mean (about $2000 per month), 132 (28.3%) an average family income, and 146 (31.2%) a family income higher than the mean. The sample, which was roughly comparable to that in our previous study [15], was representative of the Israeli population, with no differences between the above distributions and data provided by the Israel Central Bureau of Statistics [21].

Analysis of Non-Participants

Non-participants (n = 201) did not differ from participants (n = 501) on any demographic variable apart from having slightly lower income (mean ± SD 2.6 ± 1.3 vs. 2.8 ± 1.3); $t_{700} = 2.0$; $p = 0.05$) and, as in the previous study, being significantly younger (mean ± SD age, 42.0 ± 16.7 years) than participants (44.8 ± 17.1 years; $t_{700} = 2.0$; $p = 0.05$).

Data Collection

Interviews were conducted by telephone on 5 May 2004, using identical data collection procedures to those in our previous study [15]. Oral informed consent was obtained from participants at the beginning of the interview. The internal review board of Lev-Hasharon Mental Health Center approved the study.

Instruments

The research instrument was a structured questionnaire consisting of 59 questions. Most questions were drawn from questionnaires used in the previous study to assess reactions to trauma [15]. The measures drawn from these questionnaires were level of exposure, PTSD symptoms; traumatic stress-related symptoms (TSRS), depression, sense of safety, optimism, and self-efficacy. In addition, we added questions tapping the respondents' anxiety, social support, previous experience with life-threatening events and physical injury ensuing from terrorist attacks, life events in the previous year, substantial loss of income any time in the past, and experience of blatant ethnic discrimination any time in the past. Finally, we asked whether a number of major societal problems caused the respondent personal distress. Except when otherwise indicated, the participants were asked to reply with respect to the time 'since the beginning of the Intifada'. Following a pilot study of 30 people (not included in the final sample), the questionnaire was modified to make it telephone-friendly. On average, the telephone survey took 12 minutes.

Table 1: Demographic characteristics of survey participants (n = 501)

Characteristics	Number (%)
Age (years), mean ± SD (range)	44.81 ± 17.1 (18-91)
Gender	
Male	242 (48.3)
Female	259 (51.7)
Ethnicity	
Jews	430 (85.8)
Israeli Arabs	71(14.2)
Education	
Elementary school only	29 (5.8)
High school	220 (43.9)
Higher education	252 (50.3)
Religiosity (Jews, n = 426)*	
Orthodox	25 (5.9)
Religious	39 (9.2)
Traditional	122 (28.6)
Atheist	240 (56.3)
Residence	
Urban	382 (76.2)
Agricultural, village communities (including	35 (7.0)
Arab villages	71 (14.2)
Settlements outside 1967	13 (2.6)
Place of birth: (Jews; n = 430)†	
Israel	241 (56.0)
Outside of Israel	191 (44.0)
Income	
Below mean	189 (40.5)
Mean (US $2000)	132 (28.3)
Above mean	146 (31.2)

*Religiosity data were not obtained for Arab participants; †All Arab participants were born in Israel

Exposure was assessed by questions asking the participants whether they had personally witnessed a terrorist attack and whether they had been injured by it, and whether friend(s) or family members had witnessed a terrorist attack and whether any of them had been injured or died in an attack. Based on the answers given, we divided the participants into nine exposure score (ES) groups: (i) no exposure, (ii) friend/family-only exposure, uninjured; (iii) friend/family-only exposure, injured; (iv) friend/family-only exposure, killed; (v) personal exposure only, uninjured; (vi) personal exposure and friend/family exposure, uninjured; (vii) personal exposure (uninjured) and friend/family injured or (viii) killed; and (ix) personal exposure with physical injury.

TSRS, PTSD, and traumatic stress (TS) resiliency were assessed using a modified 23-item version of the Stanford Acute Stress Reaction Questionnaire (SASRQ [22]). Subjects were asked to rate on a 5-point Likert scale (0 = disagree, 1 = agree somewhat, 2 = agree, 3 = strongly agree, 4 = totally agree) whether they had each stress symptom, and to report for how long: (i) 2 days or less, (ii) less than 1 month, (iii) longer than 1 month. A symptom was considered clinically relevant for TSRS and PTSD diagnosis if the individual at least 'agreed' (third choice out of 5). The scale showed a Cronbach's α of 0.88. Because not all respondents met the full DSM-IV criteria for PTSD (e.g., actual exposure to a traumatic event) and because our observations were made on the basis of screening instruments and not comprehensive clinical evaluations, the participants were not considered to have PTSD, but rather an aggregation of symptoms that met the criteria for PTSD. This included meeting the criteria for hyperarousal, re-experiencing, avoidance and functional problems, or a high level of distress.

Participants were considered TS resilient if they endorsed no TSRS item above 'a little'. To ensure that the measure did not assess denial, we compared, using data from our previous study, the use of denial as a coping strategy by TS resilient and non-resilient individuals. The comparison showed similar use by both groups (mean ± SD items endorsed: TS resilient (n=119) 1.25 ± 0.7 vs. non-TS resilient (n = 390) 1.20 ± 0.7; $t_{508} = 0.744$; p = 0.5, NS). The same approach to assessing the absence of stress-related symptomatology was proposed by Galea et al. [3].

Depression and anxiety were assessed via the statements: 'I feel depressed or gloomy' and 'I feel anxious or tense', rated on a 5-point Likert scale from 0 (very true) to 5 (not true at all) [4]. Personal optimism and optimism about the future of Israel were queried via two items adapted from the Children's Future Orientation Scale [23], rated on a 6-point Likert scale from 1 (very much agree) to 6 (do not agree at all). A response was considered positive if the participant indicated at least moderate agreement. Sense of safety was assessed by two statements developed for our previous study, which referred to a sense of threat to oneself and one's relatives, and which were rated on a 6-point Likert scale from 1 (strongly agree) to 6 (don't agree at all). Self-efficacy was assessed by the question, 'How well would you know what to do if you were caught in a terrorist attack?,' answered on a 6-point Likert scale from 0 (not at all) to 6 (very much). Responses of 3 and above were considered positive. The statistical reliability of these measures is presented in our previous study [15].

Sense of social support was assessed by one statement adapted from the Social Support Appraisal Scale designed by Vaux et al. [24]: 'I can always rely on someone to help me when I'm in difficulty,' rated on a 6-point Likert scale from 1 (very true) to 6 (not true at all). Based on a telephone interview of a student sample, 2-week test-retest of this item was 0.92 (n = 30). A response was considered positive if the participant indicated at least moderate agreement [3].

Help-seeking was examined by asking participants two yes/no questions: (i) whether they were currently undergoing mental health treatment and (ii) whether they currently felt the need for such a treatment. To assess objective threat, we grouped together the participants who lived in high-risk areas (Jerusalem, Tel-Aviv, Netanya, Haifa, and West Bank settlements), where most of the suicide bombings had occurred, and compared their exposure with that of the participants who lived elsewhere. The comparison showed that participants residing in the high-risk areas (n = 129) had significantly higher exposure scores than those (n = 372) residing in lower-risk areas (mean ± SD 1.5 ± 2.1 versus 0.7 ± 1.6, respectively; t= 4.2; df = 499; p = 0.001).

Exposure to previous traumas was assessed by five yes/no questions: (i) life events in the previous year were tapped by asking respondents whether they had experienced a stressful or highly emotional event in the previous year; subjective economic hardship was assessed by asking whether they had ever suffered a major loss of income; subjective sense of ethnic discrimination was queried by asking whether they felt they had ever personally suffered blatant ethnic discrimination; (iv and v) previous exposure to life-threatening events was tapped by two questions: whether the respondents had ever been in a life-threatening situation due to accident, illness, terrorist attack or war; and whether they had sustained an injury of any consequence during these situations.

Distress related to major societal issues was assessed by asking the participants to rate how distressed they felt about 10 social problems: (i) terror, (ii) the economic situation, (iii) traffic accidents, (iv) ethnic discrimination, (v) the security situation, (vi) crime and violence, (vii) administration corruption, (viii) lack of leadership, (ix) the treatment of minorities (foreign workers, Israeli-Arabs, Bedouins etc.), and (x) the treatment of the Palestinians in the territories. This list represents the consensus of a panel of seven Israeli specialists in the behavioral sciences, who were asked to list all the 'social and national' issues about which Israelis get upset. Participants rated their distress about each issue on a 6-point Likert scale, from 1 (not at all) to 5 (very much). A societal distress score was computed by summing the ratings on all items except terror. In addition, respondents were asked to indicate which issue they regarded as the 'most distressing'. Based on a telephone interview of a student sample, 2-week test-retest of these items ranged from 0.75 to 0.92 (n = 30).

Statistical Analyses

Independent sample t-test, χ^2 tests, and Pearson's correlations were performed, followed by one-forward stepwise linear regressions for the continuous variables of TSR symptoms and two-forward conditional logistic regressions for categorical variables of symptom criteria of PTSD and TS resiliency. In each regression analysis, the significant predictors from nine groups of variables were tested for inclusion in the final models. Significance was set at 0.05 (two-tailed). Non-significant variables and variables that did not add to the predictive power of the model were removed from the regression to provide the most parsimonious model. No imputation of missing values was performed apart from the income variable score, which was replaced in the regression analyses with the sample mean (n = 34). Regression analysis omitting participants who did not complete the income variable did not significantly change any of the results. For other variables, cases were excluded from specific analysis when information was missing relative to the content analyzed. This did not substantially affect the size and the integrity of the sample. SPSS-PC version 11.5 (SPSS Inc, Chicago, IL, USA) was used for all analyses.

Table 2: Rate of exposure to terrorism and other life events, life threatening experiences, loss of income, and ethnic discrimination

	No.	%
No personal exposure and no exposure of friends or relative	344	68.7
No personal exposure but exposure of friends or relative who were not wounded	35	7.0
No personal exposure but exposure of friends or relative who were wounded	34	6.8
No personal exposure but exposure of friends or relative who died	32	6.4
Personal exposure: no physical wounds, but no exposure of friends or relative	25	5.0
Personal exposure: no physical wounds, and exposure of friends or relative who were not wounded	10	2.0
Personal exposure: no physical wounds, and exposure of friends or relative who were wounded	8	1.6
Personal exposure: no physical wounds, and exposure of friends or relative who died	11	2.2
Personal exposure with physical wounds but no exposure of friends or relative	2	0.4
Lifetime life-threatening experience	179	35.9
Lifetime life-threatening experience with injury	36	7.2
Substantial loss of income	175	35.0
Victim of ethnic discrimination	70	14.0
Major life event in previous year	211	42.3

Results

Exposure, Life Events, Life-Threatening Situations, Injury Following Life-Threatening Situations, Loss of Income, and Ethnic Discrimination

The percentages of people exposed to terrorist attacks at the different degrees of exposure are presented in Table 2. More than one in 10 respondents (56; 11.2%) had witnessed a terrorist attack first-hand, and more than one in five (101; 20.2%) had friends or relatives who had witnessed an attack.

In total, 211 (42.3%) reported having experienced a non-terror highly stressful or emotional event in the previous year, while 179 (35.9%) reported having been in a life-threatening situation at some time in their lives. Of these 179, 36 (20.5%) reported having been seriously injured in that event. There were 175 people (35%) who reported having suffered a significant loss of income, and 70 participants (14%) felt they had been victims of ethnic discrimination. Further calculation indicated that women reported significantly more life events in the previous year than men (women 120/258 (56.9%) vs. men: 91/241 (37.8%); $\chi^2 = 3.9$ (df = 1), $p < 0.05$), while men reported having experienced significantly more life-threatening events at some time in the past (men: 129/241 (53.5%) vs. women: 50/258 (19.4%); $\chi^2 = 63.2$ (df = 1); $p < 0.001$).

PTSD and TSR Symptoms and TS Resiliency

PTSD and TSR endorsements are presented in Table 3. With regard to PTSD symptoms, 180 (35.9%) of the participants endorsed at least one re-experiencing item (cluster B), 259 (51.7%) at least one avoidance/numbing symptom (cluster C), 239 (47.7) at least one hyperarousal symptom (cluster D), 77 (15.4%) at least one of the two functional impairment items, and 221 (44.1%) the general distress item. More than a quarter (136; 27.1%) of the participants reported having at least one of the four dissociative symptoms. The mean ± SD number of dissociative symptoms endorsed was 0.4 ± 0.4). In total, 45 respondents (9.0%) met criteria for PTSD.

Regarding TSR symptoms, respondents endorsed a mean ± of 5.00 ± 4.5 symptoms out of the 23 queried. The mean ± SD TSRS intensity was 0.7 ± 0.6 (range 0–4). In total, 72 respondents (14.4%) reported no or minimal TSRS. These respondents were regarded as TS resilient.

Table 3: Frequency of symptom criteria for PTSD.

Symptoms	May 2004 study (n = 501)		April 2002 study (n = 512)	
	Symptoms endorsed, mean ± SD (range)	Respondents with ≥ 1 symptom, no. (%)	Symptoms endorsed, mean ± SD (range)	Respondents with ≥ symptom, no. (%)
Re-experiencing (B) cluster	0.6 ± 0.9 (0–4)	180 (35.9)	0.6 ± 0.9) (0–4)	189 (37.1)
Avoidance/numbing (C) cluster	1.0 ± 1.3 (0–6)	259 (51.7)	1.1 ± 1.4 (0–6)	283 (55.5)
Hyperarousal (D) cluster	1.2 ± 1.6 (0–6)	239 (47.7)	1.1 ± 1.5 (0–6)	252 (49.4)
Functional impairment	0.2 ± 0.4 (0–2)	77 (15.4)	0.3 ± 0.5 (0–2)	116 (22.8)
General distress	0.4 ± 0.5 (0–1)	221 (44.1)	0.5 ± 0.5 (0–1)	236 (46.3)
Dissociative cluster	0.4 ± 0.8 (0–4)	136 (27.1)	0.4 ± 0.8 (0–4)	138 (26.9)
Total number of TSRS symptoms	5.0 ± 4.5 (0–23)	429 (85.6)	4.0 ± 4.5 (0–23)	391 (76.7)
Met symptom criteria for PTSD	n = 45 (9%)		n = 48 (9.4%)	
TS resiliency	n = 72 (14.4%)		n = 121 (23.3%)	

Feelings and Attitudes

Table 4 presents trauma-related mental health attitudes and emotions. In total, 147 (29.5%) participants reported at least agreement with the statement 'I feel depressed and gloomy' and 50 (10.4%) stated that they agreed 'very much' or 'totally agreed'. A similar number, 145 (29%), at least agreed with the statement 'I feel anxious and tense'. Most respondents (409; 82%) reported that they felt optimistic about their personal future, and over half, 279 (56.5%) that they felt optimistic about the future of Israel. Almost half (235; 47%) felt that their lives were in danger, and over half (270; 54.1%) that the lives of family members or acquaintances were in danger. Around three-quarters (308; 76.6%) at least agreed with the statement that they would know what to do if they were caught in a terror attack. More than three-quarters (390; 78.2%) at least agreed with the statement that 'there will always be someone there to help me when I'm having difficulty'. Smaller proportions reported that they were receiving some sort of treatment for their mental health (18; 3.6%) and/or that they felt the need for such treatment (48; 9.7%).

Table 4: Percentage of participants reporting each trauma related feelings and behaviors (n = 501).

Items	Endorsements, n (%)	
	April 2004 study, n = 501	May 2002 study, n = 512
Depression	147 (29.5)	299 (58.6)
Tension and anxiety	145 (29.0)	N/A
Optimism about personal future	409 (82.0)	421 (82.2)
Optimism about the future of Israel	279 (56.5)	337 (66.2)
Low sense of personal safety	235 (47.0)	307 (60.4)
Low sense of safety of friends and relatives	270 (54.1)	345 (67.9)
Self-efficacy in terror attack	308 (76.6)	322 (74.6)
Sense of social support	390 (78.2)	N/A
Need mental health treatment*	48 (9.7)	27 (5.3%)

N/A, not applicable. All items were endorsed at 'agree' (third choice of 5) or higher, except for those marked with *; percentages on these items reflect a positive answer to yes/no questions.

Distress about Societal Issues

As can be seen from Table 5, of all the issues that preoccupy Israelis, the economic situation was viewed as the most upsetting by the highest percentage (26.1%) of respondents. However, if we combine the 15.1% who named the security situation as the most upsetting with the 24.4% who named the terror attacks, then we see that 39.6% of the population viewed the violence and its implications as a more upsetting problem than any other in Israeli society. Very few respondents rated behavior towards Palestinians (3.5%), ethnic discrimination (2.5%) and behavior towards minorities (0.6%) as most upsetting.

Objective Threat/Exposure and Symptoms

Independent-samples t tests, χ^2 tests, and Pearson correlations showed no significant association between objective threat (high- vs. low-risk place of residence) or level of exposure and any of the independent variables. With 45 participants meeting symptom criteria for PTSD compared with 456 who did not meet the criteria, the analyses had a power of 44.7% to yield a statistically significant result. Neither was a significant difference found in the exposure to terror reported by the Jewish (n = 430) and Arab (n = 71) participants (mean ± SD 1.0 ± 1.7 vs. 0.9 ± 1.7 respectively; t_{499} = 0.4; p = 0.7).

Demographic Variables Associated with Symptoms

Meeting symptom criteria for PTSD was associated significantly with being female 12.7% (33/256) women vs. 4.5% (11/242) men; χ^2 = 10.5 (df = 1); p = 0.001), with being Arab (16.9% (12/71) Arabs vs. 7.4% (32/340) Jews; χ^2 = 6.8 (df = 1); p = 0.009), and with a somewhat lower level of education (participants who met symptom criteria for PTSD versus those who did not: mean ± SD 12.8 ± 3.1 vs. 13.8 ± 2.9 years of schooling; t_{499} = 2.2; p = 0.026). No other demographic feature was found to be significantly associated with meeting symptom criteria for PTSD. In a similar vein, significantly more TSRS were found among women (women 6.3 ± 4.6 vs. men 3.6 ± 4.0; t_{499} = 7.1, p < 0.001), Arabs (Arabs 6.4 ± 4.6 vs. Jews 4.8 ± 4.5; t499 = 2.8; p = 0.005), and among those who were less educated (r = 0.16, p < 0.001). Significantly more TSRS were also found among participants born outside of Israel than among native-born Israelis (5.7 ± 4.6 vs. 4.6 ± 4.5; t_{499} = 2.5, p=0.01), those who reported lower income (Pearson r = .15, p < 0.001), and those who were religiously observant Jews (religious Jews 5.3 ± 4.9 vs. non-religious Jews 4.4 ± 4.2); t = 2.0, p = 0.05).

TS resiliency was significantly associated with being male (23.6% (69/242) men vs. 5.8% (15/259) women); χ^2 = 32.1 (df = 1), p < 0.001), being Jewish (16.0% (69/430) Jews vs. 4.2% (3/71) Arabs); χ^2 = 6.9 (df = 1), p = 0.009), being born in Israel (17.6% (54/307) native Israelis vs. 8.9% (17/191) immigrants); χ^2 = 7.3(df = 1), p = 0.007), and higher income level (TS resilient 3.2 ± 1.20 vs. non-TS resilient 2.7 ± 1.3; t_{465} = 2.8, p = 0.006).

Regression Analyses

Two logistic regressions and one linear regression were performed to assess the relative contribution of exposure to terrorist attacks, demographic items, future orientation, sense of safety, self-efficacy, life events, social support, and distress about societal problems to meeting symptom criteria of PTSD and to TS resiliency and number of TSR symptoms. The final regression models are presented in Table 6.

Table 5: Distress about societal issues

Distress about:	Very distressed* n (%)	Most Distressing,† n (%)
The economic situation	133/499 (26.7)	126 (26.1)
The terror attacks	121/500 (24.2)	118 (24.4)
Security situation	141/499 (28.3)	73 (15.1)
Administration corruption	180/498 (36.1)	50 (10.4)
Lack of leadership	143/492 (29.1)	46 (9.5)
Violence and crime	136/498 (27.3)	24 (5.0)
Treatment of Palestinians in the territories	82/482 (17.0)	17 (3.5)
Motor vehicle accidents	158/500 (31.6)	14 (2.9)
Ethnic discrimination	27/497 (5.4)	12 (2.5)
Treatment of minorities (Arabs, Bedouins, foreign workers)	94/495 (19.0)	3 (0.6)

* Items endorsed 'very much' (fifth choice of 5).; † Forced-choice items

The three regression models showed the following significant contributions:

•   Being female and being Arab contributed significantly to meeting PTSD symptom criteria, having more TSR symptoms, and not being TS resilient

•   Being born in Israel contributed to TS resilience and fewer TSRS

•   Optimism about the future of the State of Israel contributed to being TS resilient

•   Less education contributed to more TSRS

•   Sense of safety contributed to TS resilience and less TSRS

•   A life-threatening experience with injury contributed to meeting PTSD criteria and having more TSR symptoms

•   Greater distress about societal problems contributed to more TSRS

- Sense of social support contributed to less TSRS
- A major life event in the previous year contributed to meeting PTSD criteria
- A substantial loss of income in the past contributed to meeting symptom criteria for PTSD and not being TS resilient.

Table 6: Summary of hierarchical regression analysis (TSR symptoms) and logistic regression analysis (PTSD symptoms and TS resiliency)

Variable	PTSD symptoms, OR (95% CI)	TSR symptoms, standard B ± SE	Not TS resilient, OR (95% CI)
Female	4.0 (1.8–8.6)	-0.18 ± 0.35	3.7 (1.9–7.4)
Arab (vs. Jewish) ethnicity	2.5 (1.2–5.5)	-0.15 ± 0.52	5.9 (1.6–21.2)
Born outside of Israel	N/A	-0.11 ± 0.38	2.8 (1.5–5.5)
Low optimism about state	N/A	N/A	1.4 (1.1–1.7)
Less education	N/A	0.11 ± 0.05	N/A
Low sense of safety	N/A	0.19 ± 0.09	1.8 (1.3–2.4)
Life-threatening experience with injury in the past	4.5 (1.7–12.1)	0.15 ± 0.64	N/A
Higher distress over societal problems	N/A	-0.18 ± 0.02	N/A
Lower sense of social support	N/A	0.08 ± 0.12	N/A
Major life events in previous year	2.0 (1.0–3.9)	N/A	N/A
Substantial loss of income in the past	3.1 (1.6–6.1)	N/A	2.4 (1.2–5.0)

N/A, not applicable; TS, traumatic stress. TSRS, traumatic stress-related symptoms; Total R^2 for variables predicting TSR symptoms = 38.5; Respondents meeting symptom criteria for PTSD = 45/501 (9%); TS-resilient respondents = 71/501 (14.4%). $p < 0.05$ for all variables

Discussion

Resiliency and Distress

The findings of the present survey show heterogeneous responses compared with our study 2 years previously. We found that some of the measures had improved, some worsened, and some remained unchanged, possibly due to interactive processes of habituation, stress accumulation, and the ability to compartmentalize stresses.

On the one hand, the responses on some of the measures point to an apparent reduction in distress. While around half the study participants reported feeling that their own lives (47%) and/or the lives of their friends and family were in danger (54.1%), these rates are about 13% lower than those found 2 years previously. These figures suggest that even though the ongoing terror continues to rob much of Israel's civilian population of their peace of mind and sense of safety, fewer people than previously feel significantly threatened by it. There were also substantial reductions in the percentage of respondents who reported feeling depressed (29.5% vs. 58.6%) and who reported functional impairment (15.4% vs. 22.7%).

The greater sense of safety, reduced distress, and improved functioning seem to point to a process of habituation. It cannot be ruled out, however, that the changes also stem from a reduction in the number and scope of terrorist attacks over the 2-year interval and/or from the increased visibility of preventive measures (e.g. armed guards at the entrances to pubs and restaurants) and offensive actions by the Israeli Defence Forces, which had initially adapted a more defensive stance.

Responses on some other measures, however, point to increased distress. Mean TSRS rose (5.0 vs. 4.0), TS resiliency dropped by around a third (14.4% vs. 23.3%), almost twice as many respondents reported feeling the need for professional mental-health treatment (9.7% vs. 5.3%), and fewer reported feeling optimistic about the future of the State (56.5% vs. 66.2%). This pattern of responses seems to reflect an accumulation of stress and erosion of resiliency after 4 years of ongoing terror. It highlights the need to enhance the ability of individuals and societies to withstand the psychological stress of ongoing terror, especially as terror is becoming a worldwide affliction.

Finally, responses on some measures remained unchanged. The percentage of respondents who met PTSD criteria (9%) remained roughly the same as previously (9.4%), as did their scores on the various PTSD symptom clusters. These findings are interesting, as one would expect increased rates as a result of more people being exposed over time, and the development of delayed and reactivated PTSD as a result of the repeated terror attacks.

Also unchanged were the very high percentages of respondents who reported feeling optimistic about their personal futures (82%) and feeling self-efficacy if they were caught in a terrorist attack in the future (76.6%). These findings suggest that self-confidence and abilities are not undermined by terror and may even be bolstered by it [[25], pp. 43–47] and suggesting that external threat can increase aspects of resiliency and sense of purpose [26]. At the same time, there seems to be some disparity between the respondents' optimism about their personal future and the sense of life threat, whether to themselves or to people close to them, reported by at least half the participants. This may reflect the human ability to compartmentalize.

Overall, the various patterns of responses suggest that exposure to ongoing terror may result in both habituation and erosion of resiliency. The findings point to the need to examine the long-term impact of terror, war, and other disasters on a variety of parameters [25].

As trauma studies traditionally tend to explore the pathological aspects of the consequences of trauma (e.g. PTSD, TSRS) it is important to note that resiliency is not a mere mirror reflection of PTSD. While resiliency and not PTSD is influenced by optimism, sense of safety, and immigrant status, PTSD but not resiliency is influenced by previous life-threatening experiences and major life events in the previous year.

Societal Concerns

The findings on societal concerns are also equivocal. On the one hand, two-fifths of the respondents marked either the terror attacks or the security situation as the most upsetting of the 10 societal problems listed, yet the great concern with terrorism-related issues did not prevent respondents from being very upset by more mundane social problems. Over a quarter of the respondents rated the economic situation as the most upsetting, while about a quarter to over a third reported feeling very upset about ordinary problems of civil society: corruption, lack of leadership, road accidents, and crime. These findings suggest that, for all the tension created by the ongoing terrorism, people still had energy left over for other concerns. It cannot be ruled out, however, that the tension created by terrorism did perhaps augment their distress about other matters. Further study is required to better understand this inter-relationship.

Relatively low percentages of respondents were 'very upset' about human rights issues: the treatment of Palestinians in the territories; the treatment of the country's minorities, Israeli-Arabs or foreign workers; and ethnic discrimination among Jews. It is difficult to know how much the relative unconcern stems from anger at the Palestinian terrorism and how much from a blunting of empathy and moral consciousness in the face of the survival threat posed by terrorism. Our findings are in line with the terror management theory [27] and the findings of Hobfoll et al. [28], suggesting that the threat and fear of death increases prejudice, stereotyping, and derogation of outsiders.

Risk Factors

Our findings also show that various sectors of society were affected by the terror differently. In particular, being female and being Arab both contributed significantly to the likelihood of meeting symptom criteria for PTSD, to having more TSR symptoms, and not being TS resilient.

The women in our sample were four times more likely than men to meet symptom criteria for PTSD, endorsed higher levels of TSRS, and were 3.7 times less likely to be TS resilient. Their greater vulnerability is consistent with other findings [29,30]. It may be rooted in women's higher sense of threat, lower self-efficacy, and tendency to use less effective coping strategies than men [31]. It may stem from the fact that more women than men in this study had experienced a major life event in the past year. Alternatively, it may also be anchored in gender-differentiated reporting patterns, with women more ready to report distress than men.

Arabs were 2.5 times more likely than Jews to meet PTSD criteria and 5.9 times less likely to be TS resilient. These findings contrast with those of our previous study, which did not show any ethnic differences in vulnerability. They are surprising in light of the fact that Arabs were not targeted by terrorism and proportionately fewer were killed and injured in the attacks than Jews. However, these findings are consistent with those of Hobfall et al. [28] and Somers et al. [32], and with studies of the reactions of children to continuous stress of war and terrorism in the region [33], which have shown that the Israeli Arab minority as well as the Palestinian population has become psychologically vulnerable to terrorism. Several non-exclusive explanations may be suggested. One is that the identification of Arab citizens of Israel with the suffering of the Palestinians in the territories, the tensions of dual allegiance, and mounting Jewish hostility in the wake of the violence may all have been sources of traumatogenic stress [34], the impact of which became increasingly apparent as the intifada raged on. Another possible explanation is their minority status in Israel. This explanation is consistent with findings showing that belonging to a minority group increases the likelihood of PTSD and trauma-related distress [35,36]. A third explanation lies in the resource deprivation of Arabs in Israel, where they earn less than Jews, are less educated, have low social status, and fewer opportunities for advancement. Their heightened vulnerability, in comparison both with that in our previous study and with the Jewish population, may stem from the depletion of their limited resources over time [28,37].

Resource deprivation may also help account for our findings that less educated respondents had more TSRS than their better educated peers, and that immigrants were less TS resilient than native-born Israelis. Although both findings are consistent with those of earlier studies [25,38], neither education nor immigration were found to be predictors of terror-induced distress in our previous study.

Consistent with our previous findings, level of exposure did not contribute to any of our measures of traumatic stress. This finding is inconsistent with findings of significant associations between level of exposure and traumatization [29]. It is, however, consistent with findings of traumatization in the wake of the '9/11' attacks among people who were very far from the areas targeted [4], as well as with findings in Israel showing that level of exposure was not necessarily related to symptom severity [15,39,40]. Thus, when terror assumes a national dimension, people do not have to experience it first-hand to suffer its psychological consequences. An explanation may lie in the process of social/cultural distress reappraisal or calibration [37] that accompanies a national threat of this amplitude.

In contrast to current exposure to terror, however, previous exposure to trauma or stress (e.g. prior traumatic experience, substantial income loss, and a highly stressful or emotional experience in the previous year) did contribute to vulnerability in the face of terror, while distress over societal problems contributed to increased TSRS.

Limitations

When evaluating our conclusions, it should be noted that although our questionnaires included validated, widely used questionnaires, we added study-specific questions, thus not all items in our evaluation instruments had been previously validated.

The limitations include the lack of data from before the Intifada on the psychological repercussions examined in this study. We also cannot know whether the refusal of those who declined the interview was associated with higher levels of distress. Furthermore, we cannot determine whether self-reported symptoms are clinically significant or merely reflect heightened awareness and agitation due to the threat of terrorism. Caution should be taken when generalizing findings to various subpopulations that may or may not have been exposed to the threat of terrorism and may not have been adequately represented in the strata sampling (e.g., those without homes or telephones). However, the large sample size, high response rate, and lack of significant demographic differences between participants and those who refused to participate support the credibility of our findings.

Conclusion

This study shows that Israeli society has coped with nearly 4 years of intense and continuous terror in a mixed manner, and suggests that, aside from possibly fostering habituation, continuous terror results in the erosion of resiliency. The findings also show that erosion of resiliency disproportionately affects groups with fewer basic resources, including the Arab population, the less educated, and immigrants. Finally, our findings suggest that known vulnerability factors such as gender and exposure to previous traumatic events contribute to prediction of terrorism-related distress.

Authors' Contributions and Acknowledgements

AB, MG and ZS were responsible for the study concept and design. MG was responsible for acquisition of data, and MG, AB, and ZS for analysis and interpretation of data. The drafting of the manuscript was carried out by MG and AB, and critical revision of the manuscript for important intellectual content by AB, MG, YM and ZS. Statistical expertise was provided by MG, and study supervision carried out by AB, MG, YM and ZS. MG, AB, YM and ZS had full access to all of the data in the study and take responsibility for the integrity of the data and the accuracy of the data analysis. We thank Mina Zemah PhD of the Dahaf Institute for helping us make the questionnaires telephone-friendly, and Toby Mostysser PhD and Rena Kurs for their valuable editorial assistance. We would also like to thank Sandro Galea, Simon Wessely, and Arieh Shalev for reviewing the manuscript.

References

1. Israeli Ministry of Foreign Affairs [http://www.mfa.gov.il]. Accessed 10 April 2006.

2. Schlenger W, Caddell J, Ebert L, Jordan B, Rourke K, Wilson D, et al.: Psychological reactions to terrorist attacks: Findings from the national study of Americans' reactions to September 11. JAMA 2002, 581-588.

3. Galea S, Ahern J, Resnick H, Kilpatrick D, Kilpatrick D, Bucuvalas M, Gold J, Vlahov D: Psychological sequelae of the September 11 terrorist attacks in New York City. New Engl J Med 2002, 346(13):982-987.

4. Cohen Silver R, Holman A, McIntosh DN, Poulin M, Gil-Rivas V: Nationwide longitudinal study of psychological responses to September 11. JAMA 2002, 288:1235-1244.

5. Baca E, Baca-Garcia E, Perez-Rodriguea MM, Cabanas ML: Short and long-term effects of terrorist attacks in Spain. In The Trauma of Terrorism Edited by: Danieli Y, Brom D, Sills J. Binghampton NY: The Haworth Maltreatment and Trauma Press; 2005:157-170.

6. Jehel L, Paternity S, Brunet S, Duchet C, Guelfi JD: Predictions of the occurrence and intensity of post-traumatic stress disorder in victims 32 months after bomb attack. Eur J Psychiatry 2003, 18:172-176.

7. Verger P, Dab W, Lamping D, Loze J, Deschaseaux-Voinet C, Abenhaim L, Rouillon F: The psychological impact of terrorism: An epidemiologic study of posttraumatic stress disorder and associated factors in victims of the 1995–96 bombings in France. Am J Psychiatry 2004, 161:1384-1389.

8. Curran PS: Psychiatric aspects of terrorist violence: Northern Ireland 1969–1987. Br J Psychiatry 1988, 153:470-475.

9. Khaled N: Psychological effects of terrorist attacks in Algeria. In The Trauma of Terrorism Edited by: Danieli Y, Brom D, Sills J. Binghampton, NY: The Haworth Maltreatment and Trauma Press; 2005.

10. Somasundaram D: Short and long term effects on the victims of terror in Sri-Lanka. In The Trauma of Terrorism Edited by: Danieli Y, Brom D, Sills J. Binghampton, NY: Haworth Press; 2005:157-170.

11. Wooding S, Raphael B: Psychological impact of disasters and terrorism on children and adolescents: experiences from Australia. Prehospital Disaster 2004, 19:10-20.

12. Lykes M: Terror, silencing and children: International, multidisciplinary collaboration with Guatemalan Maya communities. Soc Sci Med 1994, 38:543-552.

13. Ohtani T, Iwanami A, Kasai K, Yamasue H, Kato T, Sasaki T, Kato N: Post-traumatic stress disorder symptoms in victims of Tokyo subway attack: 5-year follow-up study. Psychiatry Clin Neurosci 2004, 624-629.

14. Rubin GJ, Brewin C, Greenberg N, Simpson J, Wesseley S: Psychological and behavioral reactions to the bombings in London on 7 July 2005: Cross sectional survey of a representative sample of Londoners. BMJ 2005:606.

15. Bleich A, Gelkopf M, Solomon Z: Exposure to terrorism, stress-related mental health symptoms, and coping behaviors among a nationally representative sample in Israel. JAMA 2003, 290:612-620.

16. Bonanno G: Loss, trauma, and human resilience. Am Psychol 2004, 20-28.

17. Hanson RF, Kilpatrick DG, Freedy JR, Saunders BE: Los Angeles County after the 1992 civil disturbance: Degree of exposure and impact on mental health. J Consult Clin Psychol 1995, 63:987-996.

18. Bryant RA, Harvey AG, Guthry RM, Moulds ML: A prospective study on psychophysiological arousal, acute stress disorder and posttraumatic stress disorder. J Abnorm Psychol 2002, 109:341-344.

19. Sutker P, Davis J, Uddo M, Ditta SR: War zone stress, personal resources, and PTSD in Persian Gulf War returnees. J Abnorm Psychol 1995, 104:444-452.

20. Bonanno GA, Rennicke C, Dekel S: Self-enhancement among high-exposure survivors of the September 11th terrorist attack: Resilience or social maladjustment? J Pers Soc Psychol 2005, 88:984-998.

21. Central Bureau of Statistics. 2004 [http://www.cbs.gov.il]. Accessed 10 April 2006.

22. Cardena E, Koopman C, Classen C, Waelde LC, Spiegel D: Psychometric properties of the Stanford acute stress reaction questionnaire (SASRQ). J Traumatic Stress 2000, 13:719-734.

23. Saigh PA: The Children's Future Orientation Scale New York: City University of New York Graduate School; 1997.

24. Vaux A, Philips J, Holly L, Thomson B, Williams D, Stewart D: The social support appraisal scale: studies of reliability and validity. Am J Comm Psychol 1986, 14:195-219.

25. Solomon Z: Coping With War Induced Stress. The Gulf war and the Israeli response. New York: Plenum Press; 1995.

26. Durkheim E: Le Suicide [English transl. 1951]. Glencoe, Il: Free Press.

27. Solomon S, Greenberg J, Pyszezynsky T: Pride and prejudice: Fear of death and social behavior. Curr Dir Psychol Sci 2000, 9:200-204.

28. Hobfoll SE, Canetti-Nisim D, Johnson RJ: Exposure to terrorism, stress-related mental health symptoms, and defensive coping among Jews and Arabs in Israel. J Consult Clin Psychol 2006, 74(2): 207- 18.

29. Kessler RC, Sonnega A, Bromet E, Hughes M, Nelson CB: Posttraumatic stress disorder in the national comorbidity survey. Arch Gen Psychiatry 1995, 52:1048-1060.

30. Stuber J, Resnick H, Galea S: Gender disparities in posttraumatic stress disorder after mass trauma. Gend Med 2006, 3:54-67.

31. Solomon Z, Gelkopf M, Bleich A: Is terrorism gender blind? Gender differences in reaction to terror events. Soc Psychiatry Psychiatr Epidemiol 2005, 40:947-54.

32. Somers E, Or-Chen K, Peled AM: When my people fight my country: Expsoure to terror, distress and coping among Israeli Arabs. In Mental Health in Terror's Shadow: The Israeli Experience Edited by: Somer E, Bleich A. Tel Aviv: Ramot-Tel Aviv University (In Hebrew); 2005.

33. Lavi T, Solomon Z: Palestinian youth of the Intifada: PTSD and future orientation. J Am Acad Child Adolesc Psychiatry 2005, 44:1176-1183.

34. Musallam N, Ginzburg K, Lev-Shalem L, Solomon Z: The psychological effects of Intifada Al Aqsa: acute stress disorder and distress in Palestinian-Israeli students. Isr J Psychiatry Relat Sci 2005, 42:96-105.

35. Brewin CR, Andrews B, Valentine JD: Meta-analysis of risk factors for posttraumatic stress disorder in trauma-exposed adults. J Consult Clin Psychol 2005, 68:748-766.

36. Norris FH, Friedman MJ, Watson PJ, Byrne CM, Diaz E, Kaniasty K: 60000 disaster victims speak: Part I and II. An empirical review of the empirical literature, 1981–2001. Psychiatry 2002, 65:207-260.

37. Hobfoll SE: The Ecology of Stress. NY: Hemisphere publishing; 1998.

38. Livanou M, Basoglu M, Salcioglu E, Kalendar D: Traumatic stress responses in treatment-seeking earthquake survivors in Turkey. J Nerv Ment Dis 2002, 190:816-823.

39. Shalev AY, Freedman S: PTSD following terrorist attacks: a prospective evaluation. Am J Psychiatry 2005, 162:1188-1191.

40. Shalev A, Tuval R, Frenkiel-Fishman S, Hadar H, Eth S: Psychological responses to continuous terror: A study of two communities in Israel. Am J Psychiatry 2006, 163:667-673.

Psychological Responses to Continuous Terror: A Study of Two Communities in Israel

Arieh Y. Shalev, M.D., Rivka Tuval, Ph.D., Sarah Frenkiel-Fishman, M.A.
Hilit Hadar, M.A., Spencer Eth, M.D.

ABSTRACT: *Objective*: The authors evaluated psychological responses to continuous terror. *Method*: Data were collected after 10 months of escalating hostilities against civilians in Israel. The study's participants were randomly selected adults living in two suburbs of Jerusalem, one that was frequently and directly exposed to acts of terrorism (N=167) and the other indirectly exposed (N=89). Participants provided information about exposure to terror-related incidents, disruption of daily living, symptoms of posttraumatic stress disorder (PTSD), and general distress (assessed with the Brief Symptom Inventory). *Results*: Residents of the directly exposed community reported more frequent exposure to terror and deeper disruption of daily living. Notwithstanding, the directly and indirectly exposed groups reported comparable rates of PTSD and similar levels of symptoms: 26.95% of the directly exposed group and 21.35% of the indirectly exposed group met DSM-IV PTSD symptom criteria (criteria B through D), and about one-third of those with PTSD symptoms (35.7% in the directly exposed group and 31.5% in the indirectly exposed group) reported significant distress and dysfunction. Subjects who did not meet PTSD symptom criteria had very low levels of PTSD symptoms, and their Brief Symptom Inventory scores were within population norms. Exposure *and* disruption of daily living contributed to PTSD symptoms in the directly exposed group. Disruption of daily routines contributed to Brief Symptom Inventory scores in both groups. *Conclusions*: Continuous terror created similar distress in proximal and remote communities. Exposure to discrete events was not a necessary mediator of terror threat. A subgroup of those exposed developed serious symptoms, whereas others were surprisingly resilient. Disruption of daily routines was a major secondary stressor.

Studies following the events of Sept. 11, 2001, have shown posttraumatic stress disorder (PTSD) symptoms and widespread anxiety among directly and indirectly exposed civilians (1–5). These studies have also shown more severe reactions among those residing near the sites of the attacks (a proximity effect) and progressive decline of symptoms with time (a time effect [6]). The clinical and public health implications of reporting early PTSD symptoms have been questioned (5).

Studies of the psychological effects of Sept. 11, however, may have limited relevance to living under continuous terror. Whereas the Sept. 11 studies evaluated the aftermath of a discrete occurrence, after which recuperation could follow undisturbed by further attacks, continuous terror may evoke other reactions. For example, scattered attacks may defy the proximity effect in that they may seem to occur everywhere. Repeated attacks may also challenge the time effect by interfering with recuperation. In addition, a degree of adjustment might be seen as people develop effective ways of coping (7). Terrorism, and the efforts to contain it, can also disrupt people's daily living (e.g., by affecting transportation and other forms of freedom) and thereby create a secondary stressor of unknown effects (8).

It is important to note that under continuous threat, the symptoms that are currently subsumed as posttraumatic and therefore purposeless and somewhat exaggerated (e.g., avoiding previously dangerous places and situations, responding emotionally to threat signals, remaining vigilant and "on guard") may reflect anticipation and self-protection. This possibility predicts that there would be a gap between reporting such "symptoms" and being outstandingly distressed or dysfunctional.

Finally, terrorism may elicit excessive distress in a subgroup of vulnerable individuals (e.g., those with previous traumatic experiences, those with lesser resources) and thereby underscore a disparity between those severely affected and others who are more resilient. This possibility predicts that the distribution of PTSD symptoms within affected communities will not be homogeneous.

From October 2000 on, Israel has faced a lengthy wave of terror. There have been 132 suicide bomber attacks between October 2000 and April 2004, causing 666 deaths and 4,447 injuries among Israeli civilians and 276 deaths and 1,843 injuries among the security forces (i.e., 0.11% of the Israeli population of 6,667,000) (9,10). Indirect exposure was also prevalent: 45% of Israelis reported having had "some exposure" to terrorism, and 60% felt that their life was in danger (11).

This work evaluates the effect of continuous terror by looking at the prevalence of PTSD, PTSD symptoms, and symptoms of general distress in two differentially exposed suburbs of Jerusalem. Data collection took place 10 months into this wave of violence. The study assessed the contributions of direct exposure and that of the disruption of daily living to symptom severity. It explored the distribution of PTSD symptoms within affected communities and the association between expressing PTSD symptoms and reporting outstanding distress and impairment.

Method

Communities Under Threat

Data for this study were collected between June and August 2001 in two suburbs of Jerusalem: Efrat (a directly exposed community) and Bét Shemesh (an indirectly exposed community). The two communities are located at similar distances from Jerusalem (11 miles for Efrat and 15 miles for Bét Shemesh). During the 8 months that preceded data collection, the directly exposed community was practically under siege, whereas the indirectly exposed community was not. Specifically, shooting incidents occurred frequently and erratically blocked the roads leading to Efrat. Stoning of cars occurred daily. Snipers killed and wounded several residents. Daily living was severely disrupted (12). Bét Shemesh, in contrast, had not experienced a single attack within its boundaries. The roads leading to it were safe and open. There had been no stoning or shooting incidents.

Data Collection

Trained interviewers used the telephone directory to identify every fifth consecutive entry for each letter of the alphabet to contact participants in each community. Following an explanation of the study and oral consent, a questionnaire was distributed to participants' homes and collected a day later. Written informed consent was obtained from each participant upon distribution of the questionnaires.

Instruments and Key Measures

Situation-specific measures. The participants' exposure to distinct, terror-related events during the 8 months before data collection was assessed by using a version of the trauma history questionnaire employed by Goodman et al. (13). The original instrument inquires about 13 specific events, and those that were irrelevant to the current situation (e.g., rape, natural disaster) were replaced by more relevant ones. Our adapted instrument included 13 situation-specific events (e.g., being stoned while driving a car; being shot at; witnessing a gunshot injury; being stuck in a road block; witnessing damage to property; being forced to evacuate one's home). Exposure items for the revised questionnaire had been derived from 30 preliminary interviews with community residents, who described the various ways in which they, and others, were exposed to terrorism.

The questionnaire also evaluated the degree of distress experienced during each exposure, using a 4-point severity scale (0=no distress; 3=extreme distress). Exposure frequency was computed as the sum of all positive endorsements of exposure. Response intensity was the average distress across positively endorsed items. The internal consistency of the response intensity scale was good (Cronbach's alpha=0.87, average inter-item correlation=0.45).

Disruption of daily routines was assessed by a nine-item questionnaire, developed from the same exploratory interviews. The instrument evaluated threat-related disruption of daily life in nine distinct areas. Each item was rated on a 5-point severity scale (0=no disruption; 4=extreme disruption). The disruption score was calculated by summing all items. The instrument's internal consistency was satisfactory (Cronbach's alpha=0.89, average interitem correlation=0.49).

Generic measures. PTSD and PTSD symptoms were assessed with the self-report Posttraumatic Symptom Scale (14). Responses to the Posttraumatic Symptom Scale items were anchored to the most severe, terrorism-related incident experienced during the previous 8 months. The Posttraumatic Symptom Scale evaluates the presence or the severity of 17 DSM-IV PTSD symptoms during the preceding month on a 4-point frequency scale (0=not at all or only once; 3=almost always or five or more times per week). The instrument yields a diagnosis of PTSD and a continuous measure of symptom severity. A score of one or higher signifies the presence of a DSM-IV PTSD symptom. A continuous score was obtained by summing all items.

General distress. The Brief Symptom Inventory (15, 16) has been previously used to evaluate general distress—including after the 9/11 attacks (2). The instrument's 53 items evaluate nine symptom domains. Their summation provides a measure of global symptom severity (the Global Severity Index). The Brief Symptom Inventory has norms for healthy adults in the United States and in Israel (17, 18) as well as gender-corrected T scores for each item. By convention, a T score above 63 (i.e., 1.3 standard deviations above the gender- and item-specific population mean) indicates a clinically meaningful symptom (15).

Functional impairment. As described in the study by Pearlin and Schooler (19), subjects' level of functioning during the month that preceded data collection was assessed by evaluating four domains: 1) the ability to pursue task performance, 2) controllability of emotions, 3) the ability to sustain rewarding interpersonal contacts, and 4) the ability to maintain positive self-value. Each domain was assessed on a 5-point Likert scale. For each domain, a score of 0 represented, respectively, being unable to assume one's roles at work, home, or socially; having no effective control of one's emotional reactions; being unable to engage in rewarding or meaningful relationships with others; and not feeling good about oneself. Conversely, a score of 4 represented, respectively, excellent functioning, good emotional control, meaningful and satisfying relationships with others, and a very good feeling about oneself. This four-item instrument has satisfactory internal consistency (Cronbach's alpha=0.74; average interitem correlation=0.41). A person was considered as being significantly impaired if his or her score was more than one standard deviation below the sample's average.

Statistical Analyses

We used two-tailed t tests and analyses of variance (ANOVAs) for group comparisons, linear regression for testing the prediction of continuous variables, and stepwise logistic regression to test the prediction of PTSD. Data are reported as means and standard deviations. Additionally, standard errors are reported.

Results

Participants and Background Characteristics

We approached 362 residents of the two communities, and 277 (76.5%) agreed to participate in the study. Subjects who declined did not differ from those who participated in gender rates. Refusal rates were similar in both communities. Comparisons between the current study group's age, education, and number of children in the household and those reported for the same communities in Israel's Central Bureau of Statistics' Population Census (10) were performed. According to the National Census, the mean age of residents in Efrat was 38.9 years and in Bét Shemesh was 41.4. In this study, the respective mean ages were 40.1 and 35.1 years. The mean number of children in a household was between 3.7 and 3.8 according to the National Census; in this study it was between 3.3 and 3.4. Education levels (data available for the directly exposed group alone) were as follows: 37.2% with college degree (B.A. or equivalent) and 39.6% with full academic degree (CM.A. or equivalent) (National Census figures) and, respectively, 42.6% and 34.6% (current study).

One subject withdrew his participation, and 20 had incomplete data. The study's final sample was N=256: 167 from the directly exposed community and 89 from the indirectly exposed community. The two groups were similar in terms of gender composition, marital status, education, and average income but differed in age (Table 1).

TABLE 1. Demographic Characteristics of Residents From Israeli Communities Directly Versus Indirectly Exposed to Continuous Terror

Characteristic	Residents of Directly Exposed Community (N=167)[a]		Residents of Indirectly Exposed Community (N=89)[b]		Analysis
	Mean	SD	Mean	SD	t
Age (years)	40.11	1.01	35.13	0.87	3.30*
Number of children in household	3.45	0.15	3.29	0.16	0.69
	N	%	N	%	χ^2
Gender					0.92
Male	56	33.53	25	28.07	
Female	111	63.47	64	71.91	
Marital status					6.50
Married	141	84.43	82	92.13	
Widowed	4	2.40	0	0.0	
Divorced	4	2.40	3	3.37	
Single	18	10.78	4	4.50	
Education					4.01
Up to high school	28	16.77	10	11.24	
B.A. or equivalent	71	42.51	44	49.44	
Higher degree	58	34.73	29	32.58	
Other	10	5.99	6	6.74	
Income					4.84
Well below average	19	11.38	5	5.62	
Below average	12	7.19	5	5.62	
Average	35	20.96	14	15.73	
Above average	75	44.91	49	55.06	
Well above average	26	15.57	16	17.97	

[a] Town of Efrat, 11 miles from Jerusalem, in which shooting incidents occurred frequently and erratically blocked the roads leading to the town. Stoning of cars occurred daily. Snipers killed and wounded several residents. Daily living was severely disrupted.
[b] Town of Bét Shemesh, 15 miles from Jerusalem, which had not had an attack within its boundaries. The roads leading to it were safe and open. There had been no stoning or shooting incidents.
*p<0.01.

Frequency and Intensity of Exposure

As expected, residents of the directly exposed community were more frequently exposed to terror-related incidents (mean=6.58 incidents per resident [SD=3.96, SE= 0.31]) than were those in the indirectly exposed community (mean=2.41 [SD=3.20, SE=0.34]) (t=8.94, df=254, p<0.001).

Men and women reported similar frequencies of exposure (men: mean=5.69 episodes [SD=4.56, SE=0.51], women: mean=4.87 [SD=4.02, SE=0.30]; t=1.41, df=254, p= 0.20). Age-corrected ANOVA for exposure frequency showed a significant main effect of site (F=59.26, df= 1, 254, p<0.0001) but a nonsignificant main effect of gender and a nonsignificant site-by-gender interaction.

The intensity of the immediate response to exposure was significantly higher in the directly exposed group (mean=1.61 [SD=0.73, SE=0.06]) relative to the indirectly exposed group (mean=1.30 [SD=0.82, SE=0.09]) (t=2.87, df=254, p<0.01). Immediate response intensity was also significantly higher in women (mean= 1.65 [SD=0.75, SE= 0.06]) relative to men (mean=1.27 [SD=0.76, SE=0.08]) (t=3.68, df=254, p<0.001). Age-corrected ANOVA for response intensity showed significant main effects of site (F=4.84, df=1, 253, p<0.02) and gender (F=7.42, p<0.01) but no site-by-gender interaction.

Disruption of Daily Living

With the exception of financial burden, daily life was significantly more disrupted in the directly exposed group (Table 2). In both communities, women reported higher disruption of daily living. Age-corrected ANOVAs for total disruption score revealed significant main effects of site (F=73.38, df=1, 253, p<0.0001) and gender (F=3.9, 1, 253, p<0.05) but no significant site-by-gender interaction.

Prevalence of PTSD

Forty-five residents of the directly exposed community (26.95%) and 19 residents of the indirectly exposed community (21.35%) met Posttraumatic Symptom Scale criteria for PTSD, a nonsignificant difference. PTSD with significant distress was observed in 31 (18.56%) of the directly exposed residents and 15 (16.85%) of the indirectly exposed residents, also a nonsignificant difference. Last, PTSD with significant distress and functional impairment was seen in 16 (9.58%) of the directly exposed residents and six (6.74%) of the indirectly exposed residents, a nonsignificant difference.

Women and men had equal rates of PTSD according to both Posttraumatic Symptom Scale criteria (N=45 or 25.71% of all women and N=19 or 23.46% of all men) and by PTSD symptom criteria with distress and dysfunction (N=13 or 7.43% of women and N=9 or 11.11% of all men). Individuals with and without PTSD had similar age, marital status, income, and education.

TABLE 2. Disruption of Daily Routine Among Residents From Israeli Communities Directly Versus Indirectly Exposed to Continuous Terror

Area of Disruption	Residents of Directly Exposed Community (N=167)[a]			Residents of Indirectly Exposed Community (N=89)[b]			t (df=254)
	Mean Score[c]	SD	SE	Mean Score[c]	SD	SE	
Work	1.06	0.97	0.69	0.24	0.69	0.07	7.04**
Leisure activities	2.44	1.16	1.04	1.28	1.04	0.11	7.99**
Relationships with friends residing elsewhere	2.24	1.24	1.10	0.89	1.10	0.12	8.61**
Relationships with family members residing elsewhere	1.93	1.31	1.07	0.76	1.07	0.11	7.21**
Relationships with immediate family	0.83	1.19	0.84	0.41	0.84	0.09	2.78*
Financial burden	0.68	1.10	0.94	0.44	0.94	0.10	1.78
Day-to-day schedule	1.27	1.03	0.58	0.35	0.58	0.06	7.85**
Mobility	2.17	1.28	0.95	0.99	0.95	0.10	7.81**
Overall quality of life	1.91	1.10	0.98	1.10	0.98	0.10	5.95**
Total disruption score	14.16	7.11	0.56	6.21	4.80	0.51	9.67**

[a] Town of Efrat, 11 miles from Jerusalem, in which shooting incidents occurred frequently and erratically blocked the roads leading to the town. Stoning of cars occurred daily. Snipers killed and wounded several residents. Daily living was severely disrupted.
[b] Town of Bét Shemesh, 15 miles from Jerusalem, which had not experienced a single attack within its boundaries. The roads leading to it were safe and open. There had been no stoning or shooting incidents.
[c] Each area of disruption was rated on a 5-point severity scale (0=no disruption; 4=extreme disruption).
*p<0.01 .**p<0.0001.

Symptoms Expressed

The two groups had comparable levels of PTSD symptoms and Brief Symptom Inventory scores (Table 3). Somatization and paranoid ideation were somewhat higher in the indirectly exposed group, but the difference was not significant when corrected for multiple comparisons. The Global Severity Index was also higher in the indirectly exposed group.

Relative to men, women tended to endorse significantly more reexperiencing symptoms (mean=2.74 [SD=2.63, SE=0.20] versus 1.58 [SD=1.61, SE=0.18]) (t=3.68, df=254, p<0.001) and more hyperarousal symptoms (mean=4.22 [SD=3.87, SE=0.29] versus 3.25 [SD=3.42, SE=0.38]) (t=1.92, df=254, p=0.053) as well as somewhat higher, but not significantly different, avoidance symptoms (mean=2.28 [SD=4.74, SE=0.36] versus 1.89 [SD=2.74, SE=0.30]) (t=1.07, df=254, p<0.30). There was no interaction between gender and community for PTSD symptoms. ANOVA for Posttraumatic Symptom Scale total score showed a significant main effect of gender (F=5.43, df=1, 252, p<0.05) but no significant main effect of site or site-by-gender interaction.

TABLE 3. Symptoms of PTSD and General Distress Exhibited by Residents From Israeli Communities Directly Versus Indirectly Exposed to Continuous Terror

Measure	Residents of Directly Exposed Community (N=167)[a]			Residents of Indirectly Exposed Community (N=89)[b]			t (df=254)
	Mean	**SD**	**SE**	**Mean**	**SD**	**SE**	
Posttraumatic Symptom Scale score							
Intrusion	2.45	2.40	0.19	2.35	2.44	0.26	0.68
Avoidance/numbing	2.32	2.91	0.23	1.84	2.27	0.24	1.35
Arousal	4.00	3.68	0.28	3.76	3.92	0.42	0.45
Total score	8.71	7.94	0.61	7.84	7.26	0.77	0.70
Brief Symptom Inventory score							
Somatization	51.25	9.66	0.75	55.16	11.50	1.22	−2.95**
Obsessiveness	57.71	10.45	0.81	58.03	11.50	1.22	−0.23
Interpersonal sensitivity	55.01	10.23	0.79	56.95	11.60	1.23	−1.41
Depression	57.65	9.77	0.76	58.54	9.41	1.00	−0.72
Anxiety	59.56	9.67	0.75	60.17	10.17	1.08	−0.48
Hostility	57.36	10.37	0.80	59.43	10.70	1.13	−1.34
Phobic anxiety	60.03	10.30	0.80	62.18	10.20	1.08	−1.64
Paranoid ideation	55.57	9.84	0.76	58.29	10.52	1.12	−2.10*
Psychoticism	56.63	9.63	0.75	59.01	10.83	1.15	−1.86
Global Severity Index	58.77	10.15	0.79	61.62	9.74	1.03	−2.23*

[a] Town of Efrat, 11 miles from Jerusalem, in which shooting incidents occurred frequently and erratically blocked the roads leading to the town. Stoning of cars occurred daily. Snipers killed and wounded several residents. Daily living was severely disrupted.
[b] Town of Bét Shemesh, 15 miles from Jerusalem, which had not experienced a single attack within its boundaries. The roads leading to it were safe and open. There had been no stoning or shooting incidents.
*p<0.05.**p<0.01.

In order to further illustrate the similarity in PTSD symptom expression between the two communities, Figure 1 displays the prevalence of each of the 17 DSM-IV PTSD symptom criteria for both sites. As

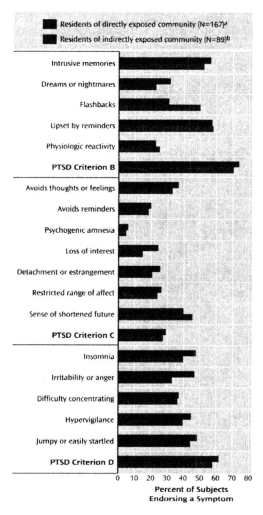

FIGURE 1. PTSD Symptom Expression Among Residents From Israeli Communities Directly Versus Indirectly Exposed to Continuous Terror

[a]Town of Efrat, 11 miles from Jerusalem, in which shooting incidents occurred frequently and erratically blocked the roads leading to the town. Stoning of cars occurred daily. Snipers killed and wounded several residents. Daily living was severely disrupted.

[b]Town of Bét Shemesh, 15 miles from Jerusalem, which had not experienced a single attack within its boundaries. The roads leading to it were safe and open. There had been no stoning or shooting incidents.

can be seen, most PTSD symptoms were equally reported. Eighty-seven percent of the participants reported at least one PTSD symptom. Intrusive thoughts/recollections and being upset by reminders were the most frequently reported symptoms. Avoidance (DSM-IV criterion C) was less frequently reported than reexperiencing (criterion B) or hyperarousal (Criterion D).

Distribution of PTSD Symptoms

A goodness-of-fit test evaluated the distribution of Post-traumatic Symptom Scale scores in the study group. Post-traumatic Symptom Scale scores were not normally distributed (distribution χ^2=64.5, df=20, p<0.0001; Kolmogorov-Smirnov d=0.14, p<0.01).

Comparison between subjects who met Posttraumatic Symptom Scale criteria for PTSD (N=64) and those who did not (N=192) revealed Posttraumatic Symptom Scale scores that were relatively high in the former (mean=18.68 [SD=6.95, SE=0.87]) and very low in the latter (mean=4.9 [SD=4.00, SE=0.29]) (t=19.20, df=254, p<0.0001). Figure 2 illustrates the distribution of PTSD symptoms among subjects with and without PTSD.

Similarly, subjects who met symptom criteria for PTSD scored abnormally high on the Global Severity Index (mean=67.78 [SD=6.18, SE=0.77]), whereas the mean Global Severity Index of those without PTSD (mean=57.07 [SD=9.61, SE=0.69]) was within one standard deviation of the normal population score. The between-group difference was statistically significant (t=8.35, df=254, p<0.0001).

Table 2: Posttraumatic Symptom Scale Score Distribution Among Subjects With and Without PTSD

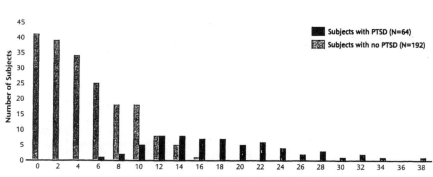

Contributors to PTSD and General Distress

Stepwise logistic regression assessed the contributions of exposure and disruption of routines (in that order) to Posttraumatic Symptom Scale-defined PTSD. In the directly exposed group, the analysis shows a significant contribution of exposure (odds ratio=1.29; maximum likelihood χ^2=13.77, df=2, p=0.001), with an additional and significant contribution of disruption of routines (odds ratio=3.30; model χ^2=36.64, df=3, p<0.00001; difference from previous fit: χ^2=26.12, df=1, p<0.00001). In the indirectly exposed group, neither exposure nor disruption of routines predicted PTSD status (exposure: odds ratio=1.09 [χ^2=2.58, df=2, p=0.28]; disruption of routines: odds ratio=1.06 [χ^2=3.42, df=3, p=0.33]).

Stepwise regression analysis evaluated the relative contribution of exposure and disruption of routines to the Global Severity Index in each group. Disruption of routines, but not exposure, contributed to the Global Severity Index in both groups (directly exposed group: R^2=0.21 [F=42.27, df=1, 164, p<0.0001]; indirectly exposed group: R^2=0.08 [F=7.46, df=1, 88, p<0.01]).

Discussion

The results of this study show comparable PTSD prevalence and comparable levels of PTSD symptom intensity and general distress in two differentially exposed communities during a wave of terror. The results also show equal exposure of men and women to terrorist incidents and equal prevalence of PTSD in both genders. They additionally demonstrate an unequal distribution of PTSD symptoms, such that a subgroup of about 25% of the population was highly symptomatic, whereas others expressed low levels of symptoms. Many subjects met DSM-IV PTSD symptom criteria without simultaneously reporting significant distress and impairment. Disruption of daily living significantly contributed to PTSD symptoms and Brief Symptom Inventory scores.

In line with previous reports (1–5), this study documented a frequent occurrence of PTSD symptoms in proximal and remote communities. Contrasting with previous research (2, 3), however, a "proximity" effect was not found. This observation was consistent across symptoms (Figure 1) and instruments (Table 2). It replicates a previous finding (11) of nonsignificant association between geographical proximity to sites of terrorist acts and PTSD symptoms among Israelis at about the same period.

A parsimonious explanation of this finding is that both communities were similarly affected by the stressfulness of living near Jerusalem—a prime target for terrorism, or living in a country besieged by terror. Terr et al. (20) refer to this phenomenon as "distant-traumatic effects not connected to personal or direct threat." The idea that the proximity to Jerusalem or an overall stressfulness of ongoing terror was sufficient to create equal responses in two differentially exposed communities raises the intriguing possibility of a ceiling effect, i.e., a saturation of responses by common threat factors. The idea of a "ceiling effect" should be further tested as a potential model for evaluating and predicting communities' responses under duress.

The immediate and vivid way in which violent attacks are currently broadcasted and communicated may also account for the lack of difference between the communities. Accordingly, repeated exposure to unpredictable, shocking, and instantly communicated sights of terror defies the perception of safety, which geographic distance would normally confer.

Another way of interpreting this effect is a shift from probabilistic and exposure-driven, risk-assessment to indiscriminate contextual-driven fearfulness and an ensuing sense of imminent threat (21). Interventions designed to help people to better discern patterns of threat may, therefore, be called for in terror-prone areas.

Several symptoms were higher in the indirectly exposed group (Table 3), and this requires further elaboration. Expressed symptoms reflect the summation of perceived threat on the one hand and perceived control and coping self-efficacy on the other (22). While this study did not measure these modulators of stress responses, it might be the case that being concretely challenged and having to actively cope with daily stressors contributes to a sense of controllability and self-efficacy. In that sense, the many ways in which residents of the directly exposed community had to concretely cope with terror threat could have contributed to better perception of controllability and self-efficacy, and thereby to a reduction in symptoms. A previous descriptive publication (7) discussed the ways in which responding to the challenge of continuous terrorism in Jerusalem could be experienced as a sequence of small daily victories (e.g., effectively organizing one's day, successfully driving to and from work) rather than defeats.

One must also remember that the current study recorded "peritraumatic" reactions, i.e., those experienced during exposure. Psychological defenses may operate at such time and mitigate the open expression of emotions. The longterm consequences of higher exposure may be different.

The results of this study suggest that terror does not equally affect every community member. Although a minority appear to be highly susceptible to terror threat, most subjects had virtually no PTSD symptoms. The idea that only a subset of residents may require help may have important implications for planning of interventions. In addition, reporting PTSD was inconsistently associated with distress and impairment. A previous study of the 9/11 attacks (2) used the Brief Symptom Inventory to independently evaluate the prevalence of "clinically significant psychological distress." However, the prevalence of probable PTSD in that study was inferred from a cutoff score on a PTSD symptom scale. Our results suggest that combining PTSD symptoms, psychological distress, and functional impairment may effectively differentiate those whose defensive reactions of vigilance, worry, and caution become ineffective and who might need help.

This study is limited by the use of ad hoc measures of exposure and disruption of routines. In addition, the choice of two stable Israeli towns may not be representative of occurrences in which community resources and structures break down. However, this work identifies several clinically meaningful patterns of the response to continuous terror, such as the existence of a subgroup with very intense reactions. Furthermore, our understanding of what exposure represents should be modified in order to account for vectors of threat other than concrete exposure to acts of terror. Our results are in line with the conclusion of Silver et al. (6) that "the psychological effects of a major national trauma are not limited to those who experience it directly, and the degree of response is not predicted simply by objective measures of exposure." The complex interplay of the experience of danger, the disruption of daily routine, the coping behaviors, and the resulting symptoms of distress and disability provides a more nuanced picture of the dynamic impact of terror.

From the Center for Traumatic Stress Studies, Department of Psychiatry, Hadassah University Hospital; the Department of Psychology, Bar Ilan University, Ramat Gan, Israel; and the Department of Psychiatry, Saint Vincent Catholic Medical Centers, New York.

Supported by NIMH grant MH-50379

References

1. Galea S, Ahern J, Resnick H, Kilpatrick D, Bucuvalas M, Gold J, Vlahov D: Psychological sequelae of the Sept 11 terrorist attacks in New York City. N Engl J Med 2002; 346:982–987

2. Schlenger WE, Caddell JM, Ebert L, Jordan K, Rourke KM, Wilson D, Thalji L, Dennis JM, Fairbank JA, Kulka RA: Psychological reactions to terrorist attacks: findings from the national study of Americans' reactions to Sept 11. JAMA 2002; 288:581–588

3. Galea S, Resnick H, Ahern J, Gold J, Bucuvalas M, Kilpatrick D, Stuber J, Vlahov D: Posttraumatic stress disorder in Manhattan, NY, after the Sept 11th terrorist attacks. J Urban Health 2002; 79:340–353

4. Schuster MA, Stein BD, Jaycox LH, Collins RL, Marshall GN, Elliott MN, Zhou AJ, Kanouse DE, Morrison JL, Berry SH: A national survey of stress reactions after the Sept 11, 2001, terrorist attacks. N Engl J Med 2001; 345:1 507–1 512

5. North CS, Nixon SJ, Shariat S, Mallonne S, McMillen JC, Spitznagel EL, Smith EM: Psychiatric disorders among survivors of the Oklahoma City bombing. JAMA 1999; 282:755–762

6. Silver RC, Holman EA, McIntosh DN, Poulin M, Gil-Rivas V: Nationwide longitudinal study of psychological responses to Sept 11. JAMA 2002; 288:1235–1244

7. Shalev AY: The Israeli experience of continuous terrorism (2000–2004), in Disasters and Mental Health. Edited by LopezIbor JJ, Christodoulou G, Maj M, Sartorius N, Okasha A. London, John Wiley & Sons (in press)

8. Brewin C, Andrews B, Valentine J: Meta-analysis of risk factors for posttraumatic stress disorder in trauma exposed adults. J Consult Clin Psychol 2000; 68:748–766

9. Israel Defense Force: Casualties Statistics. www.idf.il

10. Israel Central Bureau of Statistics: Population Census, 2004. www.cbs.gov.il

11. Bleich A, Gelkopf M, Solomon Z: Exposure to terrorism, stress related mental health symptoms and coping behavior among a nationally representative sample in Israel. JAMA 2003; 290: 612–620

12. Shalev AY, Tuval-Mashiach R, Hadar H: Posttraumatic stress disorder as a result of mass trauma. J Clin Psychiatry 2004; 65(suppl 1):4–10

13. Goodman LA, Corcoran CB, Turner K, Yuan N, Green BL: Assessing traumatic event exposure: general issues and preliminary findings for the Stressful Life Events Screening Questionnaire. J Trauma Stress 1998; 11:521–542

14. Foa EB, Riggs DS, Dancu CV, Rothbaum BO: Reliability and validity of a brief instrument for assessing post-traumatic stress disorder. J Trauma Stress 1993; 6:459–473

15. Derogatis LR, Spencer PM: The Brief Symptom Inventory (BSI): Administration, Scoring and Procedures Manual I. Baltimore, Clinical Psychometric Research, 1982

16. Derogatis LR, Melisaratos N: The Brief Symptom Inventory: an introductory report. Psychol Med 1983; 13:595–605

17. Baider L, Peretz T, Hadani PE, Koch U: Psychological intervention in cancer patients: a randomized study. Gen Hosp Psychiatry 2001; 23:272–277

18. Baider L, Walach N, Perry S, De-Nour AK: Cancer in married couples: higher or lower distress? J Psychosom Res 1998; 45: 239–248

19. Pearlin LI, Schooler C: The structure of coping. J Health Soc Behav 1978; 22:337–356

20. Terr LC, Bloch DA, Michel BA, Shi H, Reinhardt JA, Metayer S: Children's symptoms in the wake of *Challenger:* a field study of distant-traumatic effects and an outline of related conditions. Am J Psychiatry 1999; 156:1536–1544

21. Fendt M, Fanselow MS: The neuroanatomical and neurochemical basis of conditioned fear. Neurosci Biobehav Rev 1999; 23: 743–760

22. Benight CC, Harper ML: Coping self-efficacy perceptions as a mediator between acute stress response and long-term distress following natural disasters. J Trauma Stress 2002; 15:177– 186

The Continuous Trauma Phenomenon: Psychological Responses to Continuous Terror—An Exchange Between Dr. Trappler and Dr. Shalev*

Brian Trappler, M.D. and Arieh Y. Shalev, M.D.

To the Editor:
May 13, 2006

While many studies in the literature evaluate PTSD following a discrete traumatic occurrence, the recent article by Shalev and colleagues evaluates the effect of continuous terror by examining the occurrence of general distress, PTSD symptoms, and full-blown PTSD, in two suburbs of Jerusalem.[1] While Efrat (the directly exposed community) and Bet Shemesh (an indirectly exposed community) are located at similar distances from Jerusalem (11 miles for Efrat and 15 miles for Bet Shemesh), during the eight months preceding the data collection, the directly exposed community was practically under siege, whereas the indirectly exposed community was not. Specifically, shooting incidents occurred frequently, and erratically blocked the roads leading to Efrat. Stoning of cars occurred daily. Snipers killed and wounded several residents. While stress exposure was far more pervasive in the directly exposed community of Efrat, the prevalence of PTSD symptoms (26.95%) for the directly exposed community sample compared with that of 21.35% for the indirectly exposed community was not statistically significant.[1] These findings reflect a high frequency of traumatic anxiety in neighborhood communities exposed either directly or indirectly to continuous threat.

---

* *Note to Reader*: The letter above was written by Dr. Trappler to the editor of *American Journal of Psychiatry* in response to the article by Shalev et al., "Psychological Responses to Continuous Terror: A Study of Two Communities in Israel" (see the preceding article in this anthology). Following Dr. Trappler's letter is the reply by Dr. Shalev.

When comparing the effects of circumscribed catastrophic events with those of a continuous terror paradigm, a spectrum emerges representing two contrasting stress models with differing psychological, behavioral, neurobiological, and sociological implications. In fact, the fear conditioning model has guided the neurocircuitry theories of PTSD and its pathophysiology.[2,3] Previous exposure to trauma is the important risk factor for PTSD.[4] Furthermore, studies have shown that previous history of stressors may alter the HPA axis response to subsequent stressors.[3,4] Fear conditioning leads to heightened threat responsiveness, overgeneralization of fear responses, and failure of extinction.[5] Kindling and sensitization within the amygdala is the accumulative result of multiple traumas and predicts the development of PTSD.[5,6]

Examples of discrete, targeted, terrorist-attack occurrences were the attacks on the Twin Towers and Pentagon and the Brooklyn Bridge Shooting. As Associate Director of the Anxiety Disorder Clinic at the State University of New York, Brooklyn, I had the opportunity of treating survivors of two of these attacks. In the Brooklyn Bridge Shooting, four of the eleven survivors had PTSD symptoms 10 months after the attack, and none after 18 months.[7]

In contrast, in the Continuous Terror Model, as a result of sensitization to repeated fear-conditioned cues and neurological kindling, PTSD is more likely to endure.[8,9] The mechanisms involved here may include both long-term potentiation as well as lasting changes in the genetic regulation of neurotransmitters, intracellular messengers, and cellular structures.[2,8] These changes affect primarily the amygdala, hippocampus, and medial prefrontal cortex—the triad of structures implicated in fear conditioning.[2,8,9]

In the Continuous Terror study conducted by Shalev and colleagues, the investigators expressed concern regarding the implications of living under continuous terror, where recuperation may not occur as it does following a discrete occurrence.[1] In fact, in the chapter written by Dr. Shalev on "The Life Course of Post-Traumatic Stress Disorder," in a book titled, *Post-Traumatic Stress Disorder*, he writes, "Studies have examined the construct of validity of PTSD in various samples of trauma survivors, and found it to be good."[10]

Despite somewhat fluctuating individual trajectories, symptom severity in cohorts of chronic PTSD patients remain stable over time.[10] These observations are consistent with the findings of the "Cross-Sectional and Longitudinal Aging Study (CALAS)," funded by the U.S. National Institute on Aging. 1,369 Holocaust survivors interviewed from the Israel National Population Registry reported a high incidence of cumulative life events distress, a lower level of lifestyle activity, and poorer social functioning.[11] Overall, the findings indicated that older Holocaust survivors randomly approached in a nonclinical setting still endure the sequelae of their trauma. These findings are consistent with the theory of sensitization, and are particularly pertinent to the Continuous Terror model posed by Dr. Shalev and colleagues. Not only does this bode poorly for life quality on a long-term time trajectory, but raises concern for the potential impact of a major national disaster of the magnitude of a September 11th event in a pre-traumatized population. In fact, this vulnerability to retraumatization was reported by Solomon and Prager in this journal, where survivors of the Nazi Holocaust showed more pronounced psychological symptoms following the SCUD missile attacks during the Persian Gulf War than the rest of the population.[12]

Brian Trappler, M.D.
New York

References

1.   Shalev, A.Y., Tuval, R., Frenkiel-Fishman, S., Hadar, H., Eth, S. Psychological Responses to Continuous Terror: A Study of Two Communities in Israel. *Am. J. Psychiatry* 2006; 163:667-673.
2.   Kent, J., Sullivan, K.J., Rauchs, G. Neural Circuitry and Signalling in Anxiety. In: Kaplan, G., Hammer, R. (eds). Brain Circuitry and Signalling in Psychiatry. *American Psychiatric Publishing* 2002; 13-133.
3.   Southwick, S.M., Yehuda, R., Wang, S. Neuroendocrine Alterations in Posttraumatic Stress Disorder. *Psychiatric Annals* August 1998; 28:8.
4.   Resnick, H.S., Yehuda, R., Pitman, R.K., Foy, D.W. Effect of Previous Trauma on Acute Plasma Cortisol Level Following Rape. *Am. J. Psychiatry* 1995; 152:1675-1677.
5.   Post, R.M., Weiss, S.R.B., Smith, Ma. Sensitization and Kindling. Neurobiological and Clinical Consequences of Stress: From Normal Adaptation

to Post-Traumatic Stress Disorder. *Lippincott-Raven: Philadelphia* 1995; 203-24.

6.   Davis, M. The Role of Amygdala in Fear and Anxiety. *Annual Rev. Neurosc.* 1992; 15:353-375.

7.   Trappler, B., Friedman, S. Post Traumatic Stress Disorder in Survivors of the Brooklyn Bridge Shooting. *Am. J. Psychiatry* May 1996; 153:5.

8.   Mcewen, B. The Effects of Stress on Structural and Functional Plasticity in the Hippocampus. In: Charney, D., Nestler, E., Bunney, B. (eds). *Neurobiology of Mental Illness* 1999 Oxford University Press.

9.   LeDoux, J.E., Iwata, J., Cicchetti, P., Reis., D.J. Different Projections of the Central Amygdaloid Nucleus Mediate Autonomic and Behavioral Correlates of Conditioned Fear. *The Journal of Neuroscience* July 1988; 8(7):2517-2529.

10.   Shalev, A.Y. Post-Traumatic Stress Disorder, Diagnosis, Management and Treatment. In: Nutt, D., Davidson, J., Zohar, J. (eds). Post-Traumatic Stress Disorder: Diagnosis, History and Life Course. *Martin Dunitz Ltd.* 2000.

11.   Shmotkin, D., Blumstein, T., Modan, B. Tracing Long-Term Effects of Early Trauma: A Broad-Scope View of Holocaust Survivors in Late Life. *Journal of Consulting and Clinical Psychology* 2003; Vol.71, No.2, 223-34.

12.   Solomon, S., Prager, E. Elderly Israeli Holocaust Survivors During the Persian Gulf War: A Study of Psychological Distress. *Am. J. Psychiatry* 1992; 149:1707-1710.

Comments by Dr. Shalev: Dr. Trappler expands the implication of our study of the effects of continuous terror by commenting on putative biological underpinning of repeated exposure and their potential long-term effects. These are very important points, since our published study only concerned reactions recorded during adversities, whereas Dr. Trappler's comment implies that the relative resilience shown in that work might reveal itself as masking a hidden sensitizing effect. This could lead to currently resilient survivors becoming more sensitive to subsequent stressors, or developing PTSD symptoms in the future. The debate regarding the sensitizing or immunizing effect of exposure has not been resolved. A study of Israeli soldiers who served in two successive wars (the 1973 Yom Kippur and the 1982 Lebanon wars) supports both views[1]: Those who had developed combat stress reactions (CSR) during the first war were more likely to develop PTSD in 1982 (a sensitization effect). However, soldiers who had fought without developing CSR reacted to subsequent exposure with levels of stress that were lower than those of newly exposed combatants (an immunizing effect). Clarifying these issues is of particular relevance in an era where US soldiers may be called for second or third tour of duty in Iraq or Afghanistan. Moreover, some specifics of current warfare and terrorism (e.g., the rapid and vivid communication of atrocities and suffering) significantly extend the circle of those affected by extreme events. Theory suggests that controllable stress tends to be immunizing whereas uncontrollable stress sensitizes.[3] Poor social support after trauma is a major risk factor for PTSD.[4] A series of animal studies have established the role of soothing body contact in reversing the stress-sensitizing effects of early maternal separation—indeed in turning stress-sensitivity into stress-resilience.[4] In humans, appraisal of traumatic events and subsequent symptoms is a powerful moderator of the link between exposure and PTSD.[5] We, therefore, come back to the old adage: Hug a Veteran Today. Because post-exposure factors significantly contribute to the outcome of traumatic events it behooves us, particularly at these dire times, to protect those among us who might be repeatedly exposed by as much personal support and understanding as we can. This, alone, may not prevent repeated exposure. It might help those exposed.

References

1. Solomon Z, Garb R, Bleich A, Grupper D: Reactivation of combat-related posttraumatic stress disorder. *Am J Psychiatry* 1987; *144*(1):51-5

2. Foa EB, Zinbarg R, Rothbaum BO: Uncontrollability and unpredictability in post-traumatic stress disorder: an animal model. *Psychol Bull* 1992; *112*(2):218-38

3. Brewin CR, Andrews B, Valentine JD: Meta-analysis of risk factors for posttraumatic stress disorder in trauma-exposed adults. *J Consult Clin Psychol* 2000; *68*(5):748-66

4. Liu D, Diorio J, Tannenbaum B, Caldji C, Francis D, Freedman A, Sharma S, Pearson D, Plotsky PM, Meaney MJ: Maternal care, hippocampal glucocorticoid receptors, and hypothalamic-pituitary-adrenal responses to stress. *Science* 1997; *277*(5332):1659-62

5. Ehlers A, Mayou RA, Bryant B: Cognitive predictors of posttraumatic stress disorder in children: results of a prospective longitudinal study. *Behav Res Ther* 2003; *41*(1):1-10

The Effects of September 11 on Traumatized Refugees: Reactivation of Posttraumatic Stress Disorder

J. David Kinzie, M.D.,[1] James H. Boehnlein, M.D.,[1,2]
Crystal Riley, M.A.,[1] Landy Sparr, M.D.[1,3]

ABSTRACT: Secondary traumatization from the tragic events of September 11, 2001 was studied among an ethnically diverse group of refugees who had been previously traumatized in their native war torn countries. A brief clinically oriented questionnaire was developed and administered to a clinic population of Vietnamese, Cambodian, Laotian, Bosnian and Somalian refugees in the Intercultural Psychiatric Program at Oregon Health & Science University. Traumatic symptoms and responses to the widely televised images from September 11 were assessed among the five ethnic groups, and the differential responses among patients with posttraumatic stress disorder (PTSD), depression, and schizophrenia also were assessed. The strongest responses were among Bosnian and Somalian patients with PTSD, and the Somalis had the greatest deterioration in their subjective sense of safety and security. Regardless of ethnic group, PTSD patients reacted most intensely, and patients with schizophrenia the least. Although patients largely returned to their baseline clinical status after two to three months, this study shows that cross-cultural reactivation of trauma has a significant clinical impact. It is essential that clinicians anticipate PTSD symptom reactivation among refugees when they are reexposed to significant traumatic stimuli.

The observation that current stresses could activate memories of prior losses and traumatic events was made by Lindemann in 1944 (Lindemann, 1944). Reactivations, either psychological distress or physiological activity, or exposure to cues that symbolize or resemble an aspect of the traumatic event were included in posttraumatic stress disorder (PTSD) diagnostic criteria (American Psychiatric Association, 1980). Solomon et al. (1987) reported that combat-related reactivation of PTSD is a complex phenomenon and could take several forms. Furthermore, traumatized former POWs were found to be very vulnerable to the det-

[1] Department of Psychiatry, Oregon Health & Science University, 3181 S.W. Sam Jackson Park Road, UHN-80, Portland, Oregon 97201-3098. Send reprint requests to Dr. Kinzie.
[2] Veterans Administration Northwest Network, Mental Illness Research, Education, and Clinical Center (MIRECC), Portland, Oregon.
[3] Mental Health Services (P-3-MHDC), Veterans Administration Medical Center, Portland Oregon.

rimental effects of life events (Solomon, 1995). Indeed, post-disaster negative life events have been found to increase the incidence and severity of PSTD (Maes, 2001). In a recent study of Gulf War Scud missile survivors, the threat of additional Iraqi missile attacks as late as 1998 was found to have an unfavorable effect on a previously exposed population (Toren et al., 2002). This supports the view that exposure to a subsequent traumatic event serves as a reminder in vulnerable survivors.

For more than 20 years, the Intercultural Psychiatric Program at Oregon Health and Science University has been treating refugees from Southeast Asia, many of whom have been noted to suffer from effects of severe trauma. A consistent clinical finding reported in the Cambodians, but noted in all refugee groups, has been the reactivation of posttraumatic stress syndrome after experiencing current stressors such as an accident, surgery, assault, or even a violent television show (Kinzie, 1988). A related study found that the experience of violence in the United States predicted Cambodian adolescent PTSD severity and perceived level of functioning (Berthold, 1999). In a psychological study exposing subjects to traumatic video scenes, Cambodians were found (compared with control subjects and Vietnam veterans) to have a general nonspecific arousal to all traumatic scenes (Kinzie et al., 1998).

On September 11, 2001, with the terrorists' destruction of the World Trade Center, a dramatic and terrible event was repeatedly broadcast to the American public. There were widespread feelings of sadness, anger, and anxiety. In our clinical work with refugees, it soon became apparent that the television viewing of this event had profound and disturbing effects, with recurrent nightmares, intrusive memories, depressed mood, and a sense of not being safe in America, a place where most felt they had found security. Added to this was the further insecurity and vulnerability felt by two Muslim groups, Bosnians and Somalians, who felt singled out by their appearance and religious background.

Tragic as the 9/11 attack was, it did provide a unique opportunity to study the effects of secondary traumatization on a group previously severely traumatized, many of who suffered from a diagnosis of PTSD. Even though ethnicity, religion, and time from the refugee trauma were variables, all of these refugees had witnessed the same television images of the World Trade Center destruction, which provided a unique and uniform stimulus for measuring retraumatization. In this report, we describe the results of a brief clinically oriented questionnaire given to Vietnamese, Cambodian, Lao, Bosnian, and Somalian refugees attending our Intercultural Psychiatric Program. The specific goals of this report are:

a) To describe the variable responses of five ethnic patient groups to viewing the 9/11 events. Specifically, we report symptom changes for each group.

b) To describe the variable responses of patients in three major diagnostic groups—PTSD, depression, and schizophrenia.

c) To describe the sense of personal vulnerability that was affected by ethnic and religious background.

d) To assess the effects of ethnicity, religion, diagnosis, and elapsed time since the initial trauma on the responses to 9/11.

Setting

The clinical setting for this report is the Intercultural (formerly Indochinese) Psychiatric Program at Oregon Health and Science University, Portland, Oregon. The Program has existed for 24 years, originally serving refugees from Vietnam, Laos, and Cambodia. In the past 3 years, two more highly traumatized groups, the Bosnians and Somalians, were added. The total number of current patients enrolled in our clinic is now 900 (which also includes refugees from the former Soviet Union and from Latin America). Each patient has a single psychiatrist and a mental health counselor who provide psychiatric treatment and case management, often for many years. The refugee groups in the study include the following.

Vietnamese

This was the clinic's first group of refugees, arriving after the fall of Saigon in 1975. The primary traumas were related to the Vietnam War, and in some cases, multiple traumas during the escape process (the boat people), in refugee camps, or in reeducation camps. This group has the lowest percentage of PTSD, approximately 50% (Kinzie et al., 1988), reflecting the fact that many had little or no traumatization. This group is approximately 50% Buddhist and 50% Christian.

Laotians

This group followed the Vietnamese and had suffered the effects of the Indochinese war in Laos or in refugee camps. This group is mostly Buddhist.

Cambodians

This is a severely traumatized group (Boehnlein et al., 1985; Kinzie et al., 1984) because almost all of the patients went through 4 years of extreme cruelty from 1975 to 1979, during the Pol Pot regime. Most of the patients continue to have PTSD symptoms despite long-term treatment. With the exception of a few recent conversions to Christianity, this group is largely Buddhist.

Bosnians

This group came to the United States shortly after the conflicts and the ethnic cleansing that occurred in the former Yugoslavia from 1992 to 1993. All were subjected to war experiences, including indiscriminate bombing, rape, and ethnic and religious persecution. Some also experienced the Serbian-controlled concentration camps. All the patients in our study are Muslim, although less traditional and less strict in observance than the Somalis.

Somalis

The civil war and tribal conflict occurred in Somalia in 1991 and 1992 and resulted in general lawlessness, with looting, mass starvation, and indiscriminate killing. The refugees who made it to the United States usually had lived for several years in refugee camps, mostly in Kenya. All Somalian refugees lost immediate family members and were separated from others. They are the most recent arrivals to the United States, usually less than 3 years. All are strict Muslims and most of the women wear traditional Islamic clothing.

Methods

When it became apparent to us that the 9/11 events significantly impacted the patients' lives, the clinical staff (psychiatrists and counselors) met to develop a questionnaire that could assess the degree of impact.

We wanted to develop a questionnaire that could be easily administered during regularly scheduled patient visits and would be understandable to patients from a variety of ethnic groups and trauma backgrounds. The questionnaire, administered by the attending psychiatrists, included age, gender, ethnicity, current working diagnosis, and years since the major trauma. The patients were asked if they had seen the 9/11 events on the television and if any of this had had an effect on them. This latter question, and the subsequent questions about changes in nightmares, flashbacks, and depression, was structured on an analog 10-point scale, with 10 being the worst or the most effect and 0 being no effect. The visual analog scale has been found to reliably monitor pain and mood (Aitkin, 1969; Folstein and Luria, 1973) and we have used the Mood Analogue Scale in our clinic for more than 10 years. Usually, the patients could state where their reaction occurred on the 0 to 10 scale, but occasionally the psychiatrist rated the reaction based on the totality of verbal and nonverbal responses, which were sometimes pressured and emotional. Additionally, the patients were asked to judge how safe they felt before 9/11 and after. The questionnaire included an open-ended question about their major feelings since 9/11. As a part of regular clinical contact, the interviews often provided relevant clinical data that promoted important clinical intervention. Because the data were collected during regularly scheduled appointments, and because of clinical time pressures, not all patients seen during this time were given the questionnaire, nor was there an attempt to randomize. All interviews were completed within two months after September 11, 2001. We interviewed 29% of the Vietnamese, 39% of the Cambodians, 43% of the Laotians, 54% of the Bosnians, and 47% of the Somali clinic patients.

Results

Table 1 shows the numbers of each group interviewed, the average age, percent female, and the percentage with the diagnoses of PTSD, depression, and schizophrenia. The data show a largely middle-age population, with the Vietnamese being the oldest (data not in table). The gender breakdown is similar to the entire clinic population, which is predominately female. Many men from these cultures were killed during repeated wars and conflicts. The majority of patients suffer from PTSD, with depression being the second most common diagnosis. A number of patients have psychotic disorders, usually schizophrenia. Excluded from the analysis were eight patients with both schizophrenia and PTSD, all of whom were women (two Vietnamese, three Cambodians, one Bosnian, and two Somalians).

Table 1 (N = 181)

Ethnicity	N	Average Age	% Female	PTSD[a] (N)	Depression (N)	Schizophrenia (N)
Vietnamese	74	55.7	74	48	18	8
Cambodian	43	53.4	70	37	3	3
Laotian	17	50.1	62	10	5	2
Bosnian	26	48.5	69	18	3	5
Somalian	17	42.7	88	17		
Total	181	52.2 (20-80)	73%	132	30	19

[a] Posttraumatic stress disorder

Eight patients with both schizophrenia and PTSD were excluded from analysis (all female—two Vietnamese, three Cambodian, one Bosnian, two Somalian).

Virtually all (95%) saw the television images of the 9/11 disaster, and 92% of those said it affected them. Of the 14 nonaffected patients, six were diagnosed with PTSD, three with depression, and five with schizophrenia. They included eight Vietnamese, five Cambodians, and one Bosnian.

Table 2 specifically summarizes data from patients with PTSD. The analogue scale measures the patients' subjective report of how significantly the 9/11 events affected them, along with the degree of change in their nightmares, flashbacks, and depression. The patients also rated their perceived sense of safety before and after 9/11 (Table 3), with most patients reporting feeling at least very safe before 9/11. The Somalis felt the greatest decrease in security, and the Cambodians had the least change. Table 4 summarizes results based on diagnoses, irrespective of ethnicity. Results for those with either PTSD or depression were very similar. Comparing patients with the three major diagnoses, those with schizophrenia were least affected by the 9/11 events.

We asked an open-ended question to all patients about their major reactions to 9/11. The most common reaction was fear among Bosnians (75%) and Somalis (47%). Uncertainty and insecurity was most common among Vietnamese (31%) and Laotians (53%). The Cambodians showed a mixture of fear (26%) and uncertainty (23%), but 23% also stated they felt no change. Fear clearly was a predominant reaction among Bosnians and Somalis, probably representing their personal sense of vulnerability.

Table 2

Patients with Posttraumatic Stress Disorder (N = 129)

1. How much did it affect you?

Not safe at all		Mildly safe		Moderately safe			Very safe		Extremely safe
0	1	2	3	4	5	6	7	8	9	10

2. Since 9/11, how much did your nightmares change?
3. Since 9/11, how much did your flashbacks change?
4. Since 9/11, how much did your depression change?

Ethnicity	Affect you*	Nightmare change**	Flashback Change***	Depression change****
Vietnamese (N = 42)	7.33	6.13	4.65	6.09
SD	+2.34	3.13	3.26	2.45
Cambodian (N = 37)	6.65	2.57	5.05	3.92
SD	3.08	3.18	3.32	2.92
Somalian (N = 17)	9.00	6.94	8.00	6.29
SD	1.27	3.60	2.92	3.53
Laotian (N = 10)	7.10	2.40	3.50	6.20
SD	2.08	2.80	2.32	1.55
Bosnian (N = 18)	9.22	4.56	6.50	8.56
SD	1.31	3.88	3.55	1.15

ANOVA test of significance
F = 5.414, Significance = .000, **F = 9.274, significance = .000, ***F = 4.303, significance = .000, ****F = 10.384, significance = .000.

Table 3

Change in Feeling Safe

Not safe at all		Mildly safe		Moderately safe			Very safe		Extremely safe
0	1	2	3	4	5	6	7	8	9	10

Ethnicity	How Safe Before 9/11	How Safe Now	Change*
Vietnamese, N = 73 (SD)	7.92 (2.66)	3.74 (2.62)	4,19 (2.85)
Cambodian, W = 46 (SD)	9.52 (1.21)	6.54 (2.39)	2.98 (2.93
Somalian, W = 19 (SD)	9.89 (.46)	3.58 (2.85)	6.32 (2.79)
Laotian, N = 17 (SD)	8.00 (1.17)	3.99 (2.22)	4.06 (2.59)
Bosnian, N = 27 (SD)	8.93 (2.09)	4.59 (3.35)	4.33 (3.10)

*ANOVA, F = 5.17; Significance = .001.

Table 4

Results Based on Diagnosis (All Ethnicities)

Diagnosis	Affect You*	Change in Depression**	Change in Feeling Safe***
PTSD[a] (N = 124)	7.60	5.24	4.24
SD	2.51	2.81	3.14
Depression (N = 27)	7.44	5.84	4.24
SD	2.24	2.94	2.73
Schizophrenia (N = 17)	5.41	3.94	3.00
SD	3.66	2.91	3.03
Other (N = 80)	6.00	4.00	3.12
SD	3.85	3.55	3.48

[a] Posttraumatic stress disorder
ANOVA: *F = 4.048, significance = .008; **F = 2.857, significance = .039; ***NS

Discussion

Traumatized refugees in our clinic showed a strong reaction to the horrific events of 9/11. We were interested in whether there were differences in responses among patients as a function of ethnicity or diagnosis. The strongest responses were among patients with PTSD from Bosnia and Somalia. Interestingly, the Somalis also had the greatest deterioration in their sense of safety and security. These two groups experienced the most recent war atrocities, which also were highly covered by the television. It is possible that their reactions are related to their Muslim religious background and the geographic proximity of their homeland to the Middle East and Afghanistan. Both factors may contribute to a greater sense of vulnerability. Although the Cambodians also experienced massive trauma in their homeland, their more muted reaction may be related to the relative remoteness of their experiences both in time and place. Also, it is conceivable that the more muted response, despite the significant presence of chronic PTSD, is partially because of both the fatalism and acceptance at the core of Buddhism.

The differences in reactions related to diagnosis are interesting. Although patients with PTSD had a strong reaction to 9/11, so did the patients with a primary diagnosis of depression. Overall, patients with PTSD reacted more intensely, which would not be surprising because the 9/11 events could reactivate traumatic memories. Patients with schizophrenia, and even with schizophrenia and PTSD, reacted the least of the diagnostic groups, regardless of ethnicity. Most of the schizophrenic patients had little or no reaction and did not have an increase in fear or paranoia, despite viewing the 9/11 images. This may be caused by isolation of emotion in schizophrenia, a probable core symptom found in all cultures.

Although patients returned to their baseline clinical status after 2 to 3 months, this data shows that cross-cultural reactivation of PTSD symptoms from traumatic stimuli has a significant clinical impact on patients. Although some differences existed among ethnic groups, it is essential that clinicians anticipate likely PTSD symptom reactivation among refugee patients when they are exposed to significant traumatic stimuli.

Conclusion

a) Refugees showed a strong reaction to events of 9/11.

b) Those with PTSD showed more significant impact. Patients with schizophrenia showed fewer changes and effects in all areas compared with patients with PTSD and depression.

c) Somalis (all with PTSD) showed the most significant changes in symptoms, including an increase in nightmares and flashbacks, whereas Bosnians experienced more general reactions of fear and an increase in depression.

d) The Somalis were the ethnic group that showed the most significant change in their sense of security.

e) The most common open-ended response to 9/11 was fear among Bosnians (73%) and Somalis (47%). Uncertainty was most common among Laotians (53°%), whereas no one reaction stood out among Vietnamese and Cambodians.

f) Television coverage of the highly graphic and disturbing effects of 9/11 had serious psychiatric consequences for traumatized refugees (especially those with PTSD and depression) and had to be addressed in their treatment. One of the most helpful and practical clinical interventions was to encourage patients to turn off their television sets.

References

Aitkin RCB (1969) Measurement. of feelings using Visual Analogue Scale. *Proc R Soc Med* 62:989-992.

American Psychiatric Association (1980) *Diagnostic and statistical manual of mental disorders* (3rd ed). Washington, DC: American Psychiatric Association.

Berthold SM (1999) The effects of exposure to community violence on Khmer refugee adolescents. *J Trauma Stress* 12:455–471.

Boehnlein JK, Kinzie JD, Ben R, Fleck J (1985) One year follow up study of post traumatic stress disorder among survivors of Cambodian concentration camps. *Am J Psychiatry* 142:956–959.

Folstein M, Luria R (1973) Reliability, validity and clinical applications of Visual Analogue Mood Scale. *Psychol Med.* 3:479–486.

Kinzie JD, Frederickson RH, Ben R, Fleck J, Karls W (1984) Post traumatic stress disorder among survivors of Cambodian concentration camps. *Am J Psychiatry* 141:645–650.

Kinzie JD (1988) The psychiatric effects of massive trauma on Cambodian refugees. In: JP Wilson, Z Hasel, B Kehana (Eds), *Human adaptation to extreme stress*. New York: Plenum Press.

Kinzie JD, Boehnlein JK, Leung P, Moore P, Riley C, Smith D (1990) The prevalence of posttraumatic stress disorder Southeast Asian refugees. *Am J Psychiatry* 147:913–917.

Kinzie JD, Denney D, Riley C, Boehnlein J, McFarland B, Leung P (1998) A cross-cultural study of reactivation of posttraumatic stress disorder symptoms. *J Nerv Ment Dis* 186:670–676.

Lindemann E (1944) Symptomatology and management of acute grief. *Am J Psychiatry* 101:141–148.

Maes M, Mylle J, Delmerse L, Janca A (2001) Pre- and post-disaster negative life events in relation to the incidence and severity of post-traumatic stress disorder. *Psychiatry Res* 105: 1–12.

Solomon Z (1995) The effect of prior stressful experience on coping with war trauma and captivity. *Psychol Med 25:1280*—1294.

Solomon Z, Gorb R, Bleich A, Grupper D (1987) Reactivation of combat-related posttraumatic stress disorder. *Am J Psychiatry* 144:51–55.

Toren P, Wolmer L, Weizman R. Magel-Vandl, O, Loan, N (2002) Retraumatization of Israel civilians during a reactivation of the Gulf War threat. *J Nerv Ment Dis* 190:43–45.

Section III: The Enduring Effects of PTSD

Survivors: A Review of the Late-Life Effects of Prior Psychological Trauma

Joel Sadavoy, M.D., F.R.C.P.(C)

ABSTRACT: The author reviews the literature on the epidemiology, symptom picture, and treatment of elderly patients who have encountered serious psychological trauma earlier in life. Data are predominantly derived from studies of aging Holocaust survivors and combat veterans from World War II, the Korean Conflict, and Vietnam. Survivor syndromes persist into old age, but patterns of expression vary. Holocaust survivors appear to have adapted well to instrumental aspects of life, whereas combat warriors may show less functional life-adaptation. Persisting symptoms in all groups include marked disruptions of sleep and dreaming, intrusive memories, impairment of trust, avoidance of stressors, and heightened vulnerability to various types of age-associated retraumatization. There is a deficiency of controlled treatment studies of traumatized elderly patients, but successful group, individual, and family clinical interventions have been described.

From *The Australia Morning Herald*, October 28, 1995:

Age Brings Holocaust of Memories

Kitty Fischer is 68, a survivor of Auschwitz. Memories of the Auschwitz concentration camp have come flooding back now that she has time to think. She said that "it has become more difficult as I get older. I dwell a lot more on the past. I talk to the few friends I have who are all survivors. We just have to face up to it—that we are as alone now as in 1944 when we were separated from our parents."

Currently, there is a significant population of aged survivors of trauma, as well as a large group of younger individuals who will graduate later into old age with unresolved trauma-related problems. It has been proposed that previous psychological trauma produces tenacious symptoms that color the aging process, continuing to affect profoundly the areas of emotion, behavior, relationships, and the individual's sense of self. Conversely, because old age often is a time of stress, the aging process interacts with earlier trauma to affect symptom expression and complicate the management of these elderly patients. The late-life effects of prior psychological trauma are poorly studied and understood in elderly populations, and no comprehensive review of the area as it applies to elderly patients is available. This article reviews what is known about the forms of symptom expression resulting from previous psychological trauma in elderly patients, and the effects that aging may have on the conceptualization of symptom etiology and treatment.

Posttraumatic Stress Disorder (PTSD) and The Survivor Syndrome

Kardiner[1] is credited with the first modern description of PTSD in 1941. However, it was not until the 1960s that the concept began to be studied in depth, focusing on concentration camp survivors of the Nazi Holocaust.[2] Research blossomed in the 1980s, when the chronic effects of war trauma on Vietnam veterans became the object of study.

The term *survivor syndrome* is attributed to Neideriand.[2] Although the terms are similar, PTSD seems to be a more general form of survivor syndrome, the latter having characteristics (e.g., guilt, unresolved grief, and an emphasis on physical symptoms) that are somewhat more specific to Holocaust trauma. In the following summary of the survivor syndrome as Neiderland described it, the related DSM-IV[3] PTSD items are italicized in parentheses. The survivor syndrome is characterized by increased arousal *(persistent symptoms of increased arousal);* persistent multiple symptoms of both psychological and physiological disruption, including anxiety and cognition/memory changes—that is, amnesias *(inability to recall an important aspect of the trauma)*; hypermnesia *(intrusive recollections);* and confusion between the present and the period of persecution *(acting or feeling as if the traumatic event were recurring);* chronic depressive states characterized by guilt and often focused on specific traumas, such as loss of children, parents, or siblings; isolation and withdrawal *(detachment/estrangement from others and avoidance of thoughts* or *conversations associated with the trauma);* psychotic and psychotic-like symptoms *(illusions, hallucinations);* alterations of personal identity, that is changes in body image, sense of time and space, and self-image *(dissociative flashback episodes);* psychosomatic symptoms, particularly gastrointestinal, headache, and cardiac; nightmares *(traumatic dreams);* what Neiderland called "the appearance of being a living corpse;" and inability to verbalize the nature of the events.

It is now apparent that massive trauma can produce a chronic syndrome of varying intensity that includes the features of PTSD, survivor syndrome, and other variations. These features appear to be lifelong in many individuals and to affect not only elderly survivors, but their families and even subsequent generations.[4] The chronicity and extent of persistent symptoms makes this an important and relevant study in the elderly population.

Epidemiology of Late-Life Effects of Trauma

There have been no specific studies of the epidemiology of PTSD in the general population of elderly individuals,[5] but some data are available for war veterans.

According to a Department of Veterans Affairs report,[6] 52% of World War II veterans and 35.2% of Korean Conflict veterans were exposed to combat. This means that about 25% of the then-current population of older Americans had been exposed to combat. On the basis of these data, it has been suggested that combat trauma effects on both physical and psychological health are so pervasive as to be a crucial "hidden variable" in the health of the current cohort of older men.[7]

Studies of aging cohorts of war veterans consistently show high persisting levels of PTSD-related symptoms. Over time, prevalence rates of PTSD decrease, perhaps because of selective mortality and the memory bias inherent in retrospective studies. Kulka et al.[8] estimated that 31% of the 3.1 million men who served in the Southeast Asian theater during the Vietnam War have a lifetime history of PTSD. Among those exposed to heavy combat, 36% demonstrated persisting PTSD, with lifetime prevalence estimates as high as 70%.[9]

In a study of Department of Veterans Affairs medical patients in 1990, 18.5% of World War II veterans had current PTSD.[10] PTSD often coexists with other psychiatric diagnoses,[11] and prevalence rates for PTSD soar among veterans who have other psychiatric disorders. Rosen et al.[12] found a lifetime prevalence rate for the diagnosis of PTSD of 54% and a current diagnosis of 27% in World War II veteran psychiatric patients.

Late-Life Effects of Earlier Trauma: Holocaust Survivors

General clinical picture. Although clinical studies of the lasting effects on geriatric survivors of Holocaust trauma are sparse, some data are available. Kuch and Cox[13] retrospectively studied the data from German compensation assessments of 124 community-dwelling older adults (mean age 62) who had survived the Holocaust. They found that gross indicators of adjustment were favorable; that is, 80% were married, and 83% had children. Despite these indicators of favorable adjustment, however, the symptom profile was highly significant, particularly for physiological symptoms. Of the Auschwitz survivors, 65% fulfilled criteria for PTSD, although only 22% of the survivors of other forms of Holocaust trauma fulfilled these criteria. In those with PTSD, sleep disturbances and nightmares were almost universal, and the majority exhibited hypervigilance, physiologically intense distress to reminders of the events, avoidance, intrusive ideation, impaired concentration, reduced interest, and irritability.

Robinson et al.[14] examined 103 Israeli survivors of the Nazi Holocaust who were under 13 years of age when the persecution began in their country and who were 50-69 years old at the time of study. They used a questionnaire that they designed for use with Holocaust survivors. Subjects' war experiences included death camps and death marches, various forms of hiding, and resistance-fighting with the partisans. Results were similar to those of Kuch and Cox.[13] Those who survived a death camp suffered from depression and anhedonia to a significantly greater degree than survivors of other forms of persecution. Despite persistent and significant symptoms, gross indicators of adjustment were favorable. Eighty-five percent had married, and subjects described a warm family atmosphere. Ninety-five percent had children and rated their adjustment to (Israeli) society as good or very good. In another uncontrolled cohort study, using the same questionnaire, Robinson et al.[15] examined a nonclinical sample of 86 Israeli Holocaust survivors (41 men and 45 women; average age 68.3 years). Holocaust-related physical symptoms persisted in 60%; 75% considered themselves still suffering from the Holocaust; and death camp survivors were significantly more affected than survivors of other forms of persecution on measures of 13 symptoms of the survivor syndrome. Despite their symptoms, however, other indicators of coping and adjustment were favorable. Eighty-seven percent reported good assimilation into Israeli society; 75% were still married, 94% had children, and 91% described their home atmosphere as warm.

Carmil and Carel[16] examined 1,150 Israelis (mean age 59 years) who had lived under Nazi occupation in Europe and 2,159 matched control subjects (mean age 61) with a questionnaire based on the Cornell Medical Index. Data were divided into three categories: emotional distress, general satisfaction, and psychosomatic complaints. This study was the only one to report a gender difference in symptom expression. Emotional distress was significantly greater in female survivors of the Holocaust. There was no difference in life satisfaction scores between the two groups, and, surprisingly, there also were no differences in psychosomatic complaints. One weakness of this study is its failure to identify the specific type and severity of war-related experiences in survivors or inquire about past trauma experiences in control subjects, making fuller interpretation of the data problematic.

The symptom picture in later life may present with different emphases. In an uncontrolled study sample of 200 community-dwelling individuals claiming compensation for the Nazi Holocaust, on average 20 to 30 years after the war, 85% demonstrated a survivor syndrome.[17] The author observed five nuclear syndromes: depression, anxiety, somatization, intellectual disturbance, and "contact abnormalities" (i.e., aggression, paranoid ideation, or sociopathic behavior). The severity of the symptoms varied with the nature of the trauma and, again, was most pronounced in survivors of extermination camps; next were concentration camp, labor camp, ghetto, and illegal hiding experiences. He concluded that the survivor syndrome reflects a permanent personality change.

These studies suffer from significant methodological flaws, the most important of which are biased sampling and absent control groups. Despite these flaws, the studies are consistent in reporting the persistence of formal PTSD or "Holocaust-related symptoms" in the majority of death-camp survivors. Symptoms in this subgroup were more severe than in those who had suffered other forms of persecution.

Overall, the studies of community-dwelling nonclinical survivor populations support the contention that after the war, survivors adapted well during their adult lives to instrumental aspects of life, such as working, maintaining economic stability, marrying, and procreation. Some nongeriatric studies have concluded from data of this type that there is no serious psychological impairment in survivors or their children.[18-20]

However such survey studies are weakened by the difficulty of examining disordered emotional and cognitive states that may be masked by apparently good instrumental adaptation. The more convincing data suggest that emotional reactivity often may remain intense and dysphoric without affecting measures of adaptation and overt behavior. The idea that deeper psychological problems may remain hidden unless specifically sought out is illustrated by Matusek.[21] Writing in 1969 about 130 patients who were believed to show no after-effects of the concentration camp experience, he observed that, on closer inquiry, he did not see a single person in this group who was without pathology.[21]

Sleep disturbance. Sleep disturbance is one of the hallmarks of the survivor syndrome in late life[13] and should be distinguished from the normative changes in sleep architecture that occur with advancing age. Rosen et al.[22] studied sleep in three groups of elderly individuals: survivors of the Nazi Holocaust (n = 42, mean age 69); depressed elderly patients (n = 37, mean age 70); and healthy control subjects (n = 54, mean age 54). Sixty-four percent of survivors scored in the moderate-to-severe range of sleep disorder, as did 96% of depressed patients, but 94% of the healthy control subjects scored in the normal range. In contrast to the depressed group, the survivors reported significantly more frequent awakenings due to "bad dreams," and "being unable to breathe comfortably." The duration of time spent in the concentration camp correlated with the severity of sleep impairment.

Other studies, on younger subjects, have concluded that the effects of trauma include either near-complete suppression of dream recall or persistent nightmares incorporating memories of the actual trauma.[23-25] If the low rate of dream recall in younger persons persists into old age, it is important clinically, because many elderly patients, on clinical inquiry, will deny the presence of traumatic dreams. The absence of recall may be a component of the avoidance symptoms of the syndrome. The author's clinical experience with several hundred survivors of the Holocaust suggests that the persistence of traumatic dreams into old age is variable, with some elderly subjects reporting continued vivid dreaming, whereas others state that over time their dreams have moderated and occasionally have disappeared.

Trust and trauma. Of great importance to the geriatric group is an observation that in survivors there is a lasting erosion of basic trust.[4] Such trust is especially difficult for those who have been victimized willfully by others.[26] Indeed, it has been suggested that what is destroyed in individuals traumatized in this way is their belief in the very possibility of good. From this perspective, the most traumatic events are those perpetrated by others, when compared with the effects of accidents or natural disasters.[4]

Themes of mistrust arise frequently among trauma victims.[27,26] Lifton has suggested that these problems with trust arise from the victims' recognition of their own vulnerability and mortality.[29-31] Elderly persons, more often than those in other age groups, must put their trust in others, sometimes family, but often health care workers who are strangers providing necessary life-sustaining services. Impaired trust can have obvious deleterious effects on such dependent elderly individuals, who may reject or avoid essential care. Institutionalization, for example, may evoke feelings of being held, incarcerated, trapped, tortured, or otherwise victimized—feelings that, in turn, lead to withdrawal from, and mistrust of, needed medical or social support personnel, to the detriment of the patient.

In psychotic states, the content of the psychosis may be filled with tormentors from the past. A Holocaust survivor who was hospitalized on a geriatric psychiatry ward for psychotic depression violently resisted electroconvulsive therapy, screaming his terrified conviction that he was being dragged to his death by Nazis.

The symptom of avoidance of potential triggers of trauma-related symptoms may remain prominent into old age, although studies are somewhat silent on this issue. For example, a 79-year-old man, on initial history-taking, became repeatedly resistive and agitated each time the therapist asked about family relations and losses that had occurred during the war 55 years earlier. Whenever he was questioned in this area, he protested that he had to go home. He revealed that he had always put such intrusive thoughts out of his mind because, in his words, "they can make you go crazy."

What is being avoided by survivors? A 68-year-old successful businessman tearfully revealed the recurrent vivid image of his last glimpse of his little brother before the Germans took him forever. An 80-year-old survivor recounted memories of a forced march that he said were as alive as the day they happened. His memories were of brutal beatings, shooting of the weak and sick, and dismembered bodies by the side of the road.

Despite frequent avoidance defenses, old age sometimes becomes a time when victims and survivors are prepared to discuss previously avoided memories for the first time. For example, 50 years after his experiences in the Holocaust, a man in his late 70s revealed to his therapist the existence of massive trauma during the war. He felt deep shame and guilt over what had happened, but wanted finally to speak of it. The only way that he could cope with speaking his memories aloud was to stand facing the wall in the therapist's office while recounting his traumatic story.

Combat Veterans

General clinical picture. Although most survivors of the Vietnam War are not yet in the geriatric age range, the course of symptoms almost 30 years after the war is instructive. Referring to this group, Goderez[32] described what he called the "warrior syndrome." It is characterized by belligerence, violence, suspiciousness, poor work history, severely disrupted interpersonal relationships, drug and alcohol abuse, risk-taking behaviors, psychopathological disorders, and self-destructive, marginal lifestyles. This picture contrasts dramatically with the relatively effective adaptation and apparently functional overt interpersonal relationships of the survivors of the Holocaust. He attributed some of the differences to the fact that Vietnam combat veterans coped actively with their stress by using deadly force to survive, rather than having to resort to passive suppression of rage or other emotions, as did the concentration camp survivors.

Archibald and Tuddenham's[33] controlled, comparative study of combat veterans supports Goderez's contention that the lifestyles and social adaptation of "warriors" are significantly disturbed. In general, combat veterans have reported more chronic health problems and diagnosed illnesses, engaged more often in risky behaviors such as drinking and smoking, and had poorer self-rated health.[8,34,35]

A subset of combat veterans who were subjected to prolonged incarceration under exceptionally harsh prisoner-of-war conditions demonstrate patterns of late-life social adaptation and psychological symptoms that are more similar to those of Holocaust survivors than other combat veterans.[36] The "warrior" experience alone, therefore, does not seem to necessarily predict poor social and lifestyle adaptation. Rather, we may hypothesize that encounters with massive trauma associated with help-lessness will produce a late-life picture closer to the survivor syndrome, whereas trauma associated with active combat may produce a warrior-type syndrome.

Sleep disturbance. Sleep disturbance emerges repeatedly as the most commonly reported symptom in aging survivors of combat trauma, and, as in many Holocaust survivors, combat-related nightmares appear to persist into old age.[12,36,37] In addition to disturbances of sleep and dreaming, other symptoms that persist frequently into old age are feelings of detachment or estrangement from others, memory impairment, intensification of symptoms by exposure to reminders of the traumatic events, hyperalertness, avoidance symptoms, guilt, diminished interest, and suddenly acting or feeling as if the traumatic event were recurring.[36]

Retraumatization and delayed emergence of symptoms. Clinical reports suggest that symptoms of massive trauma can lie dormant for many years, only to be reactivated in later life. Several case studies describe combat-related psychiatric symptoms emerging in previously asymptomatic war veterans, even 50 years after combat .[38-42]

Vulnerability to retraumatization may be particularly relevant to elderly persons because the effect of aging may compromise coping capacities. In a controlled study of a nonclinical group of elderly Israelis (Holocaust survivors: n = 61, mean age 68.3; control subjects: n = 31, mean age 72.9) conducted during the Persian Gulf War, those with a history of surviving the Nazi Holocaust had more pronounced psychological symptoms.[43] Similar retraumatization effects were noted during the notorious Demjaniuk trial in Israel[44] and in other circumstances.[45]

Mejo[46] reported the case of an 84-year-old woman who functioned well until her involvement in a motor vehicle accident that apparently reactivated traumatic memories of the bloody death of her sister during childbirth. Retraumatization effects may help to explain the higher level of distress found in cancer patients with a history of concentration camp survival vs. cancer patients without such a history.[47]

Case Report

Mrs. A, an inpatient in a hospital psychiatric unit, was admitted for treatment of depression. As a young woman of 26, while in a concentration camp, she had been subjected to torture in the form of freezing experiments on her legs. She came to psychiatric attention for the first time in her mid-70s, presenting with apparent depression and severe agitation. Her symptoms had begun apparently in response to emotional conflict over needing a hip operation. She had been given a video of the procedure to educate and prepare her for surgery; the tape had been emotionally distressing for her to watch because it evoked memories of the war. After her subsequent hip surgery, she returned home to an empty house with no one to turn to and became depressed. She rapidly improved with supportive therapy in a psychiatric day-hospital environment where, in her words, "they listened and cared." Not long after, she again became depressed after gynecological surgery and was admitted for inpatient psychiatric care.

Although the symbolic meaning and evocative retraumatizing power of her surgeries was crucially important to the emergence of depressive symptoms, hidden in her history was a more profound dynamic.

During the war, Mrs. A. had lost every one of her close, loving family. Her only surviving relative had been a Canadian physician, a cousin who found her and rescued her from Europe. In Canada she forged a home and a life, but it was clear that her cousin remained her constant beacon, a savior who was her key symbol of security and hope. What emerged on more careful history-taking was the fact that at about the same time as her hip surgery, her cousin had died.

Although many factors were operative, the death of her cousin seemed to be the most central factor in opening wide her survivor wounds in old age, leading to 3 years of depressive decompensation. With the loss of her savior, she had to face the aggressive assault of her illness, surgeries, and solitary confrontation with death. Moreover, old age had diminished her capacity to utilize previously sustaining defenses. In particular, this patient had always used rigid avoidance of thoughts and memories, presenting an aristocratic, somewhat narcissistic, remote, and polite appearance to the world, never speaking about the war outside her family, and denying dreams or other negative thoughts.

Physical illness may be retraumatizing in other circumstances of relevance to elderly patients. In a nongeriatric study of delirium in burn victims, Blank and Perry[48] evaluated psychological processes during and after delirium. Two groups emerged: Group One demonstrated much greater evidence of posttraumatic psychological disruption and reliving of their trauma. During the height of their delirium, they were retraumatized by reliving the trauma in the hallucinations and delusions that then led to subsequent pervasive preoccupation with their injury and fear of reinjury. Group Two, in contrast, were relatively unconcerned about their injuries, possibly because they were unconscious or drunk when burned. This study is worthy of comment when considering retraumatization experiences because delirium is so common in aged, medically ill, hospitalized patients. Further research is necessary to support the relevance of this study to elderly patients. However, two important issues for traumatized aged patients may be suggested: 1) that the presence of an underlying posttraumatic state may be a risk factor for increased agitation or morbidity during delirium and 2) that delirium, per se, may be a retraumatization experience.

Etiology of Posttraumatic States

A key issue in the etiology of trauma symptoms is how much is due to stress and how much to preexisting factors. The Task Force on War-Related Stress[49] has proposed a two-factor model of trauma: Factor 1, based on the severity of the stress (e.g., threat to life), and Factor 2, based on premorbid coping resources. They, like most others, suggest that one trauma "piggybacks" on another, and among the risk factors for PTSD, they list previous exposure to trauma. Also, they recognize the importance of environmental factors, such as recent life upheavals and social isolation. These factors are associated with old age in the form of losses and physical changes that may reactivate earlier loss and trauma. Old age is a life context that often is specifically unsupportive to dealing with trauma.[50] The view that old age is especially stressful to groups with earlier trauma has not been researched, but there is some support for the concept. Robinson et al.[15] and Dasberg[51] both suggested that some symptoms of the survivor syndrome are greater 50 years after the war. Others, similarly, have suggested that older individuals are more vulnerable to the sequelae of trauma and that events such as retirement and loss exacerbate PTSD symptoms in combat veterans.[7,52]

Kluznik et al.[53] found that although the frequency of formal PTSD in a group of former prisoners of war (n = 188) diminished with age, 40 years after the end of World War II, other features (i.e., generalized anxiety, affective disorder, and alcohol abuse) had increased.

Although early life experience and character development may be important modifiers of trauma symptom expression, the characteristics of intensity and duration of the trauma are prime determinants of long-term symptom production. Posttraumatic states are not due to a flaw, weakness, or neurotic element in the victim.[32] This formulation does not deny the importance of personality strengths or vulnerabilities deriving from developmental and psychodynamic factors that may strongly influence the intensity and forms of expression of the stress disorder.[54] However, from a practical therapeutic perspective, it is important to try to accurately identify the key traumatic source of the symptoms, so that therapeutic intervention may be directed appropriately. Clinical experience with elderly patients suggests that attempting to treat the symptoms of massive trauma as though they result primarily from early life conflicts fails; although to tailor the treatment to the unique aspects of the individual, it is important to incorporate key psychodynamic features of each patient.[54,55]

It appears that the severity of the trauma response may be modified or worsened by immediate posttrauma experiences.[26] For example, the Vietnam veterans encountered unexpected rejection and hostility upon coming home. The notion that significant personality change could result from trauma was controversial at that time, and symptoms often were attributed to preexisting character flaws.[32] Not surprisingly, veterans easily interpreted the stance of therapists toward their symptoms as "blaming," engendering further feelings of isolation, anxiety and projection. Holocaust survivors encountered a similar response after World War II,[26] and more recent survivors of trauma are often misunderstood for cultural reasons,[36] although no data are yet available for "ethno-racial" senior subjects.

Beyond the nature of the stress itself, several intrapsychic mechanisms have been proposed to explain the symptom picture generated by traumatic experience. Psychodynamic explanations abound. Key elements include premorbid vulnerabilities, the meaning of the event to the individual, and the impact of the events on psychic structures and functions such as attachment, self-esteem, or trust.[54,55,57-60] Also, massive trauma may overturn normal early development.[32,58] Clinical observations suggest that one outcome of these major psychological changes is the formation of what may be termed a traumatically induced "false self" (i.e., the effective coping skills that are observed in many survivors may be conceptualized as a form of character armor, protecting the victim's vulnerable true self that was impinged upon by the trauma). The false self meets the world successfully when supported by life circumstances such as stable marriage, having and raising children, immersion in activities and friendships, work, and good health. But the traumatically affected part of the self lies vulnerable beneath the surface; emotions and thoughts are waiting to be triggered by everyday experiences such as movies or news reports. Using Holocaust survivors as a paradigm, this identity disorder derives from a variety of factors, important elements of which are unresolved and unresolvable grief in conjunction with guilt, awareness of vulnerability, and destroyed trust. Although superficially adjusted, the vulnerable, traumatically affected "true self" often dominates emotional life, imposing the need to live a pleasureless life and provoking unusual fears of separation, inner feelings of emptiness predisposing to depression, intolerance of strong emotions, and intense longing for those who were lost. Affected individuals remain emotionally vulnerable, in part, because of the failure of their mourning processes, perhaps because, as Roth[61] pointed out, mourning is designed for loss, not for catastrophe.

Aging often produces a sense of alienation and disengagement from those who are younger. This leads to various attempts to maintain continuity and self-esteem by turning to past memories (i.e., reminiscence). However the supportive elements of reminiscence often are not available to victims, survivors, and veterans. In many cases, such reminiscence taps into traumatic memories and evokes anxiety, depression, or desperation.

The enduring neurobiological effects of psychological trauma are said to include alterations in function of the noradrenergic and serotonergic systems, the hypothalamic-pituitary-adrenocortical axis, endogenous opioid system, and the sleep-wake cycle.[62] Van Der Kolk et al.[63] have proposed a theory of "inescapable shock," which leads to depletion of the noradrenergic system. They suggest further that trauma victims with PTSD become addicted to stress to avoid endogenous opioid withdrawal. Kolb has theorized that the excess stimulation from psychic trauma leads to neuronal conditioning characterized by neurophysiologic sensitization. One result is impairment of learning responses.[64] These theories pose intriguing questions about the relationship between the natural course of PTSD symptoms into old age and normal age-related declines in neurotransmitters. One theoretical outcome might be blunting of symptom intensity with aging. Although there are no clear data, the long-term clinical course suggests some moderation of symptom expression in old age.

Management Issues

Treatment of geriatric patients with a history of massive psychological trauma requires careful diagnosis and flexible, often multifaceted interventions, recognizing the frequency of comorbidities and the effects on family systems.

Management begins with the taking of a careful history, including collateral information, and a physical evaluation. On the basis of the data now available, it seems important for the clinician to examine not only for a history of trauma, but also its nature, intensity, duration, and context. Special inquiry is made into sleep and dreams, remembering that absence or avoidance of traumatic dream recall is common. Here, collateral information from spouse or bed partner is helpful to determine whether the patient has nocturnal awakenings or other signs of agitation. Daytime response to dreams is important because dreams may be intense and retraumatizing. Because of the potential for retraumatization in old age, inquiry is most complete when it contains questions about current triggers of traumatic memories, such as physical illness, institutionalization, threatened or real losses and grief, and anniversaries or apparent positive events, such as the birth of a grandchild or a child's wedding.

When we examine for the effects of trauma, emphasis is placed on the nature of current relationships, keeping in mind the lasting power of psychic numbing and avoidance that may restrict pleasurable involvement with others and produce avoidance of strong affect states and heightened feelings of alienation.[65,66] The presence of an intimate relationship with a confidant may reflect survivors' capacity to tolerate affect and memories of their experience. Similarly, it is helpful to know if the patient is a member of a survivors' group or tends to deal with experiences alone. This information aids in the decision about whether group therapy (or other group experiences) vs. individual therapy, is more appropriate. Specific cultural variables may affect presentation and should be sought out—for example, guilt and shame, minimizing of events, or religious or cultural beliefs about symptoms.[67,68]

The stage of life in which the trauma occurred has relevance to late-life symptomatology. Silence about war experiences has been especially noted among aging child survivors of the Holocaust.[69] An integrated approach to diagnosis is especially relevant to trauma victims because comorbid diagnoses of depression, generalized anxiety, substance abuse, and personality disorder are common. Sorting out an Axis I disorder from physical illness and chronic, trauma-related symptoms is often difficult in the diagnosis of elderly patients.

Pharmacologic treatment. There are no available studies of medication therapy for trauma related symptoms in elderly patients. However the general goals of drug therapy probably will be similar to those for other age groups and include reducing intrusive memories and hyperarousal symptoms, improving sleep, reducing self-destructive or destructive impulses (especially in combat syndromes), treating comorbid conditions (e.g., depressive disorder), and controlling psychotic symptoms.[70]

In younger populations, partial benefits from tricyclic antidepressants and monoamine oxidase inhibitors have been demonstrated (mostly in Vietnam veterans), primarily in diminishing nightmares and intrusive thoughts.[71] Fluoxetine has been shown to ameliorate PTSD symptoms, especially avoidant symptoms.[72] Minor tranquilizers and sedative-hypnotics are commonly used, but easily become problematic for elderly patients because symptoms, especially sleep disturbance, generally are chronic. When situational stress reactivates previously controlled anxieties or dreams, brief pharmacotherapy, adjunctive to psychotherapy, is often helpful. Other potentially useful medications are propranolol,[73] carbamazepine,[74] lithium, and alprazolam.[73] Overall, the demonstrated response to pharmacotherapy in adult patients with PTSD is modest at best. With increasing age, patients become more vulnerable to medication side effects, further complicating routine use of these agents.

Psychotherapy techniques. Psychotherapeutic interventions must be individualized because the late-life presentation of early life trauma is so varied. Here, the data already cited suggest that a climate of trust, safety, consistency, and tolerance of the patient's affect in the therapy milieu, are crucial basic starting points. The therapy will be further strengthened if an integrated approach is taken to formulation of treatment modalities.[75]

Group psychotherapy has been reported as effective in relieving PTSD symptoms and improving social comfort in older war veterans.[76] Boehlein and Sparr[77] treated eight geriatric prisoners of war from the European theater in group psychotherapy. They concluded that recovery from PTSD in the geriatric population is a social process involving support, education, and provision of a forum to work through suppressed thoughts and emotions. Both group and individual therapy formats can provide such a forum.

Therapists may encounter unique problems when dealing with the victims because one component of psychotherapeutic work with this population is the need for the therapist to remain open to hearing and tolerating the patient despite the horror of his or her pain and suffering.[56] Counterreactions and countertransferences experienced by therapists may include withdrawal from the patient's emotional pain, as revealed by boredom or loss of interest, premature closure of issues stemming from therapist anxiety, and, especially with elderly patients, experiencing the need to act as the patient's savior (a response to the patient's conveyed pain and vulnerability).[26] All of these matters have been noted as general issues in geriatric psychotherapy,[76] but they take on special importance in traumatically injured patients.

It is known that psychotherapy is probably underutilized for elderly patients. This may be compounded by the presence of trauma pathology. Commenting on their data from a community study of survivors of the Holocaust, Levav and Abramson[78] wondered why so few survivors had received psychotherapy and suggested more careful research on the use of psychiatric services by survivors of trauma. For survivors of hostage-taking and torture, psychotherapy techniques are similar. Allodi[79] points out that supporting structures of the self are damaged under torture and that dynamic psychotherapy of various types is appropriate for these victims. However, there are no data for aging victims per se.

There is one case report of successful amelioration of some PTSD symptoms in an elderly man, by use of eye-movement desensitization,[80] but evidence for the efficacy of this treatment is still anecdotal.

There have been no reports on cognitive-behavioral therapy in elderly patients with trauma-related symptoms. In a study of young rape victims, exposure and stress inoculation therapies (SIT) have been effective,[81] although other researchers have reported that the effect of SIT is transient.[82] Brom et al.[83] conclude from a review of PTSD treatment studies that the strongest evidence for efficacy favors behavioral techniques.[83]

The following vignette briefly describes the value of cognitive reframing in the psychotherapy of a patient with traumatically induced anxiety and depression.

Clinical Report

Mrs. W, a 70-year-old woman, spent the war years from age 12 to 18 "hiding and running" through Poland as a member of the resistance. After the war, she married and raised a successful family but was plagued throughout her life by anxiety, sleep disorder, and traumatic dreams of the Germans coming for her. In her early 60s, she developed the first of several severe recurrent depressive episodes. Of note is the fact that these depressions were preceded by family events—the marriage of two of her children and the engagement of her youngest. She described her depressions as agonizing, "worse than the war," during which the intensity and frequency of dormant traumatic dreams and memories escalated. Treatment was directed at the depression. She was only partially responsive to antidepressants, but concurrent cognitive therapy approaches reduced symptom intensity and enhanced her feelings of control. The working hypothesis was that her anxiety and depression arose from her unconscious fear that if she failed to watch over and control her children, they would be doomed to the same fate that she had suffered. The patient was encouraged to vent her feelings and then received focused educational interventions to counter unrealistic distortions, for example, that catastrophe would befall her children if they pursued their plans of marriage. Efforts also focused on mobilizing acceptance, that is, helping her adopt a quality of fatalism and giving up the need to be so watchful, which she seemed prepared to accept. This acceptance took the form of "What can you do? Children must live their own lives. What will be will be." When she could revert to this stance, it diminished her anticipatory anxiety, which seemed rooted in chronic feelings of helplessness and loss of control stemming from her war trauma.

Family therapy. "Enmeshment"[84]—overinvolvement, guilt, and overconcern with the welfare of children[15]—have been reported in trauma survivors. Adult children of survivors may respond by attempting to compensate for their parent's lost family, restricting expression of their emotional pain, believing it can never compare with the pain of their parents, carrying on the incomplete mourning of the parent by denying themselves pleasure, and identifying with the trauma experience to the extent they develop elements of a survivor syndrome. The burden on the children of survivors of the Holocaust is poignantly brought to life by Ginsberg-McEwan.[85] In her clinical report, she details the successful intergenerational family therapy she conducted with aging survivors, their children and grandchildren. During therapy, special emphasis was placed on understanding how the Holocaust distorted the relationships of three generations and on repairing the damage. For example, the daughter lived with intense guilt about pleasure-seeking desires that caused her to suppress them. In turn, she unwittingly imposed the same restrictions on her own daughter every time she sought to express the natural joy of childhood.

Conclusions

It is clear from the data that the effects of trauma often persist into late life. The symptom picture may vary considerably, depending on the nature, duration, and intensity of the trauma, environmental factors, and strengths or weaknesses in the psychological make-up of the individual. Factors associated with aging may be retraumatizing. As Kastenbaum[50] has observed, all elderly people are survivors, facing increasing experiences of isolation, marginalization, and feelings of being viewed as burdens on society. On the other hand, the passage of time, various therapeutic interventions, and healing life experience can promote the healthy integration of traumatic experiences and modification of the trauma. The scope of these problems is widespread, and, unfortunately, new cohorts of future elderly survivors are created daily.

Research specific to the elderly group is exceedingly sparse, considering the public health implications of posttraumatic disorders and symptoms in this age group. We require basic epidemiological research with a multicultural perspective on the nature and frequency of symptoms in late life. To correct deficiencies in earlier studies, methodology should use blinded control groups drawn from both clinical and nonclinical samples and take into account the significant modifiers of intensity, multiplicity, duration, and context of the trauma, appreciation of the role of pretrauma psychological development and make-up of the subjects, and the presence of posttrauma environmental factors that may modify symptom expression. Some specific geriatric issues include the relationship of trauma to the first episode of the late-life comorbidities, such as depressive disorders and dementia; how these groups adapt to physical illness; trust and dependency issues that are raised in institutional care; and the use of various biological and psychological treatment modalities.

Despite the difficulties, horrors, and stresses encountered in treating traumatized elderly patients, therapists may take hope from the sometimes unimaginable strength and resilience of survivors in overcoming adversity, recreating lives, and living in old age.

References

1. Kardiner A: The Traumatic Neuroses of War. New York, P Hoeber, 1941
2. Neiderland EG: Clinical observations on the survivor syndrome. Int J Psychoanal 1968; 49:313-315
3. American Psychiatric Association: Diagnostic and Statistical Manual of Mental Disorders, 4th Ed. Wash., DC, American Psychiatric Association, 1994
4. Garland C: The lasting trauma of the concentration camp. BMJ 1993; 77-78
5. Flint AJ: Epidemiology and comorbidity of anxiety disorders in the elderly. Am J Psychiatry 1994; 151:640-649
6. Department of Veterans Affairs: Survey of veterans, III. Wash., DC, 1989
7. Elder G, Clipp E: Combat experience and emotional health: impairment and resilience in later life. J Pers 1989', 57:311-341
8. Kulka R et al: Trauma and the Vietnam War Generation: Report of Findings from the National Vietnam Veterans Readjustment Study. New York, Brunner-Mazel, 1990
9. Eberly R, Engdahl B: Prevalence of somatic and psychiatric disorders among former prisoners of war. Hosp Community Psychiatry 1991; 42: 807-813
10. Blake D et al: Prevalence of posttraumatic stress disorder symptoms in combat veterans seeking medical treatment. J Trauma Stress 1990; 3:15-27
11. Sierles F, Chen J. McFarland R: Posttraumatic stress disorder and concurrent psychiatric illness: a preliminary report. Am J Psychiatry 1983; 1177-1179
12. Rosen J, Fields R, Hand A, et al: Concurrent posttraumatic stress disorder in psychogeratrics patients. J Geriatr Psychiatry Neural 1989; 2:65-69
13. Kuch K, Cox B J: Symptoms of PTSD in 124 survivors of the Holocaust. Am J Psychiatry 1992; 149:337-340

14. Robinson S, Rapaport-Bar-Sever M, Rapaport J: The present state of people who survived the Holocaust as children. Acta Psychiatr Scand 1994; 89:242-245

15. Robinson S, Rapaport J, Durst R et al: The late effects of Nazi persecution among elderly Holocaust survivors. Acta Psychiatr Scand 1990; 311-315

16. Carmil D, Carel R: Emotional distress and satisfaction in life among Holocaust survivors: a community study of survivors and controls. Psychol Med 1986; 16:141-149

17. Bower H: The concentration camp syndrome. Aust N Z J Psychiatry 1994; 28:391-397

18. Butcher L, Kleinman M, et al: Survivors of the Holocaust and their children: current status and adjustment. J Pers Soc Psychol 1981; 41: 503-516

19. Robinson S, Hemmendinger J: Psychosocial adjustment of those who were in Nazi concentration camps as children: thirty years later, in Stress and Anxiety. Eds. Spielberger C, Saranson J, Milgram N. Wash., DC, Hemisphere, 1982

20. Eaton J et al: Impairment in Holocaust survivors after 33 years: data from an unbiased community sample. Am J Psychiatry 1982; 139:773-777

21. Marussek P: Die Kozentrationslagerhaft a/s Belastrungs situation. Nervenarzt 1961; 32:538-542

22. Rosen J, Reynolds C, Yeager A, et al: Sleep disturbances in survivors of the Nazi Holocaust. Am J Psychiatry 1991; 148:62-66

23. Hefez A, Metz L, Lavie P: Longterm effects of extreme situational stress on sleep and dreaming. Am J Psychiatry 1987; 144:344-347

24. Hartmann E: The Nightmare: The Psychology and Biology of Terrifying Dreams. New York, Basic Books, 1984

25. Van der Kolk B. Blitz R, Burr W, et al: Nightmares and trauma: a comparison of nightmares after combat with lifelong nightmares in veterans. Am J Psychiatry 1984; 141:187-190

26. Jucovy M: Psychoanalytic contributions to Holocaust studies. Int J Psychoanal 1992; 73:267-282

27. Kinzie JD, Fleck J: Psychotherapy with severely traumatized refugees. Am J Psychother 1987; 41:82-94

28. Glover H: Themes of mistrust and the posttraumatic stress disorder in Vietnam veterans. Am J Psychother 1984; 37:445-452

29. Lifton RJ: The sense of immortality on death and the continuity of life. Am J Psychoanal 1973; 33:3-15

30. Lifton RJ: The broken connection. New York, Simon & Schuster, 1996

31. Lifton RJ: The psychology of the survivor and the death imprint. Psychiatr Ann 1982; 12:1011-1020

32. Goderez B: The warrior syndrome. Bull Menninger Clin 1987; 51:96-113

33. Archibald H, Tuddenham R: Persistent stress reaction after combat; a 20-year follow-up. Arch Gen Psychiatry 1965; 12:475-481

34. Boyle C, Decoufle P, O'Brien T: Long-term health consequences of military service in Vietnam. Epidemiol Rev 1989; 11:1-27

35. Shalev A, Blaich A, Ursano R: Posttraumatic stress disorder, somatic co-morbidity and effort tolerance. Psychosomatics 1990; 31:197-203

36. Goldstein G et al: Survivors of imprisonment in the Pacific theatre during World War II. Am J Psychiatry 1987; 144:1210-1213

37. Guerrero J, Crocq M: Sleep disorders in the elderly: depression and posmaumatic stress disorder. J Psychosom Res 1994; 38:141-150

38. Christenson R, Walker J, Ross D, et al: Reactivation of traumatic conflicts. Am J Psychiatry 1981; 138:984-985

39. Hamilton J: Unusual longterm sequelae of a traumatic war experience. Bull Menninger Clinic 1982; 46:539-541

40. Pomerantz A: Delayed onset of posttraumatic stress disorder: delayed recognition or latent disorder? (letter). Am J Psychiatry 1991; 148;1609

41. Richmond J, Beck J: Posttraumatic mess disorder in a World War II veteran (letter). Am J Psychiatry 1986; 143:1485-1486

42. Van Dyke C, Zilberg M, McKinnon J: Posttraumatic stress disorder: a 30-year delay in a World War II veteran. Am J Psychiatry 1985; 1070-1073

43. Solomon S, Prager E: Elderly Israeli Holocaust survivors during the Persian Gulf War: a study of psychological distress. Am J Psychiatry 1992; 149:1707-1710

44. Dasberg H, Robinson S: The impact of the Demjaniuk trial on the psychotherapeutic process. Israeli Journal of Medicine and Law 1991; 395-399

45. Robinson S, Hemmendinger J, Nentel R, et al: Retraumatization of Holocaust survivors during the Gulf War and SCUD missile attacks on Israel. Br J Med Psychol 1994; 67:353-362

46. Mejo S L: Posttramatic stress disorder: an overview of three etiological variables and psychopharmacologic treatment. Nurse Pract 1990; 15:41-45

47. Balder L, Peretz T, Kaplan de-Note A: Effect of the Holocaust on coping with cancer. Soc Sci Med 1992; 43:11-15

48. Blank K, Perry S: Relationship of psychological processes during delirium to outcome. Am J Psychiatry 1984:141:843-847

49. Hobgoll S, Spielberger C, Bregnitz S, et al. (Task Force on War Related Stress): War-related stress. Am Psychol 1991; 46:848-855

50. Kastenbaum R: Death, suicide and the older adult. Suicide Life Threat Behav 1992; 22:1-14

51. Dasberg H: Psychological stress of Holocaust survivors and offspring in Israel forty years later a review. Israeli Journal of Psychiatry 1987; 24: 243-256

52. Hyer L, Walker C, Swanson G, et al: Validation of posttraumatic stress disorder measures for older combat veterans. J Clin Psychol 1992; 579-588

53. Kluznik J, Speed N, Van Valkenberg C, et al: Forty-year follow-up of United States prisoners of war. Am J Psychiatry 1986; 143: 1443-1446

54. Hendin H, Haas AR, Singer P, et al: The influence of precombat personality on posttrauntatic stress disorder. Compre Psychiatry 1983; 24:530-534

55. Emery P, Emery O: The defense process in posttraumatic stress disorder. Am J Psychother 1985; 34:541-552

56. Kinzie J, Fleck J: Psychotherapy with severely traumatized refugees. Am J Psychother 1987; 41:82-94

57. Hoppe K: The psychodynamics of concentration camp victims. Psychoanalytic Forum 1966; 1: 76-80

58. Berger D: The survivor syndrome: a problem of nosology and treatment. Am J Psychother 1977: 31:238-251

59. Gubrich-Simitis I: Extreme traumatization as cumulative trauma. Psychoanal Study Child 1981; 36:415-450.

60. Krystal H: Aging survivor of the Holocaust. J Geriatr Psych. 1981,165-189

61. Roth S: The shadow of the Holocaust. Presented at the 4th Conference of the Sigmund Freud Centre of Hebrew University, Jerusalem, May 24-26,1988

62. Solomon S, Gerritz E, Muff A: Efficacy of treatments for posttraumatic stress disorder. JAMA 1992; 268:633-638

63. Van Der Kolk B, Greenberg M, Boyd H, et al: Inescapable shock, neurotransmitters, and addiction to trauma: toward a psychobiology of posttraumatic stress disorder. Biol Psychiatry 1985;20:314-325

64. Kolb LC: A neuropsychological hypothesis explaining posttraumatic stress disorders. Am J Psychiatry 1987; 144:989-995.

65. Shipko S, Alvarez W, Novello N: Towards a teleological model of alexithymia: alexithymia and posttraumatic stress disorder. Psychother Psychosom 1983; 39:122-126.

66. Horowitz M: Stress Response Syndrome. New York, Jason Aronson, 1976

67. Kripper S, Colodzin B: Multicultural methods of treating Vietnam veterans with posttraumatic stress disorder. Int J Psychosom 1989; 36:79-85.

68. Kinzie J, Frederickson R, et al: Posttraumatic stress disorder among survivors of Cambodian concentration camps. Am J Psychiatry 1984; 645-650.

69. Krell R: Child survivors of the Holocaust—strategies of adaptation. Can J Psychiatry 1993; 38: 384-389

70. Davidson J, Nemeroff C: Pharmacotherapy in posttraumatic stress disorder: historical and clinical considerations and future directions. Psychopharmacol Bull 1989; 25:423-425

71. Davidson T: Drug therapy of posttraumatic stress disorder. Br J Psychiatry 1992; 160:309-314.

72. Davidson J, Roth S, Newman E: Treatment of posttraumatic stress disorder with FLuoxetine. J Trauma Stress 1991; 4:419-423

73. Silver J, Sandbag D, Hales P: New approaches in the pharmacotherapy of posttraumatic stress disorder. J Clin Psychiatry 1990; 51(supp):33-38

74. Keck P, McElroy M, Friedman L: Valproate and carbamazepine in the treatment of panic and posttraumatic stress disorder, withdrawal states, and behavioral dyscontrol syndromes. J Clin Psychopharmacol 1992; 365-415.

75. Sadavoy J: Integrated psychotherapy for the elderly. Can J Psychiatry 1994; 39:519-526

76. Lazarus L, Sadavoy J: Psychotherapy of the elderly, in Comprehensive Review of Geriatric Psychiatry, 2nd Edition. Edited by Sadavoy J, Lazarus L, Jarvik L, et al. Washington, DC, American Psychiatric Press, 1996

77. Boehlein J, Sparr LF: Group therapy with WWII ex-POWs: long-term posttraumatic adjustment in a geriatric population. Am J Psychother 1993; 47:273-282.

78. Levav L, Abramson J: Emotional distress amongst concentration camp survivors: a community study in Jerusalem. Psychol Med 1984: 14:215-218

79. Allodi F: Posttraumatic stress disorder in hostages and victims of torture. Psychiatr Clin North Am 1994; 17:279-288

80. Thomas R, Gafner G: Posttraumatic stress disorder in an elderly male: treatment with eye movement desensitization and reprocessing. Clin Gerontol 1993; 57-9

81. Fairbank J, Gross R, Keane T: Treatment of posttraumatic stress disorder. Behav Modif 1983; 7:557-568

82. Kilpatrick D, Veronen L, Resick P: Psychological sequelae to rape: assessment and treatment strategies, in Behavioral Medicine: Assessment and Treatment Strategies (Eds. Delay D, Meredith R.) NY, Plenum, 1982, pp 473-479.

83. Brom D, Kleber R, Defares P: Brief psychotherapy for posttraumatic stress disorder. J Consult Clin Psychol 1989; 57:607-612.

84. Sigal J, Weinfeld M: Mutual involvement and alienation in families of Holocaust survivors. Psychiatry 1987; 50:280-288.

85. Ginsberg-McEwan E: The whole grandfather: an intergenerational approach to family therapy, in Treating the Elderly With Psychotherapy. Edited by Sadavoy J, Leszcz M, Madison, CT, International Univ. Press, 1987, pp 295-324

Holocaust Survivors in a Primary Care Setting: Fifty Years Later

Brian Trappler, Jeffrey W. Braunstein,
George Moskowitz, and Steven Friedman

SUNY Health Science Center at Brooklyn

ABSTRACT: *Summary*—Past studies have not assessed the prevalence of emotional disturbances in Holocaust survivors seeking medical treatment in a family practice environment. The present study examined the prevalence of lifetime (the presence of symptomatology at any time) and current posttraumatic stress disorder (PTSD) symptoms, general anxiety, and depression in Holocaust survivors seeking medical treatment in a primary care setting. 20 of the 27 Holocaust survivors in our sample received a current diagnosis of PTSD and reported significant symptoms of depression and general anxiety. Although 74% of the survivors were currently diagnosed with PTSD, participants in this study had reported an overall decline in reexperiencing, hyperarousal, and overall PTSD symptoms but exhibited increased avoidance and numbing symptoms throughout the lifespan. These preliminary results suggest that removing avoidance as a defense mechanism during the course of psychotherapy may leave these survivors without an adequate way for coping with their trauma, subsequently increasing their vulnerability to psychopathology. Implications for psychological interventions are provided.

There is considerable interest in the long-term effects of trauma throughout the lifespan of survivors (Averill & Beck, 2000). Although numerous studies have examined emotional disturbances in war veteran and civilian populations, few studies have examined the long-term prevalence and symptoms profile of emotional disturbances in Holocaust survivors of Nazi concentration camps. Kuch and Cox (1992) were the first to apply DSM criteria to the examination of emotional disturbances. They reported that 46% of their sample of Holocaust survivors (N=58) met the DSM-III-R criteria for PTSD. Yehuda, Kahana, Schmeidler, Southwick, Wilson, and Giller (1995) noted that after 50 years, 57% of Holocaust survivors still met criteria for PTSD. In addition, these investigators concluded that the presence and severity of current PTSD symptoms was related to experiencing additional stressful events throughout life.

Hyer, Summers, Braswell, and Boyd (1995) compared survivors of World War II with survivors of the Korean and Vietnam wars and reported that younger veterans had greater elevations in PTSD symptomatology than older veterans, although older veterans experienced a diminished interest in daily activities. These older veterans were prone to all PTSD symptoms when exposed to trauma-related triggers. Yehuda, Kahana, Southwick, and Giller (1994) reported that Holocaust survivors also currently experienced significant depressive symptomatology. Solomon and Prager (1992) found that Holocaust survivors living in Israel reported greater perceptions of danger, more psychological distress, and higher state and trait anxiety during the SCUD missile attack of the Gulf War than age-matched citizens who were not Holocaust survivors. These findings suggest that in the absence of hyperarousal symptoms and fewer intrusive symptoms, older trauma survivors are more likely to be diagnosed with major depression because they show avoidance and emotional numbing.

The purpose of this study was to examine the prevalence of lifetime and current PTSD symptoms, general anxiety, and depression in Holocaust survivors seeking medical treatment in a primary care setting. Past studies have not assessed the prevalence of emotional disturbances in Holocaust survivors seeking only medical treatment in a family practice environment. We wished to identify a subgroup of survivors who had not routinely sought mental health services to gain an understanding of how they coped with trauma during their lifetime.

Method

Participants

The population for this study was limited to Holocaust survivors seeking medical services in a community-based family medical practice. Each participant had been forced into either labor or concentration camps during their childhood or early adulthood at the time of the Holocaust (1939-1945) and experienced a significant threat to life. In this medical practice 27 patients were identified as Holocaust survivors. All 27 patients agreed to participate. Their mean age was 75.3 yr. (SD=5.7, range=66 to 91 years). Fourteen participants were men, and 13 were women. Regarding marital status, 16 were married, 8 were widowed, 2 were divorced, and 1 was single. Eight participants were disabled (four medically disabled, three psychiatrically disabled, and one both medically and psychiatrically disabled). Participants were not seeking mental health treatment at the time of the study. Ten participants had received past outpatient mental health treatment. None of the participants reported any past psychiatric hospitalizations. Of participants 70.4% or 19 were receiving treatment for a variety of chronic medical problems such as diabetes, hypertension, cancer (skin, colon, breast) and emphysema in a community-based family medical office.

Scales

Clinician-administered PTSD Scale for DSM-IV (CAPS).—This scale (Blake, Weathers, Nagy, Kaloupek, Charney, & Keane, 1998) is a structured clinical diagnostic interview based on DSM-IV criterion for PTSD. It consists of standard questions and behavioral ratings, evaluating both the frequency and intensity of posttraumatic stress disorder symptoms. The CAPS assesses current (past week and past month) and lifetime symptoms of PTSD. Its items are rated for both frequency and intensity on a scale with anchors of 0: never/none and 4: daily/extreme. The interviewer assesses the validity of responses, considering issues such as compliance with the interview mental status, and efforts to exaggerate or minimize symptoms. The administration time is about 90 minutes.

An earlier version of the scale, the CAPS-1 (Blake, Weathers, Nagy, Kaloupek, Klauminzer, Charney, & Keane, 1990; Blake, Weathers, Nagy, Kaloupek, Gusman, Charney, & Keane, 1995), was based on DSM-III-R criterion and has been replaced by the current version, updated for DSM-IV. For CAPS-1 excellent test-retest reliability (.90 to .98 for the total score) and above average internal consistency (alpha=.94) were reported in a study of combat veterans (Weathers, Blake, & Litz, 1991; Weathers, Blake, Krinsley, Haddad, Huska, & Keane, 1992). The CAPS-1 has also shown excellent convergent validity with other diagnostic measures.

Impact of Event Scale.—This scale is a 15-item self-report device designed to measure current posttraumatic stress disorder symptoms associated with a specific traumatic life event. The scale provides a total score and subscales measuring reexperiencing and avoidance symptoms related to PTSD (Horowitz, Wilner, & Alvarez, 1979). Seven items load on the Intrusion subscale and eight on the Avoidance subscale. Participants rate items on a 4-point scale measuring the frequency of symptoms during the last week on a scale with anchors of 0: not at all and 5: often. Zilberg, Weiss, and Horowitz (1982) reported scores on the Intrusion and Avoidance subscales had adequate internal consistency (.79 to .91 and .82 to .91) and test-retest reliability (.86 to .89 and .88 to .90).

Beck Depression Inventory.—The Beck Depression Inventory (Beck, Ward, Mendelsohn, Mock, & Erbaugh, 1961) is a 21-item self-report inventory measuring symptoms of depression during the last seven days. Participants rate symptoms severity on a 4-point scale with anchors of 0 and 3. Total scores range from a minimum of 0 to a maximum of 63. Beck, Steer, and Garbin (1988) reviewed 25 years of research on the inventory, providing evidence of excellent reliability and validity.

Beck Anxiety Inventory.—This inventory (Beck, Epstein, Brown, & Steer, 1988; Wilson, de Beure, Palmer, & Chambless, 1999) is a 21-item self-report procedure measuring symptoms of anxiety during the last seven days. Participants rate symptom severity on a 4-point scale using numbers of 0 to 3. Total scores range from a minimum of 0 to a maximum of 63. It has high internal consistency and above average test-retest reliability over 1 wk. (Beck, et al., 1988). In addition, it has adequate concurrent, convergent, and discriminant validity (Beck & Steer, 1991; Fydrich, Dowdall, & Chambless, 1992). Gillis, Haaga, and Ford (1995) conducted extensive normative research with the Beck Anxiety Inventory, closely matching the demographic information of the normative sample with the U.S. national census of 1990.

Procedure

A board certified psychiatrist and family practice physician evaluated the participants within a community-based, primary care medical office. A general psychiatric interview, structured diagnostic clinical interview (CAPS) and the above self-report inventories were completed during the evaluation. Participants were informed of the purpose for the evaluation before consenting to the study. They received instructions for completing all self-report inventories and were offered psychiatric and psychological treatment upon the completion of the evaluation. Participants were instructed to complete the self-report scales without assistance.

Results

The CAPS Past Week Total Score, measuring DSM-IV PTSD diagnostic criterion, indicated that 20 of 27 participants met current and lifetime diagnostic criterion for PTSD. The seven participants without PTSD did not meet the criterion for PTSD at anytime in their lives as assessed on the CAPS. Four participants not diagnosed with PTSD received primary diagnoses of psychosis (n =1), intermittent explosive disorder (n = 1), and other non-PTSD anxiety disorders (n = 2) based on both a general psychiatric evaluation and the psychometric testing used in the study. Only three participants were not diagnosed with a current DSM-IV psychiatric disorder.

Table 1 presents the means and standard deviations of the total scores on the Beck Depression Inventory, Beck Anxiety Inventory, Impact of Event Scale Total score, Impact of Event Scale Intrusion subscale, Impact of Event Scale Avoidance subscale, and CAPS Total score as a function of PTSD status. The diagnosis of PTSD and subsequent group designation for the analysis was based on positive findings from the general psychiatric evaluation and the CAPS. Six Mann-Whitney tests were conducted to analyze the effects of PTSD on participants' scores for the Beck Depression Inventory, Beck Anxiety Inventory, Impact of Event Scale Total score, Impact of Event Scale Intrusion subscale, Impact of Event Scale Avoidance subscale and the CAPS Total score (see Table 1). There was a significant difference between PTSD (n = 20) and non-PTSD (n = 7) participants on all measures with participants in the PTSD group exhibiting significantly greater symptoms of depression, general anxiety, intrusive thought, avoidance, and overall PTSD symptomatology when compared to the non-PTSD group (Beck Depression Inventory, U = 4.0, p <.001; Beck Anxiety Inventory, U = 1.0, p <.001; IES Total score, U = 1.0, p <.001; TES Intrusion subscale, U = 0.0; IES Avoidance subscale, U = 0.0; and CAPS Total score, U = 0.0, p <.001).

Four case-controlled paired sample t-tests measuring differences between past week and lifetime symptoms of PTSD on the CAPS were conducted for all participants (see Table 2). There was a significant decrease in reexperiencing symptoms (t_{26} = −15.65, p < .001), hyperarousal symptoms and overall PTSD symptoms (t_{26} = −5.88, p < .001) throughout the survivors' lifetime, although a significant increase in avoidance and numbing symptoms was also reported (t_{26} = −6.48, p < .001).

Table 1

Means, Standard Deviations, and Group Differences on Measures of
Emotional Disturbances as a Function of Participants' PTSD Status

Measure	PTSD (n = 20)		Non-PTSD (n = 7)		Total (N = 27)		U
	M	SD	M	SD	M	SD	
Beck Depression Inventory	18.3	8.8	2.7	1.6	14.2	10.3	4.0*
Beck Anxiety Inventory	20.0	8.8	3.9	2.7	15.8	10.5	1.0*
Impact of Event Scale							
Total	59.8	12.4	16.1	6.1	48.5	22.4	1.0*
Intrusion	27.0	6.9	5.3	1.7	21.3	11.4	0.0*
Avoidance	33.4	5.8	10.9	5.1	27.5	11.5	0.0*
CAPS Total	64.1	12.2	7.0	10.7	49.3	28.0	0.0*

*p<.001.

Table 2

Symptom Differences Between Past Week and Lifetime Symptoms of PTSD Criterion
And Total Scores on Caps Measures for Participants

CAPs Measure	Past Week Symptoms		Lifetime Symptoms		Difference		t_{26}
	M	SD	M	SD	M	SD	
Criterion B	12.1	8.7	21.8	9.7	-9.7	3.2	-15.65*
Criterion C	26.2	14.7	19.8	11.2	6.4	6.5	5.17*
Criterion D	11.0	7.2	17.7	9.6	-6.7	5.9	-5.88*
CAPS Total	49.3	28.0	59.4	28.3	-10.2	8.1	-6.48*

Note.—CAPS = Clinician-administered PTSD Scale for DSM-IV, Criterion B = Reexperiencing
symptoms, Criterion C = Avoidance and numbing symptoms, Criterion D = Hyperarousal symptoms. *P<.001.

Discussion

Our results suggest that after more than fifty years, Holocaust survivors
continue to exhibit symptoms of posttraumatic stress with 74% of our
sample of participants attending a primary care family practice receiving
a diagnosis of PTSD. Although our participants reported an overall decline in reexperiencing, hyperarousal, and overall PTSD symptomatol-

ogy throughout the lifespan, over time there was some increase in avoidance and numbing. This is consistent with another study (McFarlane, 1990) suggesting an increase in avoidance and social estrangement as PTSD survivors age. In addition, these PTSD survivors become more somatically preoccupied and present more frequently in medical settings as they age (Lyons & McClendon, 1990).

The avoidance exhibited by Holocaust survivors has apparently served as an adaptive function, allowing many of these survivors to control hyperarousal symptoms and maintain adequate functioning. A supporting clinical observation was that most of our patients never shared the details of their trauma with their children (avoidance), and frequently requested sleep medication and sedatives during periods of hyperarousal.

Regarding the determination of pharmacotherapy, case-by-case decisions need to be made based on the patients' chronicity of PTSD symptoms. Patients without chronic physiological hyperarousal symptoms may benefit from short-term use of benzodiazepines or hypnotics, whereas patients with chronic hyperarousal symptoms might instead benefit from serotonergic antidepressant and mood stabilizing medications given the addiction potential of benzodiazepines.

Holocaust survivors may have found other adaptive ways to avoid and cope with their trauma, such as actively engaging in work, community and religious activities, and raising children. In contrast to the theory of thought rebound (Salkovskis & Campbell, 1994; Rutledge, Hancock, & Rutledge, 1996), which hypothesizes that the suppression of unwanted ideation leads to increased intrusive ideation, these trauma survivors have effectively used avoidance, suppression, and sublimation (religious, community, family values) to cope with PTSD symptoms. These findings have direct implications for psychological treatment.

Cognitive-behavioral interventions have been effective in the treatment of PTSD for other trauma populations (Keane, Fairbank, Caddell, Zimering, & Bender, 1985; Resick, Jordan, Girelli, Hutter, & Marhoefer-Dvorak, 1988), helping patients increase their capacity to tolerate cognitive, affective, and physiological symptoms. Many cognitive-behavioral interventions for the treatment of PTSD are exposure-based, encouraging survivors to discuss and confront distressing images, places, and situations related to the traumatic event that they avoid. Although these interventions have been helpful to alleviate symptoms in sexual assault victims and war veterans, these techniques may be contraindicated for Holocaust survivors who rely heavily on defenses such as suppression and avoidance. Removing avoidance as a defense mechanism in these victims may leave survivors without an adequate mechanism for coping with their trauma, subsequently increasing their vulnerability to psychopathology. Cognitive-behavioral coping skills such as relaxation training and rhythmic breathing may be a better choice for treatment if a survivor has partially succeeded in using avoidance to cope.

Research could be more useful were several of the limitations in design and measurement in this study improved. Utilizing both a geriatric patient control group and a larger non-PTSD survivor group may allow increased generalizability of findings. In addition, although the CAPS assesses for both current and lifetime symptomatology, the procedure does not measure symptomatology from a longitudinal perspective. Our clinical observations suggest that a subtle bimodal distribution of symptomatology may exist, with the most prominent avoidance symptoms occurring during the initial aftermath (1945-1950) and again later in life (1990–present).

Assessing the influence of a supportive community and familial environment on the manifestation of symptomatology during the lifespan needs to be more thoroughly assessed. In addition, examining personality traits as a function of PTSD status may provide insight into predisposing factors for developing emotional disturbances after experiencing traumatic events. With Holocaust survivors nearing the upper limits of life expectancy, such research needs to be conducted as soon as possible.

Although the generalizability of these findings to the population of Holocaust survivors is limited given the small sample, these results suggest that a careful assessment of symptomatology throughout the lifespan is needed before treatment is planned or implemented. In conclusion, the present findings are evidence that Holocaust survivors seeking medical treatment in a family practice setting may experience significant emotional disturbances requiring mental health treatment. When patients experience a temporary breakdown in their compensatory mechanisms for controlling their PTSD symptoms, targeted mental health treatment may be indicated.

References

AVERILL, P. M., & BECK, J. G. (2000) Posttraumatic stress disorder in older adults: a conceptual review. *Journal of Anxiety Disorders, 14,* 133-156.

BECK, A. T, EPSTEIN, N., BROWN, G., & STEER, R. A. (1988) An inventory for measuring clinical anxiety: psychometric properties. *Journal of Consulting and Clinical Psychology, 56,* 893-897.

BECK, A. T., & STEER, R. A. (1991) Relationship between the Beck Anxiety Inventory and the Hamilton Anxiety Rating Scale with anxious outpatients. *Journal of Anxiety Disorders, 5,* 213-223.

BECK, A. T., STEER, R. A., & GARBIN, M. G. (1988) Psychometric properties of the Beck Depression Inventory: twenty-five years later. *Clinical Psychology Review, 8,* 77-100.

BECK, A. T., WARD, C. H., MENDELSOHN, M., MOCK, J., & ERLBAUGH, J. (1961) An inventory for measuring depression. *Archives of General Psychiatry, 4,* 561-571.

BLAKE, D. D., WEATHERS, F. W., NAGY, L. M., KALOUPEK, D. G., CHARNEY, D. S., & KEANE, T. M. (1988) *Clinician-administered PTSD Scale for DSM-IV.* Boston, MA: National Center for Posttraumatic Stress Disorder-Behavioral Science Division.

BLAKE, D. D., WEATHERS, F. W., NAGY, L. M., KALOUPEK, D. G., GUSMAN, E. D., CHARNEY, D. S., & KEANE, T. M. (1995) The development of a clinician-administered PTSD scale. *Journal of Traumatic Stress, 8,* 75-90.

BLAKE, D. D., WEATHERS, F. W., NAGY, L. M., KALOUPEK, D. G, KLAUMINZER, G., CHARNEY, D. S., & KEANE, T. M. (1990) A clinician rating scale for assessing current and lifetime PTSD: the CAPS-1. *The Behavior Therapist, 13,* 187-188.

FYDRICH, T., DOWDALL, D., & CHAMBLESS, D. L. (1992) Reliability and validity of the Beck Anxiety Inventory. *Journal of Anxiety Disorders, 6,* 55-61.

GILLIS, M. M., HAAGA, D. A., & FORD, G. T. (1995) Normative values for the Beck Anxiety Inventory, Fear Questionnaire, Penn State Worry Questionnaire, and Social Phobia and Anxiety Inventory. *Psychological Assessment, 7,* 450-455.

HOROWITZ, M. J., WILNER, N., & ALVAREZ, W. (1979) Impact of Event Scale: a measure of subjective stress. *Psychosomatic Medicine, 41,* 209-218.

HYER, L., SUMMERS, M., BRASWELL, L., & BOYD, S. (1995) Posttraumatic stress disorder: silent problem among older combat veterans. *Psychotherapy*, 32, 348-364.

KEANE, T. M., FAIRBANK, J. A., CADDELL, J. M., ZIMERING, R. T., & BENDER, M. E. (1985) A behavioral approach to treating posttraumatic stress disorder in Vietnam veterans. In C. R. Figley (Ed.), *Trauma and its wake. Vol.* 1. New York: Brunner/Mazel. Pp. 257-294.

KUCH, K., & Cox, B. J. (1992) Symptoms of PTSD in 124 survivors of the Holocaust. *American Journal of Psychiatry*, 149, 337-340.

LYONS, J., & MCCLENDON, O. (1990) Changes in PTSD symptomatology as a function of aging. *Nova-Psy Newsletter*, 8, 13-18.

MCFARLANE, A. (1990) Posttraumatic stress disorder. *International Review of Psychiatry*, 3, 203-213.

RESICK, P. A., JORDAN, C. G., GIRELLI, S. A., HUTTER, C. H., & MARHOEFER-DVORAK, S. (1988) A comparative outcome study of behavioral group therapy for sexual assault victims. *Behavior Therapy*, 19, 385-401.

RUTLEDGE, P. C., HANCOCK, R. A., & RUTLEDGE, J. H. (1996) Predictors of thought rebound. *Behaviour Research and Therapy*, 34, 555-562.

SALKOVSKIS, P. M., & CAMPBELL, P. (1994) Thought suppression induces intrusion in naturally occurring negative intrusive thoughts. *Behaviour Research and Therapy*, 32, 1-8.

SOLOMON, Z., & PRAGER, E. (1992) Elderly Israeli Holocaust survivors during the Persian Gulf War: a study of psychological distress. *American Journal of Psychiatry*, 149, 1707-1710.

WEATHERS, P. W., BLAKE, D. D., KRINSLEY, K., HADDAD, W., HUSKA, J., & KEANE, T. M. (1992) The Clinician-administered PTSD Scale-Diagnostic Version (CAPS-1). Paper presented at the annual meeting of the International Society for Traumatic Stress Studies, Los Angeles, CA, October.

WEATHERS, F. W., BLAKE, D. D., & LITZ, B. T. (1991) Reliability and validity of a new structured interview for PTSD. Paper presented at the 99th Annual Convention of the American Psychological Association, San Francisco, CA, August.

WILSON, K. A., DE BEURE, E., PALMER, C. A., & CHAMBLESS, D. L. (1999) The Beck Anxiety Inventory. In M. Maruish (Ed.), *The use of psychological testing for treatment planning and outcome assessment.* (2nd ed.) Hillsdale, NJ: Erlbaum. Pp. 971-992.

YEHUDA, R., KAHANA, B., SCHMEIDLER, J., SOUTHWICK, S., WILSON, S., & GILLER, E. (1995) Impact of cumulative lifetime trauma and recent stress on current posttraumatic stress disorder symptoms in Holocaust survivors. *American Journal of Psychiatry,* 152, 1815-1818.

YEHUDA, R., KAHANA, B., SOUTHWICK, S. M., & GILLER, E. L., JR. (1994) Depressive features in Holocaust survivors with posttraumatic stress disorder. *Journal of Traumatic Stress,* 7, 4.

ZILBERG, N. J., WEISS, D. S., & HOROWITZ, M. J. (1982) Impact of Event Scale: a cross-validation study and some empirical evidence supporting a conceptual model of stress responses syndromes. *Journal of Consulting and Clinical Psychology,* 50, 407-414.

Tracing Long-Term Effects of Early Trauma: A Broad-Scope View of Holocaust Survivors in Late Life

Dov Shmotkin, Tzvia Blumstein, Baruch Modan

ABSTRACT: This study addressed long-term effects of extreme trauma among Holocaust survivors ($N = 126$) in an older (75–94 years) sample of the Israeli Jewish population. Survivors were compared with European-descent groups that had immigrated either before World War II ($n = 206$) or after ($n = 145$). Participants in the latter group had had Holocaust-related life histories but did not consider themselves survivors. Controlling for sociodemographics, the results indicated that survivors fared worse than prewar immigrants in certain psychosocial domains, mainly cumulative distress and activity, rather than in health-related ones. Survivors and postwar immigrant comparisons had almost no differences. The study highlights the need for a wide view of functioning facets and comparison groups in delineating late posttraumatic effects.

The study of Holocaust survivors poses conceptual and methodological dilemmas. Most of those who survived the mass extermination of Jews by the Nazis in World War II have become elderly. Their physical and mental status mingles long-term effects of extreme trauma, extensive efforts to reconstruct their lives, and the current aging processes. The interplay of vulnerability and resilience in these survivors may provide clues to how damages of traumatization coincide with resourceful coping along the life course. Using a wide-spectrum assessment strategy, the present study sought to delineate long-lasting traumatic aftereffects among randomly sampled Holocaust survivors in late life.

Dov Shmotkin, Department of Psychology and Herczeg Institute on Aging, Tel-Aviv University, Tel-Aviv, Israel; Tzvia Blumstein, Gertner Institute for Epidemiology and Health Policy Research, Chaim Sheba Medical Center, Tel-Hashomer, Israel; Baruch Modan, Department of Clinical Epidemiology, Chaim Sheba Medical Center, Tel-Hashomer, and the Sackler Faculty of Medicine, Tel-Aviv University. Baruch Modan passed away on November 17, 2001, after a revision of this article had been completed. We gratefully acknowledge his important contributions to this study.

This study was supported in part by the Herczeg Institute on Aging, Tel-Aviv University. The Cross-Sectional and Longitudinal Aging Study, on which the current data are based, was funded by U.S. National Institute on Aging Grants RO1–5885–03 and RO1–5885–06, with Baruch Modan as Principal Investigator. We acknowledge the helpful suggestions offered by Adrian Walter-Ginzburg, Laurence Freedman, Ilya Novikov, and Menachem Ben-Ezra.

Research on Holocaust survivors has indicated a host of physical and mental disturbances lasting decades after World War II (see reviews by Dasberg, 1987; Eitinger & Major, 1993; Levav, 1998; Sadavoy, 1997). The sequelae of the trauma were observable particularly among survivors diagnosed or treated in clinical settings and were characterized as "the concentration camp syndrome" or "the survivor syndrome" (Chodoff, 1963; Eitinger, 1964; Krystal, 1968; Niederland, 1968). Since the 1980s, the diagnosis of posttraumatic stress disorder (PTSD; American Psychiatric Association, 1994) has increasingly served as a framework for clinicians in the evaluation of Holocaust survivors (Kuch & Cox, 1992; Marmar & Horowitz, 1988; Yehuda, Schmeidler, Siever, Binder-Brynes, & Elkin, 1997).

The psychological study of Holocaust survivors traditionally has emphasized pathological dysfunction and intrapsychic dynamics, mainly because it has approached survivors through clinics and health care providers (Lomranz, 1995). However, there has also been an increasing interest in the ways that community-based, nonclinical populations of Holocaust survivors endure their long-lasting plight while living an apparently normal life. A great many of the community-oriented studies revealed higher levels of emotional distress and psychological difficulties among survivors as compared with controls (Antonovsky, Maoz, Dowty, & Wijsenbeek, 1971; Carmil & Carel, 1986; Eaton, Sigal, & Weinfeld, 1982; Fenig & Levav, 1991; Levav & Abramson, 1984; Nadler & Ben-Shushan, 1989). Other studies found only limited evidence that survivors were more psychologically impaired (Harel, Kahana, & Kahana, 1988; Leon, Butcher, Kleinman, Goldberg, & Almagor, 1981; Shanan, 1989; Weinfeld, Sigal, & Eaton, 1981). A few studies even found survivors to be higher in specific aspects of coping, social adjustment, and hope (Carmil & Breznitz, 1991; Harel, Kahana, & Kahana, 1993; Shanan, 1989).

Subjective well-being, relating to positive terms such as life satisfaction and happiness, is particularly pertinent to vulnerable populations (Shmotkin, 1998). Certain studies found that the subjective well-being of Holocaust survivors was significantly lower than that of controls (Antonovsky et al., 1971; Harel et al., 1988; Harel et al., 1993), but other studies indicated no significant differences between survivors and controls in this respect (Carmil & Carel, 1986; Landau & Litwin, 2000; Leon et al., 1981). Using a variety of subjective well-being measures and a number of comparison groups, Shmotkin and Lomranz (1998) revealed a differentiation between survivors and counterparts mainly on measures that directly address older people rather than on commonly used measures designed for the general population.

A mixed picture also emerged in the few controlled studies that have addressed the physical health of Holocaust survivors. Although greater problems and lower ratings of health were reported among survivors (Antonovsky et al., 1971; Harel et al., 1988; Landau & Litwin, 2000; Yaari, Eisenberg, Adler, & Birkhan, 1999), certain studies of large community samples showed no differences between survivors and controls in psychosomatic complaints and various medical parameters (Aviram, Silverberg & Carel, 1987; Carmil & Carel, 1986). Taken together, the controlled studies on Holocaust survivors have provided ample evidence of mental and physical health problems lasting decades after the trauma, but this evidence is definitely not uniform.

Lack of longitudinal data on Holocaust survivors is an obstacle to tracking the transformations of the early trauma in older age. However, clinical observations show that the trauma can be stirred up by normal aging processes, which involve increasing illness, frailty, dependency, isolation, institutionalization, loss of significant others, and near-coming personal death. These experiences may resonate traumatic memories of similar themes and hamper adaptation to old age (Brandler, 2000; Danieli, 1981; Harel, 1995; Safford, 1995). In addition to their sensitivity to normal processes of late life, aging Holocaust survivors may be particularly vulnerable to exceptional stress. Thus, elderly Holocaust survivors in Israel were more distressed than controls during the Gulf War when facing missile attacks accompanied by the threat of poisonous gas (Robinson et al., 1994; Solomon & Prager, 1992). As another example, Holocaust survivors having cancer manifested higher psychological distress compared with cancer patients who had not gone through the Holocaust (Baider, Peretz, & Kaplan-De-Nour, 1992).

Those who endured the Holocaust as young adults and have reached late and particularly very late life are not representative of the whole population that survived the Holocaust. Rather, they are the "surviving survivors" (Shanan, 1989), whose advanced age in itself probably attests to survival capabilities (Perls, 1995). Thus, we may expect older survivors to be endowed with high levels of physical and psychological rigor relative to younger Holocaust survivors as well as to nonvictim counterparts of a similar age. With this presumed potency notwithstanding, the handling of past trauma in late life appears intriguingly complicated when self-preservation is challenged and ultimate concerns of life and death converge so closely. Despite the interest and the urgency in approaching very old Holocaust survivors while they are still alive, the studies that have so far addressed them are extremely rare (Landau & Litwin, 2000).

According to Erikson's (1982) theory, a major developmental task of old age is gaining integrity, defined as the sense of coherence and wholeness about one's life while facing finitude. Butler (1975) postulated that older people achieve this state of mind through a life review, in which they reminisce about their past and thus revise its interpretation. Working on the congruence of their self-narrative, older people strive to bring closure to unresolved issues of the past, integrating them into a life story that embodies the identity and the unity of the self (Cohler, 1982; McAdams, 1990). These self-processes impose heavy demands for older Holocaust survivors. As described by Krystal (1981, 1991), survivors have to resolve the devastating repercussions of evil-inflicted loss, suffering, mourning, guilt, humiliation, and rage as a prerequisite for self-reconciliation. The long-standing memory of the trauma may play a highly dialectical role in this mental processing: Although memories may be painfully persistent and intrusive, they are imperative for maintaining a unified self. Thus, Holocaust survivors reaching old age may face new weighty challenges concerning their mental health.

The remembered past also contains cumulative life experiences since the focal trauma, and their influence on the present mental health, should be taken into account. Studies have shown that accumulation of both positive and negative occurrences along life allow for numerous pathways of resilience and vulnerability among people with suffering in their past (Singer, Ryff, Carr, & Magee, 1998; Turner & Lloyd, 1995). These pathways become particularly challenging in older age (Ryff, Singer, Love, & Essex, 1998). Accumulation of positive or negative events since the trauma may spark either gain or loss spirals by which the individuals' resources are interactively restituted and enhanced or, alternatively, further debilitated and depleted (Hobfoll, 1991). The few studies relating to this issue among Holocaust survivors found that cumulative lifetime stress of survivors was associated with lower subjective well-being (B. Kahana, Harel, & Kahana, 1988) and with greater PTSD symptoms (Yehuda et al., 1995, 1997).

The extant psychological literature on Holocaust survivors invites some cautionary notes on methodology. Empirical studies constitute a minority in this literature, and they exhibit a variety of methodological flaws such as very small samples of survivors, questionable procedures of sampling, lack of comparison groups or the use of inappropriate ones, and a failure to adequately inquire into the characteristics of the participants (see critical reviews by Harel et al., 1993; Lomranz, 1995; Solkoff, 1992). In addressing issues of sampling and comparison groups, Shmotkin and Lomranz (1998) found higher subjective well-being among study participants who were purposely sampled as Holocaust survivors through membership lists of relevant community organizations or by personal acquaintance networks than they found among study participants who were incidentally sampled for studies unrelated to the Holocaust and identified as survivors only as a by-product. In another finding, Holocaust survivors differed mainly from a group of European-born Jews who had immigrated with their parents before World War II to prestate Israel rather than from European-born Jews who either had immigrated before the war with their parents staying in Europe and eventually being killed in the Holocaust or had otherwise managed to avoid the Holocaust and immigrated to Israel after the war. This finding suggests that Holocaust survivors should be compared with more than one group so that their status can be appreciated in a larger historical and psychological context of their cohort fellows.

In view of the literature reviewed above, this study fills a number of evident gaps in the extant research on Holocaust survivors: It focuses on the status of old and very old survivors; uses a nationwide random sample of the older Jewish population in Israel; relies on a comprehensive assessment of health and psychosocial domains; and compares the survivors with two different groups representing contemporary life courses, with adjustments being made for sociodemographic differences among the groups.

Our first hypothesis was that Holocaust survivors would fare worse than comparative participants in an array of domains. This relied on the ample evidence, albeit not entirely consistent, that Holocaust survivors have been impaired in their physical and mental health for decades after their trauma. A second hypothesis was that Holocaust survivors would differ from European-born counterparts who immigrated to prestate Israel before World War II more than they would differ from other European-born counterparts who immigrated to Israel after the war but who were not similarly persecuted by the Nazis. The basis for this hypothesis was provided by Shmotkin and Lomranz's (1998) study that raised the need for a more refined differentiation between Holocaust survivors and potential comparison groups. A third hypothesis was that the differentiation between older Holocaust survivors and their comparison groups would be more salient in mental health and cumulative life-event distress than in physical health aspects. This hypothesis is grounded in the large body of studies where the plight of Holocaust survivors appears primarily emotional. Also, in line with Erikson and later theorists, older survivors face the developmental task of putting their past in order, and thus, they may be in a heightened psychological risk at this stage in late life.

Method

Participants

Cross-Sectional and Longitudinal Aging Study (CALAS) database. The current participants took part in the baseline interview of the CALAS. The CALAS data gatherers conducted a random sampling of the older Jewish population in Israel stratified by age group (75–79 years, 80–84 years, 85–89 years, 90–94 years), gender, and place of birth (Europe–America, Asia–Africa, and Israel). The initial sample of the CALAS was drawn from the Israel National Population Registry on January 1, 1989, and interviews were conducted during 1989–1992. Out of the 2,400 sampled individuals, 15.7% had died before the sampling day or were not located despite extensive efforts, and 8.5% refused to be interviewed. In the 1,820 interviews that actually took place, 1,369 individuals were interviewed as self-respondents, whereas 451 were interviewed by proxy (either because they could not respond by themselves or because they had passed away between the sampling day and the interview date). Two follow-ups have been conducted for baseline interviewees remaining alive in 1993–1994 and in 2001–2002. The follow-up data were not analyzed for the present article and will be reported separately (for more details on CALAS, see Fuchs et al., 1998; Prager, Walter-Ginzburg, Blumstein, & Modan, 1999; Ruskin et al., 1996; Walter-Ginzburg, Blumstein, Chetrit, Gindin, & Modan, 1999; Walter-Ginzburg, Chetrit, et al., 2001; Walter-Ginzburg, Guralnik, Blumstein, Gindin, & Modan, 2001).

The study groups. This study compared a survivor and two comparison groups drawn from the 1,369 self-respondents in the CALAS baseline database. The study groups were formed according to preset criteria.

Participants in all three groups had been born in European countries that were later occupied or dominated by the Nazi regime during World War II (including the former Soviet Union). Group 1 ($n = 126$) consisted of Holocaust survivors who (a) answered "Yes" to the question "Do you define yourself a Holocaust survivor?" (b) reported that during 1939–1945 they had actually been in any European country occupied or dominated by the Nazi regime, and (c) immigrated to Israel after World War II (1945 onward). The survivors most frequently reported having been in Poland, the Soviet Union, Romania, Hungary, and Germany during the war. Ten percent of the survivors, however, were scattered in Czechoslovakia, Austria, Western Europe, and Balkan countries. The median year of immigration to Israel in Group 1 was 1950.

Rudimentary knowledge about the survivors' experiences in the Holocaust could be obtained from a checklist in which the CALAS respondents were asked to indicate war-related experiences they underwent in the World War II (1939–1945) period. Relating to specific Holocaust-related experiences on the checklist, 35.7% of all participants in Group 1 reported they had been in concentration camps, 46.0% in forced-labor camps, 19.0% in ghettos, 9.5% in hiding, and 4.0% in partisans' activity. In addition, 23.8% chose an "other" category for which the interviewers' subcodes were specific about an additional 6.3% who had lived as fugitives, but the subcodes were obscure or unspecific about the other participants. Although most participants (57.9%) checked one of the six Holocaust-related experiences specified above, 20.6% checked two experiences, and 7.1% checked three. A subgroup of 14.3%, however, declined to check any of these experiences.

The comparison groups (Group 2 and 3) included participants that answered "No" to the question "Do you define yourself a Holocaust survivor?" Group 2 ($n = 206$) included prewar immigrants who arrived in prestate Israel before World War II (not later than 1939; median year of immigration, 1933). Group 3 ($n = 145$) included postwar immigrants who arrived in Israel after World War II (1945 onwards; median year of immigration, 1959).

A restrictive group assignment. As noted, 14.3% of the self-defined survivors in Group 1 did not report at least one of the core Holocaust experiences. Failures to report might indicate experiences not fitting into any of the preset categories (e.g., escaping transportation of Jews to killing sites, living with a false Christian identity) or be otherwise associated with reasons that could not be ascertained. In the comparison groups,

100% of Group 2 and 80.7% of Group 3 did not report any of the core Holocaust experiences. Among the 19.3% in Group 3 who reported such experiences, 22 of 28 reported having been in a forced-labor camp (none reported a concentration camp). On the basis of their countries of stay during the war, it is plausible that some of them actually meant Soviet labor camps. Thus, whereas the self-definition criterion of the study groups (as supported by the additional factual criteria; see *The study groups* section) allows for a more comprehensive sampling of participants who lived during World War II in Europe, it also involves certain cases with unclear war-related experiences.

To clarify the effect of the marginal gaps between the self-perceived status of survivor and the report on relevant experiences, we formulated a more restrictive grouping in which Group 1 included only 108 participants who reported at least one of the core Holocaust experiences specified previously (concentration camp, forced-labor camp, ghetto, hiding, living as partisan, and living as fugitive), thus excluding 18 participants who did not report a core experience and yet defined themselves as Holocaust survivors. Group 3 included only 117 participants who did not report any of the core Holocaust experiences, thus excluding 28 who apparently reported at least one core experience (not including concentration camp) and yet did not define themselves as Holocaust survivors. Group 2 remained intact.

Sociodemographic characteristics of the study groups. The stratified sampling in the CALAS ensured comparable numbers of women and men as well as of four age categories within the older age range (75–94 years). As shown in Table 1, the three study groups did not differ significantly in the participants' age, the grand mean for all groups being 83.5 years ($SD = 5.4$). There were, however, significant differences in gender distribution: Whereas Group 2 approximated the stratified distribution in the overall CALAS self-respondent sample (53.7% men and 46.3% women), Group 1 included a larger proportion of men than women, and Group 3 included more women than men. These gender effects do not interact with age: In each group, the respective age distributions of men and women were nearly identical.

Table 1

Sociodemographic Characteristics of the Study Groups

	Survivors Group 1 (n = 126)	Comparison group		Difference test
Characteristic		Group 2 (n = 206)	Group 3 (n = 145)	
Age				F(2, 474) = 1.58
M	83.8	83.0	83.9	
SD	5.2	5.5	5.4	
Gender (%)				χ^2 (2, N = 477) = 15.86***
Women	31.7	45.1	55.9	
Men	68.3	54.9	44.1	
Years of education				F(2, 460) = 12.44***
M	8.3	10.7	8.7	
SD	5.6	4.1	5.3	
Marital status (%)				χ^2 (6, N = 477) = 13.22*[a]
Never married	0.8	1.9	3.4	
Married	47.6	43.7	29.0	
Divorced	4.0	2.9	4.1	
Widowed	47.6	51.5	63.4	
Place of living (%)				χ^2 (2, N = 477) = 1.07
Home	88.1	85.0	88.3	
Institution	11.9	15.0	11.7	
Income (%)				χ^2 (2, N = 457) = 23.24***
National insurance pension only	31.7	26.2	50.7	
Other income sources	68.3	73.8	49.3	

Note. Group 2 was made up of prewar immigrants and Group 3 was made up of postwar immigrants. Data were missing for 14 and 20 cases in the questions about education and income, respectively.
[a] When marital status is collapsed into married versus presently unmarried, χ^2 (2, N=477)=11.54.**
*p < .05. **p < .01. ***p < .001.

Table 1 also presents other sociodemographic characteristics of the study groups. Group 2, compared with the other groups, appears to have a higher socioeconomic standing as indicated by more years of education and more sources of income. Group 3 has a higher proportion of widowed participants. There is no significant difference among the groups in the proportion living at home versus in institutions (sheltered housing and homes for the aged). The parallel sociodemographic comparisons among the restrictive groups yielded nearly the same results as those of the original study groups.

Measures

The CALAS measures were adapted from multidimensional studies of functioning in older populations (Cornoni-Huntley, Brock, Ostfeld, Taylor, & Wallace, 1986; Kovar & Fitti, 1987). In this study, the measures were grouped into nine domains of functioning (e.g., physical health problems, lifestyle activity) or experience (e.g., subjective health, life-event distress). Each domain was assessed by either three or four measures. The choice of the current measures from the large number available was guided by their salience in the literature (for reviews see Lawton & Teresi, 1994), their ability to represent different aspects of each domain, and their validity in prior analyses of the CALAS (see the citations given earlier). To facilitate subsequent comparisons, the measures were coded in the same direction within each of the domains that follow.

Physical health problems were assessed by four indicators: the number of major health problems on a checklist of 26 major diseases and medical conditions (e.g., heart diseases, arthritis, diabetes) that the participant ever suffered from or had ever been informed by a physician of having (adapted from Cornoni-Huntley et al., 1986); the number of medications that the participant was taking at the time the interview took place; the number of hospitalizations in the past five years; and the number of visits to doctors in the past month.

Physical functioning was assessed by three indicators. The Activities of Daily Life Scale measured activity by Katz, Downs, Cash, & Grotz's (1970) scale with Branch, Katz, Kniepmann, & Papsidero's (1984) addition. This measure consisted of seven items, each rating the difficulty in performing a certain activity (crossing a small room, washing, dressing, eating, grooming, transferring, and toileting) on a scale of 0 (*complete disability*), 1 (*severe difficulty*), 2 (*some difficulty*), and 3 (*no difficulty*). The Instrumental Activities of Daily Life Scale is an adaptation of Lawton and Brody's scale (1969). This measure consisted of seven items, each rating the difficulty in performing a certain activity (preparing meals, daily shopping, shopping for clothes, doing light housekeeping, doing heavy housework, taking the bus, and doing laundry) on a scale of 0 (*complete disability*), 1 (*severe difficulty*), 2 (*some difficulty),* and 3 *(no difficulty).* Physical performance was measured with an adaptation of Nagi (1976) with an addition from Rosow and Breslau (1966). This measure consisted of seven items, each rating the difficulty in performing a certain activity which required physical motion and vigor (pulling or pushing heavy objects, bending or kneeling, walking 1 km, climbing 10 stairs without resting, lifting or carrying weight up to 5kg, stretching the right and the left arm above the shoulder) on a scale of 0 *(complete disability),* 1 *(severe difficulty),* 2 *(some difficulty),* and 3 *(no difficulty).* For each of the above three measures, the sum score ranged from 0 to 21 with higher scores meaning better functioning. Cronbach's alpha coefficients of these measures in the CALAS self-respondent sample were .95, .88, and .91, respectively.

Health behavior was assessed by three indicators. Physical activity was measured by the frequency of performing activities such as walking up to 2 km without rest, gardening, and any kind of sport on a scale of 1 *(not at all),* 2 *(rarely),* 3 *(once or twice a week),* and 4 *(three or more times a week).* The score was the mean rating of the reported activities (mean was computed for at least the first two activities). Taking care of own health was self-rated as 1 *(badly),* 2 *(fairly well),* or 3 *(well).* Smoking behavior was coded on a scale of 0 *(more than 20 cigarettes a day),* 1 *(11–20 cigarettes a day),* 2 *(1–10 cigarettes a day),* or 3 *(does not smoke).* In line with the scoring direction in this domain, higher scores meant little or no smoking.

Mental health problems were assessed by four indicators. Depressive symptoms were measured by the Center for Epidemiological Studies—Depression Scale (CES-D; Radloff, 1977). Respondents were asked to rate the frequency they experienced each of 20 depressive symptoms in the past month on a scale of 0 *(not at all),* 1 *(sometimes),* 2 *(most of the time),* and 3 *(almost every day).* The score was the respondent's mean rating (with positive items recoded). Cronbach's alpha of the CES-D in the CALAS self-respondent sample was .88 (see Ruskin et al., 1996). Suffering from mental disease, whether presently or ever, referred to any self-report about a mental disease with no further specification and was coded as either 0 *(no)* or 1 *(yes).* The use of psychoactive medications was rated as 0 *(no use at all),* 1 *(a use of tranquilizers only),* and 2 *(a use of antidepressive or antipsychotic medications).* Current life evaluation was measured by the answer to the question, "Is your life today 1 *(good),* 2 *(pretty good),* 3 *(difficult),* or 4 *(very difficult). "* In line with the scoring direction in this domain, higher scores meant a negative evaluation.

Cognitive functioning was assessed by three indicators that compose Katzman et al.'s (1983) mini-mental instrument. Time orientation was measured by three questions that respectively asked about the year, the month, and the time of day when the interview took place. Memory was measured by a question that asked the participant to repeat a certain name and an address (changed from the original into recognizable Israeli ones). Concentration was measured by two questions that, respectively, asked the participant to count backward from 20 to 1 and to recite the months of the year in reverse order (permitting the Hebrew as well as Gregorian months). For scoring, we multiplied errors by prefixed weights and added them. In the current analyses the original scores were reverse-coded so that higher scores meant better cognitive functioning.

Lifestyle activity was assessed by three indicators: everyday activities, measured by the frequency of performing six activities (watching TV; listening to radio or music; reading newspapers, books, or the Bible; talking with family or friends; going out to cinema, restaurant, concert or theater; and playing cards or other games) and scored as the mean of the activities' ratings on a scale of 0 (*never*), 1 (*rarely*), 2 (*frequently*), and 3 (*every day*); having a hobby, measured by a 0 (*no*) or 1 (*yes*) answer to the question, "Do you have any hobbies?"; and formal volunteering, measured by a 0 (*no*) or 1 (*yes*) answer to the question of whether the participant takes part in volunteering activities conducted for social causes in an organizational framework.

Social support was assessed by three indicators: the reported number of people providing emotional support to the participant, with the question giving space for listing up to three people and hence being scored from 0 to 3; having somebody outside the home who can be contacted for immediate help in emergency, scored 1 (*yes*) or 0 (*no, don't know,* or *no answer*); and the number of close relationships, measured by the question, "Who of your relatives, friends or neighbors are close to you and you talk with them on personal matters and trust them?," with the question giving space for listing up to five people and hence being scored from 0 to 5.

Cumulative life-event distress was assessed by three indicators. The number of traumatic events was measured by the question, "Have you ever undergone a traumatic event that has influenced all your life?" As space was given for listing up to three events, the score ranged from 0 to 3. The number of happy events was measured by the question, "Can you tell about things that have given you great joy during your life?" As in the previous question, the score ranged from 0 to 3, but to conform with the scoring direction of the other measures in this domain, the coding was reversed, with the highest score (3) meaning that no happy event was mentioned. The number of deaths of first-degree relatives was measured by counting the deaths of parents, siblings, spouses, and children that ever took place during the participant's lifetime. This measure was meant to estimate the extent of significant losses experienced by the participants.

Procedure

Participants were interviewed in their residence (home or institution) by multilingual trained interviewers. When necessary, the interviews were conducted in the native language of the respondent and, in some cases, with the help of a translator. The interviewers read aloud the questions as phrased in a preordered form and recorded the participants' responses. The interview lasted approximately 2 hr. Although most of the data were based entirely on self-report, a few measures also involved certain performances by the participants (e.g., the mini-mental instrument, the arm-stretching items in the physical performance measure) or additional verification by the interviewer (e.g., checking the actual presence of reported medications). The study procedure was formally approved in accordance with the Helsinki Committee's ethical requirements. The participants signed an informed consent, and the confidentiality of their records has been strictly secured.

Data Analysis

Due to their role in the sample stratification of the CALAS, both age and gender were included as covariates in all the hypothesis-testing statistics. As we dealt here with a subsample (survivors and comparisons) derived from the larger CALAS dataset on the basis of specific attributes, the incorporation of the initial sampling weights into the analyses could not guarantee a higher precision in estimating the parameters of the target subpopulation. Another consideration for not using sampling weights in this circumstance was the bias caused by the increased variability of weighted estimators (for a discussion of these issues see Korn & Graubard, 1995; Pfeffermann, 1996; Winship & Radbill, 1994). In addition to age and gender, three other sociodemographic variables (education, marital status, and income) served as covariates in all analyses because they yielded significant differences among the study groups (see Table 1).

Results

Multivariate and Univariate Comparisons of the Study Groups

The study groups were compared in nine multivariate analyses of covariance (MANCOVA) in which each domain of functioning or experience provided a set of dependent variables with five covariates (specified in the *Data Analysis* section). Table 2 presents the MANCOVA results for health-related domains and Table 3 for psychosocial domains. As indicated by Wilks's Lambda (an inverse multivariate index of variance not explained by the independent variable), none of the four health-related domains yielded an overall significant difference among the study groups, whereas three of five psychosocial domains yielded such differences. The univariate comparisons pointed to the specific variables within each domain that significantly differentiated the study groups. The post hoc Scheffe´ tests that followed these comparisons guaranteed a most conservative analysis of pairwise differences among the groups (Bray & Maxwell, 1985).

The results showed that the survivors (Group 1) fared worse in certain indicators when they were compared with prewar immigrants (Group 2). In these comparisons, the survivors reported more cumulative life-event distress (indicated by more traumatic events), a lower level of lifestyle activity (indicated by less frequent everyday activities), and weaker social support (indicated by less availability of somebody to help in an emergency). Notably, the only significant difference found between the survivors and the comparison postwar immigrants (Group 3) was the report of more traumatic events by the former. When the two comparison groups are compared between themselves, the postwar immigrants fared significantly worse than the prewar immigrants in cumulative life-event distress (indicated by less happy events), a lower level of lifestyle activity (indicated by less frequent everyday activities), and weaker social support (indicated by less availability of somebody to help in an emergency). On the variables of physical activity and having a hobby, the ANCOVA result was significant at the .05 level, whereas the Scheffe´ test was not.

Table 2
Multivariate Analyses of Covariance Comparing Groups in Health-Related Domains

Domain and variables	Survivors Group 1[a] M/Adj. M	SD	Group 2[a] M/Adj. M	SD	Group 3[a] M/Adj. M	SD	Multivariate comparison (Wilks's Λ)	Univariate comparison and Scheffé results[b]
Comparison groups								
Physical health problems							.98	
No. of major health problems	4.30/4.40	2.72	3.82/3.77	2.54	4.12/4.07	2.48		$F(2, 424) = 2.02$
No. of medications	3.55/3.65	2.27	3.21/3.14	2.29	3.37/3.34	2.33		$F(2, 424) = 1.69$
No. of hospitalizations	1.04/1.05	1.16	0.90/0.86	1.03	0.94/0.97	1.06		$F(2, 424) = 0.07$
No. of visits to doctors	1.16/1.20	0.95	1.12/1.09	0.88	1.32/1.30	1.00		$F(2, 424) = 1.83$
Subjective health							.99	
Self-rated health (high: good health)	1.97/1.96	0.85	2.02/1.98	0.83	1.85/1.90	0.82		$F(2, 424) = 0.34$
Concern about health[c] (high: no concern)	2.05/2.03	0.73	2.11/2.08	0.71	1.91/1.95	0.75		$F(2, 424) = 1.06$
Health today compared with last year (high: better)	1.69/1.67	0.68	1.71/1.69	0.63	1.71/1.75	0.61		$F(2, 424) = 0.53$
Physical functioning							.99	
Activities of daily life (high: no difficulties)	20.27/20.21	2.05	20.06/20.08	2.81	20.03/20.17	2.54		$F(2, 414) = 0.33$
Instrumental activities of daily life (high: no difficulties)	16.83/16.56	5.44	17.12/17.03	5.12	17.04/17.41	5.47		$F(2, 414) = 0.88$
Physical performance (Nagi) (high: no difficulties)	15.66/15.28	5.11	15.58/15.40	4.95	14.88/15.44	5.40		$F(2, 414) = 0.04$
Health behavior							.98	
Frequency of physical activity	1.90/1.84	1.30	2.19/2.14	1.41	1.69/1.81	1.17		$F(2, 419) = 3.17*$
Taking care of own health	2.35/2.37	0.55	2.51/2.49	0.56	2.39/2.40	0.58		$F(2, 419) = 1.63$
Smoking behavior[c] (high: no smoking)	2.25/2.33	1.04	2.28/2.30	1.01	2.46/2.36	0.95		$F(2, 419) = 0.12$

Note. Group 2 was made up of prewar immigrants and Group 3 was made up of postwar immigrants. The original group *n*s are 126, 206, and 145, respectively ($N = 477$). Data were missing for 0–23 cases in particular variables. All results are controlled for the following covariates: age, gender, education, marital status and income. Adj. = adjusted.   [b] Scheffé post hoc test indicated pairs of groups significantly different at the .05 level (after controlling for all covariates). No post hoc pair comparison in this table yielded a significant result.   [c] Reverse-coded variable.
[a] Entries present the group's mean, mean adjusted for all covariates after the slash.
* $p < .05$.

In sum, our first hypothesis that Holocaust survivors would fare worse than comparative participants was confirmed in a modest number of domains and in comparison with prewar, but not postwar, immigrants. The contrast of the survivors with the two comparison groups was even more differential than expected, thus clearly supporting our second hypothesis that Holocaust survivors would differ most clearly from prewar immigrants who did not go through the ordeal of living in Europe during World War II. We found partial support for our third hypothesis: The survivors expressed high cumulative life-event distress by reporting a higher number of traumatic events than participants in both comparison groups, but their difference in reporting mental health problems did not reach significance. However, in line with the third hypothesis, survivors were found to differ from counterparts in certain psychosocial characteristics rather than in physical health conditions.

Results of the Restrictive Group Assignment

The statistical analyses, when run with the restrictive grouping, provide findings that are highly similar to those of the original grouping. In the MANCOVAs (Table 2 and 3), there were minor changes: The variables of physical activity and having a hobby, whose differences among the original groups reached significance, make no significant differences among the restrictive groups. On the other hand, the variable of depressive symptoms, whose difference among the original groups was slightly below significance level, makes a significant difference among the restrictive groups, $F(2, 373) = 3.03$, $p < .05$, although a Scheffe′ test did not indicate significant pairwise comparisons of the higher scores of Group 1 and 3 with the lower score of Group 2.

Discriminant Analysis of the Study Groups

Our aim in performing a discriminant analysis was to obtain an integrative view of both the unique and the combined effects of the 7 variables that had been found in the domain-specific MANCOVAs, whether in the original or the restrictive grouping, to differ significantly among the study groups. The five covariates were also included in the analysis. Altogether, 12 discriminating variables were included in the equation simultaneously and, in another analysis, were also subject to a stepwise inclusion.

The results for the original groups are shown in Table 4. The discriminant analyses yielded two significant discriminant functions. Inspection of distances between the centroids, which are the mean scores of the groups on the discriminant functions, showed that the first function maximally separated between Group 2 and the others. This function reflects the advantage of Group 2 in socioeconomic status (education, income), lifetime happy events, level of everyday activities, and availability of help in emergency. The second function maximally separated between Group 1 and the others, predominantly reflecting the former's high number of lifetime traumatic events. With particular contrast with Group 3, this function also reflects that Group 1 had a higher proportion of men and relatively more income sources (probably due to the survivors' compensation payments). Relative to the other groups, the function also shows Group 1 to be low in having a hobby. In sum, both the simultaneous and the stepwise solutions highlighted the predominant as well as the distinct roles of indicators that respectively pertain to cumulative life-event distress and lifestyle activity. Clearly demonstrated in the stepwise solution was the ineffective or redundant contribution by age and marital status (among the covariates) as well as by physical activity and depressive symptoms. Similar levels of effects by the discriminating variables were obtained in a parallel analysis of the restrictive grouping.

Discussion

This study investigated Holocaust survivors drawn from a national sample of the older Jewish population in Israel. When compared with their counterparts who had immigrated before World War II, the survivors fared worse in certain psychosocial domains than they did in health-related domains. More similarity was found between the survivors and counterparts who had immigrated after the war. Overall, these findings indicate that older Holocaust survivors, randomly approached in a nonclinical setting, still endure the sequelae of their trauma in certain domains of life. The findings also put into a new perspective the status of European Jews who do not consider themselves Holocaust survivors but underwent Holocaust-related afflictions.

Group 1, whose participants defined themselves as Holocaust survivors, experienced a wide range of traumatic experiences during World War II. In our data, survivors who were incarcerated in concentration camps did not differ from survivors who were not: After controlling for the sociodemographic effects of age, gender, education, marital status, and income, none of the 29 indicators we used yielded a significant difference between the two subgroups. Also, the reported number of core Holocaust experiences correlated with the number of deaths of first-degree relatives, $r(106) = .35$, $p < .001$, but not with the other indicators. These findings suggest that over a long time, the sequelae of traumatization may not maintain a differentiation among types and amounts of exposure to the trauma. Thus, although certain studies have found camp survivors in worse conditions than noncamp survivors (Fenig & Levav, 1991; Robinson et al., 1990), other studies have found no differences (Leon et al., 1981; Yehuda et al., 1997). It may be that specific effects of certain traumatic conditions undergo modifications as they interact with an individual's life courses of adaptation and coping (E. Kahana, Kahana, Harel, & Rosner, 1988; Kessler, 1997).

Table 3

Multivariate Analyses of Covariance Comparing Groups in Psychosocial Domains

	Survivors Group 1[a]			Comparison group							
				Group 2[a]			Group 3[a]			Multivariate comparison (Wilks's Λ)	Univariate comparison and Scheffé results[b]
Domain and variables	M/Adj. M	SD		M/Adj. M	SD		M/Adj. M	SD			
Mental health problems										.96	
Depressive symptoms (CES-D)	0.78/0.80	0.44		0.69/0.72	0.41		0.88/0.83	0.45			$F(2, 418) = 2.66$
Ever suffering from a mental disease	0.24/0.24	0.43		0.16/0.16	0.36		0.21/0.19	0.41			$F(2, 418) = 1.36$
Use of psychoactive medications	0.51/0.51	0.69		0.33/0.35	0.56		0.43/0.41	0.62			$F(2, 418) = 2.28$
Current life evaluation[c] (high: negative)	2.15/2.17	0.96		2.15/2.23	0.92		2.26/2.16	0.99			$F(2, 418) = 0.23$
Cognitive functioning										.99	
Time orientation	9.25/9.28	2.15		9.34/9.18	1.87		9.18/9.32	2.27			$F(2, 430) = 0.20$
Memory	5.76/5.85	3.65		6.83/6.52	3.11		6.07/6.30	3.50			$F(2, 430) = 1.46$
Concentration	5.21/5.30	2.75		5.89/5.66	2.54		5.53/5.68	2.68			$F(2, 430) = 0.85$
Lifestyle activity										.94***	
Everyday activities	1.64/1.64	0.52		1.87/1.83	0.42		1.56/1.61	0.53			$F(2, 427) = 9.80***$ 1 ≠ 2, 2 ≠ 3
Having a hobby	0.23/0.24	0.42		0.40/0.38	0.49		0.35/0.36	0.48			$F(2, 427) = 3.25*$
Formal volunteering	0.09/0.10	0.29		0.18/0.17	0.39		0.09/0.09	0.29			$F(2, 427) = 2.52$
Social support										.96*	
Number of people providing emotional support	0.90/0.90	0.69		0.90/0.88	0.55		0.79/0.80	0.60			$F(2, 419) = 0.99$
Having somebody to help in emergency	0.66/0.67	0.47		0.86/0.84	0.35		0.68/0.69	0.47			$F(2, 419) = 6.47**$ 1 ≠ 2, 2 ≠ 3
Number of close relationships	1.22/1.25	1.15		1.38/1.31	1.17		1.05/1.11	1.24			$F(2, 419) = 0.99$
Cumulative life-event distress										.90***	
Number of traumatic events	1.04/1.07	1.00		0.66/0.66	0.75		0.60/0.57	0.79			$F(2, 398) = 11.91***$ 1 ≠ 2, 1 ≠ 3
Number of happy events[c] (high: no happy event mentioned)	1.71/1.72	0.98		1.42/1.46	0.95		1.98/1.93	0.94			$F(2, 398) = 8.51***$ 2 ≠ 3
Number of deaths of first-degree relatives	6.99/6.87	3.25		6.30/6.43	2.55		6.36/6.35	2.50			$F(2, 398) = 1.24$

Note. Group 2 was made up of prewar immigrants and Group 3 was made up of postwar immigrants. The original groups' *n*s are 126, 206, and 145, respectively (total *N* = 477). Data were missing for 0–31 cases in particular variables. All results are controlled for the following covariates: age, gender, education, marital status and income. Adj. = adjusted; CES-D = Center for Epidemiological Studies–Depression Scale.
[a] Entries present the group's mean, mean adjusted for all covariates after the slash. [b] Scheffé post hoc test indicates pairs of groups significantly different at the .05 level (after controlling for all covariates). [c] Reverse-coded variable.
*$p < .05$. **$p < .01$. ***$p < .001$.

Group 2 emerges as the most robust of the three study groups. The participants' immigration to prestate Israel before World War II often reflected a resolute, ideologically driven affiliation with a pioneering society. However, some of them were not separated from the infliction of the Holocaust because they lost close family members who had remained in Europe. Information on these circumstances proved influential in Shmotkin and Lomranz's (1998) study but could not, unfortunately, be ascertained in the current database.

Group 3 reported fewer traumatic events than did the survivor group, but they did not differ from the latter on other indicators of the various domains. Although Group 3 participants did not consider themselves survivors, most of their biographies were related in some way to the Holocaust. An attempt to track their life histories revealed that during World War II, 19.3% of them lived in free Europe or outside of Europe, 27.6% lived in the former Soviet Union, 49.0% in Nazi-occupied dominated countries with partial extermination policy (Romania, Bulgaria, France, Italy), and 4.1% lived in countries with a full extermination policy (Poland, Czechoslovakia, Hungary, Yugoslavia). Many of them had migrated one or several times preceding their final immigration to Israel, either before the war or as refugees from territories left during the war. Those staying under Nazi or pro-Nazi rule were probably not captured for various reasons (e.g., serving as required workers, living in secrecy, assuming a false identity). Thus, although serving as a comparison to the survivors, Group 3 is likely to represent Holocaust-related experiences of a stressful or traumatic nature, such as migrations, deportation, separation from families, economic hardship, and other harsh and risky conditions.

The complementary procedure of restrictive group assignment included only the participants who maintained consistency between their self-definition as survivors (or not as survivors) and their reports of undergoing (or not undergoing) core Holocaust experiences. Inconsistencies between self-definitions and reports constituted relatively small portions of the original groups and might be due either to ambiguities in the questionnaire format or to the participants' response biases. As found here, the restrictive grouping did not change the statistical results substantially. We suggest, then, that the self-perceived status of survivor usually comes with certain traumatic experiences and is likely to represent a long-standing identity with both personal and social implications. Further study is needed to delineate the survivor identity in more detail, including the interplay between subjective (i.e., self-definition) and objective (i.e., factual) constituents and the ways they correspond to the multifaceted experience of survivorship.

Table 4

Discriminant Analysis of the Study Groups

Variables and discriminant statistics	First discriminant function		Second discriminant function	
	Simultaneous inclusion	Stepwise inclusion[a]	Simultaneous inclusion	Stepwise inclusion[a]
Standardized discriminant coefficients[b]				
Covariates				
Age	.07		.04	
Gender[c]	**-.22**	-.19	**.43**	**.53**
Education	**.31**	**.33**	-.17	-.16
Marital status[d]	.02		-.14	
Income	**.33**	**.31**	**.38**	**.40**
Discriminating variables				
Physical activity	.14		.06	
Depressive symptoms	-.02		-.12	
Everyday activities	**.41**	**.43**	.01	.08
Having a hobby	-.04	-.00	**-.42**	**-.41**
Having somebody to help in emergency	**.31**	**.32**	-.14	-.12
Number of traumatic events	-.20	-.22	**.73**	**.70**
Number of happy events[e]	**-.43**	**-.44**	-.05	-.11
Discriminant function information				
Canonical correlation	.40		.36	
Significance of function	.0000		.0000	
Percentage of explained variance	56.0		44.0	
Centroids of				
Group1	-.26		.59	
Group2	.49		-.08	
Group3	-.47		-.42	

Note. N = 394 after a listwise deletion of cases with missing data.
[a]Variables were entered into the equation by minimizing Wilks's Lambda at the .05 significance level. [b] Coefficients higher than .30 appear in bold. [c] Coded 1=female, 2=male. [d]Coded 1=married, 2=presently unmarried. [e] Reverse-coded variable (high: no happy event mentioned).

The scrutiny of the study groups calls for a differential look that weighs strengths versus weaknesses. This balanced appreciation is particularly warranted in face of the compelling similarity of survivors with postwar immigrant counterparts. Reasonably, the ability of the survivors to align themselves with peers who did not undergo the same persecution indicates resourceful coping. Notably, a no-difference result is a success for those whose life and world were totally devastated and had to start their rehabilitation from scratch. As observed (Harel et al., 1993; Helmreich, 1992; Lomranz, 2000), the search for pathology makes researchers overlook the fact that normal life is an achievement for survivors. Even posttraumatic disturbances may be regarded a normal reaction to the abnormal ordeal that the survivors underwent (Lifton, 1993). We should expect, then, that trauma survivors simultaneously exhibit distress and functional impairment along with coping and restorative adjustment (Berger, 1988; Calhoun & Tedeschi, 1998; Harel et al., 1993; B. Kahana, 1992; B. Kahana et al., 1988; Shmotkin & Lomranz, 1998).

The finding pointing to the special role of cumulative life-event distress suggests that the present impact of the past trauma should be considered in a life-span perspective (B. Kahana & Kahana, 1998). In conformity with Yehuda et al. (1995), cumulative distress in life cannot solely account for differences between survivors and comparisons, but it has a unique contribution to these differences. In the discriminant analysis, the respective enumeration of traumatic and happy events related to different functions: Although the former differentiated Group 1 (with most traumatic events) from Group 3, the latter differentiated Group 3 (with least happy events) from Group 2. This dual effect corroborates evidence on the separate impact of positive and negative events on well-being (Zautra & Reich, 1983). The cross-sectional findings, however, confuse causal links. Thus, the focal trauma possibly led the survivors into lives with more perceived anguish or otherwise may retrospectively color the older survivors' review of their life.

Also central was the role of lifestyle activity, referring to a functioning domain that has rarely been elaborated in studies on Holocaust survivors. Two of its indicators, namely everyday activities (e.g., using the mass media, reading, socializing) and having a hobby, each had an independent contribution in the discriminant analysis. Unlike cumulative distress, which refers to the past, lifestyle activity is present oriented and, thus, relates to the normative imperative of all ages to be primarily engaged with the present (Shmotkin, 1991a). Activity is linked with vitality and capability to enjoy life, which observers often found diminished among Holocaust survivors (Eitinger & Major, 1993). It may also be linked to the "zest-via-interest" approach of being curious about one's surroundings (Shmotkin, 1991b), which was found to be lower among Holocaust survivors (Shmotkin & Lomranz, 1998). Thus, lifestyle activity is sensitive to the survivors' ability to sustain involvement in common engagements as well as in more personalized pursuits such as hobbies. On a clinical level, curtailed lifestyle activity corresponds to the posttraumatic syndrome of avoidance, which includes diminished interest in significant activities.

The availability of somebody to help in an emergency proved problematic among the survivors. Although social support in terms of emotional and close relations was not hampered significantly for the survivors (cf. Harel et al., 1993; Landau & Litwin, 2000), their concern about being helped in an emergency may be a reminder of the traumatic helplessness in the past and possibly points to a continued sense of insecurity.

Notably, despite the aforementioned aspects of distress among the survivors, the major indicator of mental health problems, namely depressive symptoms, had a borderline effect in the MANCOVA and a negligible effect in the discriminant analysis. Perhaps depressive feelings are partly diffused into other potent discriminators such as life-event distress (viewing life in traumatic and unhappy colors), level of lifestyle activity (reduced energy and increased withdrawal), and whether one has someone to help in emergency (helplessness). It may also be that the depressive tendencies among the survivors are masked by intriguingly high depression rates among the Israeli elderly at large (Ruskin et al., 1996). Thus, using the relatively elevated clinical cutoff of 20 in the additive score of CES-D (Himmelfarb & Murrell, 1983), we found 31.9% of the survivor group (original grouping) above this score. This group did not differ significantly from the postwar immigrant group, in which 39.1% scored higher than 20; however, both groups differed significantly from the prewar immigrant group, in which 21.4% scored that high, respectively, $\chi^2(1, N = 317) = 4.30, p < .05$, and $\chi^2(1, N = 339) = 12.60, p < .001$. These figures suggest that the likelihood of clinical depression in Group 1 and 3 may be twice as high as expected among populations of similar age in the United States and Europe (Gatz & Hurwicz, 1990; Haynie, Berg, Johansson, Gatz, & Zarit, 2001; Radloff & Teri, 1986).

The evaluation of the current findings involves a number of methodological considerations. A major methodological strength of this study is the random, nonclinical sample of Holocaust survivors and two comparison groups, drawn from a larger national database. Another strength is the multidomain assessment of physical and mental health. However, dealing with an old and very old population whose participation in large-scale surveys is particularly problematic (e.g., Soldo, Hurd, Rodgers, & Wallace, 1997), the findings are limited to those who were willing and able to be personally interviewed. The reliance on the participants' self-reports rather than on alternative sources such as informant reports and behavioral indicators (for some exceptions see *Procedure* section) constitutes another limitation. Self-report methods may involve special biases in late-life populations due to higher rates of verbal and sensory difficulties, prevalent declines in attention and memory, and motivational aspects (e.g., social desirability, suspiciousness) that may be sensitized among some older respondents (Carp, 1989).

A major weakness is the lack of longitudinal data on the participants up to their baseline interviews analyzed here. Thus, the cross-sectional design prevents any conclusion as to whether the difficulties of the Holocaust survivors have lingered since younger age or are reactivated in this period of late life. Nevertheless, it is instructive that these difficulties barely relate to physical health and functioning, whose declines in this age may be stressful. This supports the notion that old and very old survivors have had an innately robust constitution that facilitated their survivorship in the first place. Such conclusion needs further examination in view of the mixed literature about the survivors' physical health (cf. Landau & Litwin, 2000).

The adjustment for five sociodemographic covariates in the current analyses has turned certain group differences (notably in depressive symptoms and cognitive functioning) into nonsignificant, thus probably helping to avoid undue confounding. It appears that the potential confounding by gender should be a reason for particular caution in other studies of Holocaust survivors. The unexpectedly high number of men in the survivor group (68.3%) is beyond the proportion expected by the stratified design. Interestingly, a similarly high percentage of men (64.8%) was also observed in Landau and Litwin's (2000) community sample of older (aged 75+) Holocaust survivors. As presented by these authors, explanations for such gender difference still need substantiation. It is noteworthy, however, that although sociodemographics (e.g., education, marital status , income) are considered "noise" that needs to be controlled, they are inherent characteristics of the typical life courses that each of the study groups has unfolded.

This study raises the need for further research on life-span variability in posttraumatic aftereffects, as by comparing older survivors with younger ones who endured the war as children and may bear other developmental deficits (Krell, 1985). Also, our differential outlook on functioning domains leaves open the question of the processes by which traumatized people may subsequently function well in one domain independent of, or even at the expense of, other domains (Lyons, 1991). Such processes may be analogous to ways in which older people maintain adaptive functioning in the presence of declines and losses. Future studies may implement models grounded in the psychology of aging, such as Baltes's (1997) theory of selective optimization with compensation, to better understand how older survivors prioritize and regulate their resources in ways that cope best with both the lingering trauma and the aging-related impairment. Despite the increasing time distance from World War II, the Holocaust continues to haunt both laypersons and scientists (Suedfeld, 2000). Several decades had passed before public opinion and professional circles ripened enough to fully appreciate the phenomena of victimization and survivorship and, thus, to recognize the ordeal of the Holocaust survivors (Nadler, 2001; Solomon, 1995). Presently, the investigation of these survivors contributes to greater insight into the repercussions of extreme trauma in other populations undergoing ethnopolitical, social, and domestic persecution. As survivors, people who have endured a trauma gain a hope for recovery and often achieve a newly restored life. The current study of older survivors suggests that handling the past trauma and maintaining a new life after it are ceaselessly intertwined endeavors.

References

American Psychiatric Association. (1994). *Diagnostic and statistical manual of mental disorders* (4th ed.). Washington, DC: Author.

Antonovsky, A., Maoz, B., Dowty, N., & Wijsenbeek, H. (1971). Twenty-five years later: A limited study of the sequelae of the concentration camp experience. *Social Psychiatry, 6,* 186–193.

Aviram, A., Silverberg, D. & Carel, S. (1987). Hypertension in European immigrants to Israel—The possible effect of the Holocaust. *Israel Journal of Medical Sciences, 23,* 257–263.

Baider, L., Peretz, T., & Kaplan-De-Nour, A. (1992). Effect of the Holocaust on coping with cancer. *Social Science and Medicine, 34,* 11–15.

Baltes, P. B. (1997). On the incomplete architecture of human ontology: Selection, optimization, and compensation as foundation of developmental theory. *American Psychologist, 52,* 366–380.

Berger, L. (1988). The long-term psychological consequences of the Holocaust on the survivors and their offspring. In R. L. Braham (Ed.), *The psychological perspectives of the Holocaust and its aftermath* (pp. 175–221). New York: City University of New York and Columbia University Press.

Branch, L. G., Katz, S., Kniepmann, K., & Papsidero, J. A. (1984). A prospective study of functional status among community elders. *American Journal of Public Health, 74,* 266–268.

Brandler, S. (2000). Understanding aged Holocaust survivors. *Families in Society, 81,* 66–75.

Bray, J. H., & Maxwell, S. E. (1985). *Multivariate analysis of variance.* Beverly Hills, CA: Sage.

Butler, R. N. (1975). *Why survive? Being old in America.* NY: Harper & Row.

Calhoun, L. G., & Tedeschi, R. G. (1998). Beyond recovery from trauma: Implications for clinical practice and research. *Journal of Social Issues, 54,* 357–371.

Carmil, D., & Breznitz, S. (1991). Personal trauma and world view—Are extremely stressful experiences related to political attitudes, religious beliefs, and future orientation? *Journal of Traumatic Stress, 4,* 393–405.

Carmil, D., & Carel, R. S. (1986). Emotional distress and satisfaction in life among Holocaust survivors—A community study of survivors and controls. *Psychological Medicine, 16,* 141–149.

Carp, F. M. (1989). Maximizing data quality in community studies of older people. In M. P. Lawton & A. R. Herzog (Eds.), *Special research methods for gerontology* (pp. 93–122). Amityville, NY: Baywood.

Chodoff, P. (1963). Late effects of the concentration camp syndrome. *Archives of General Psychiatry, 8,* 323–333.

Cohler, B. J. (1982). Personal narrative and life course. In P. B. Baltes & O. G. Brim, Jr. (Eds.), *Life-span development and behavior* (Vol. 4, pp. 205–241). New York: Academic Press.

Cornoni-Huntley, J. C., Brock, D. B., Ostfeld, A. M., Taylor, J. O., & Wallace, R. B. (1986). *Established populations for epidemiologic studies of the eld-*

erly: Resource data book (1st ed., NIH Publication No. 86–2443). Bethesda, MD: National Institutes of Health.

Danieli, Y. (1981). On the achievement of integration in aging survivors of the Nazi Holocaust. *Journal of Geriatric Psychiatry, 14,* 191–210.

Dasberg, H. (1987). Psychological distress and Holocaust survivors and offspring in Israel, forty years later: A review. *Israel Journal of Psychiatry and Related Sciences, 24,* 243–256.

Eaton, W. W., Sigal, J. J., & Weinfeld, M. (1982). Impairment in Holocaust survivors after 33 years: Data from an unbiased community sample. *American Journal of Psychiatry, 139,* 773–777.

Eitinger, L. (1964). *Concentration camp survivors in Norway and Israel.* Oslo, Norway: Oslo University Press.

Eitinger, L., & Major, E. F. (1993). Stress of the Holocaust. In L. Goldberger & S. Breznitz (Eds.), *Handbook of stress: Theoretical and clinical aspects* (2nd ed., pp. 617–640). New York: Free Press.

Erikson, E. H. (1982). *The life cycle completed: A review.* New York: Norton.

Fenig, S., & Levav, I. (1991). Demoralization and social supports among Holocaust survivors. *Journal of Nervous and Mental Disease, 179,* 167–172.

Fuchs, Z., Blumstein, T., Novikov, I., Walter-Ginzburg, A., Lyanders, M., Gindin, J., et al. (1998). Morbidity, comorbidity, and their association with disability among community-dwelling oldest-old in Israel. *Journal of Gerontology: Medical Sciences, 53A,* 447–455.

Gatz, M., & Hurwicz, M. L. (1990). Are old people more depressed? Cross-sectional data on Center for Epidemiological Studies Depression Scale factors. *Psychology and Aging, 5,* 284–290.

Harel, Z. (1995). Serving Holocaust survivors and survivor families. *Marriage and Family Review, 21,* 29–49.

Harel, Z., Kahana, B., & Kahana, E. (1988). Psychological well-being among Holocaust survivors and immigrants in Israel. *Journal of Traumatic Stress, 1,* 413–429.

Harel, Z., Kahana, B., & Kahana, E. (1993). Social resources and the mental health of aging Nazi Holocaust survivors and immigrants. In J. P. Wilson & B. Raphael (Eds.), *International handbook of traumatic stress syndromes* (pp. 241–252). New York: Plenum.

Haynie, D. A., Berg, S., Johansson, B., Gatz, M., & Zarit, S. H. (2001). Symptoms of depression in the oldest old: A longitudinal study. *Journal of Gerontology: Psychological Sciences, 56B,* 111–118.

Helmreich, W. B. (1992). *Against all odds: Holocaust survivors and the successful lives they made in America.* New York: Simon & Schuster.

Himmelfarb, S., & Murrell, S. A. (1983). Reliability and validity of five mental health scales in older persons. *Journal of Gerontology, 38,* 333–339.

Hobfoll, S. E. (1991). Traumatic stress: A theory based on rapid loss of resources. *Anxiety Research, 4,* 187–197.

Kahana, B. (1992). Late-life adaptation in the aftermath of extreme stress. In M. L. Wykle, E. Kahana, & J. Kowal (Eds.), *Stress and health among the elderly* (pp. 151–171). New York: Springer.

Kahana, B., Harel, Z., & Kahana, E. (1988). Predictors of psychological well-being among survivors of the Holocaust. In J. P. Wilson, Z. Harel, & B. Kahana (Eds.), *Human adaptation to extreme stress: From Holocaust to Vietnam* (pp. 171–192). New York: Plenum.

Kahana, B., & Kahana, E. (1998). Toward a temporal-spatial model of cumulative life stress: Placing late-life stress effects in a life-course perspective. In J. Lomranz (Ed.), *Handbook of aging and mental health: An integrative approach* (pp. 153–178). New York: Plenum.

Kahana, E., Kahana, B., Harel, Z., & Rosner, T. (1988). Coping with extreme trauma. In J. P. Wilson, Z. Harel, & B. Kahana (Eds.), *Human adaptation to extreme stress: From Holocaust to Vietnam* (pp. 55–79). New York: Plenum.

Katz, S. C., Downs, T. D., Cash, H. R., & Grotz, R. C. (1970). Progress in development of the index of ADL. *The Gerontologist, 10,* 20–30.

Katzman, R., Brown, T., Fuld, P., Peck, A., Schechter, R., & Schimmel, H. (1983). Validation of a short orientation–memory–concentration test of cognitive impairment. *American Journal of Psychiatry, 140,* 734–739.

Kessler, R. C. (1997). The effects of stressful life events on depression. *Annual Review of Psychology, 48,* 191–214.

Korn, E. L., & Graubard, B. I. (1995). Examples of differing weighted and unweighted estimates from a sample survey. *The American Statistician, 49,* 291–295.

Kovar, M. G., & Fitti, J. F. (1987). *The longitudinal study of aging: A description of the study* (Working Paper No. 31). Hyattsville, MD: National Center for Health Statistics.

Krell, R. (1985). Child survivors of the Holocaust: 40 years later. *Journal of the American Academy of Child Psychiatry, 24,* 378–380.

Krystal, H. (Ed.). (1968). *Massive psychic trauma.* New York: International Universities Press.

Krystal, H. (1981). The aging survivor of the Holocaust: Integration and self-healing in posttraumatic states. *Journal of Geriatric Psychiatry, 14,* 165–189.

Krystal, H. (1991). Integration and self-healing in post-traumatic states: A ten-year retrospective. *American Imago, 48,* 93–118.

Kuch, K., & Cox, B. J. (1992). Symptoms of PTSD in 124 survivors of the Holocaust. *American Journal of Psychiatry, 149,* 337–340.

Landau, R., & Litwin, H. (2000). The effects of extreme early stress in very old age. *Journal of Traumatic Stress, 13,* 473–487.

Lawton, M. P., & Brody, E. M. (1969). Assessment of older people: Self-maintaining and instrumental activities of daily living. *The Gerontologist, 9,* 179–186.

Lawton, M. P., & Teresi, J. A. (Eds.). (1994). *Annual review of gerontology and geriatrics: Focus on assessment techniques.* New York: Springer.

Leon, G. R., Butcher, J. N., Kleinman, M., Goldberg, A., & Almagor, M. (1981). Survivors of the Holocaust and their children: Current status and adjustment. *Journal of Personality and Social Psychology, 41,* 503–516.

Levav, I. (1998). Individuals under conditions of maximum adversity: The Holocaust. In B. P. Dohrenwend (Ed.), *Adversity, stress, and psychopathology* (pp. 13–33). New York: Oxford University Press.

Levav, I., & Abramson, J. H. (1984). Emotional distress among concentration camp survivors—A community study in Jerusalem. *Psychological Medicine, 14,* 215–218.

Lifton, R. J. (1993). From Hiroshima to the Nazi doctors: The evolution of psychoformative approaches to understanding traumatic stress syndromes. In J. P. Wilson & B. Raphael (Eds.), *International handbook of traumatic stress syndromes* (pp. 11–23). New York: Plenum.

Lomranz, J. (1995). Endurance and living: Long-term effects of the Holocaust. In S. E. Hobfoll & M. W. de Vries (Eds.), *Extreme stress and communities: Impact and intervention* (pp. 325–352). Dordrecht, the Netherlands: Kluwer.

Lomranz, J. (2000). The skewed image of the Holocaust survivor and the vicissitudes of psychological research. *Echoes of the Holocaust, 6,* 45–57.

Lyons, J. A. (1991). Strategies for assessing the potential for positive adjustment following trauma. *Journal of Traumatic Stress, 4,* 93–111.

Marmar, C. R., & Horowitz, M. J. (1988). Diagnosis and phase-oriented treatment of post-traumatic stress disorder. In J. P. Wilson, Z. Harel, & B. Kahana (Eds.), *Human adaptation to extreme stress: From Holocaust to Vietnam* (pp. 81–103). New York: Plenum.

McAdams, D. P. (1990). Unity and purpose in human lives: The emergence of identity as a life story. In A. I. Rabin, R. A. Zucker, R. A. Emmons, & S.

Frank (Eds.), *Studying persons and lives* (pp. 148 –200). New York: Springer.

Nadler, A. (2001). The victim and the psychologist: Changing perceptions of Israeli Holocaust survivors by the mental health community in the past 50 years. *History of Psychology, 4,* 159–181.

Nadler, A., & Ben-Shushan, D. (1989). Forty years later: Long-term consequences of massive traumatization as manifested by Holocaust survivors from the city and the kibbutz. *Journal of Consulting and Clinical Psychology, 57,* 287–293.

Nagi, S. Z. (1976). An epidemiology of disability among adults in the United States. *Milbank Memorial Fund Quarterly, 54,* 439–467.

Nelson, E. A., & Dannefer, D. (1992). Aged heterogeneity: Fact or fiction? The fate of diversity in gerontological research. *The Gerontologist, 32,* 17–23.

Niederland, W. G. (1968). Clinical observations of the "survivor syndrome." *International Journal of Psychoanalysis, 49,* 313–315.

Perls, T. T. (1995). The influence of demographic selection upon the oldest old. *Journal of Geriatric Psychiatry, 28,* 33–56.

Pfeffemann, D. (1996). The use of sampling weights for survey data analysis. *Statistical Methods in Medical Research, 5,* 239–261.

Prager, E., Walter-Ginzburg, A., Blumstein, T., & Modan, B. (1999). Gender differences in positive and negative self-assessments of health status in a national epidemiological study of Israeli aged. *Journal of Women and Aging, 11,* 21–41.

Radloff, L. S. (1977). The CES-D scale: A self-report depression scale for research in the general population. *Applied Psychological Measurement, 1,* 385–401.

Radloff, L. S., & Teri, L. (1986). Use of the Center for Epidemiological Studies-Depression scale with older adults. *Clinical Gerontologist, 5,* 119–136.

Robinson, S., Hemmendinger, J., Netanel, R., Rapaport, M., Zilberman, L., & Gal, A. (1994). Retraumatization of Holocaust survivors during the Gulf War and SCUD missile attacks on Israel. *British Journal of Medical Psychology, 67,* 353–362.

Robinson, S., Rapaport, J., Durst, R., Rapaport, M., Rosca, P., Metzer, S., & Zilberman, L. (1990). The late effects of Nazi persecution among elderly Holocaust survivors. *Acta Psychiatrica Scandinavica, 82,* 311– 315.

Rosow, I., & Breslau, N. (1966), A Guttman health scale for the aged. *Journal of Gerontology, 21,* 556–559.

Ruskin, P. E., Blumstein, Z., Walter-Ginzburg, A., Fuchs, Z., Lusky, A., Novikov, I., & Modan, B. (1996). Depressive symptoms among community-dwelling oldest-old residents in Israel. *American Journal of Geriatric Psychiatry, 4,* 208–217.

Ryff, C. D., Singer, B., Love, G. D., & Essex, M. J. (1998). Resilience in adulthood and later life: Defining features and dynamic processes. In J. Lomranz (Ed.), *Handbook of aging and mental health: An integrative approach* (pp. 69–99). New York: Plenum.

Sadavoy, J. (1997). A review of the late-life effects of prior psychological trauma. *American Journal of Geriatric Psychiatry, 5,* 287–301.

Safford, F. (1995). Aging stressors for Holocaust survivors and their families. *Journal of Gerontological Social Work, 24,* 131–153.

Shanan, J. (1989). Surviving the survivors: Late personality development of Jewish Holocaust survivors. *International Journal of Mental Health, 17,* 42–71.

Shmotkin, D. (1991a). The role of time orientation in life satisfaction across the life-span. *Journal of Gerontology: Psychological Sciences, 46B,* 243–250.

Shmotkin, D. (1991b). The structure of Life Satisfaction Index A in elderly Israeli adults. *International Journal of Aging and Human Development, 33,* 131–150.

Shmotkin, D. (1998). Declarative and differential aspects of subjective well-being and implications for mental health in later life. In J. Lomranz (Ed.), *Handbook of aging and mental health: An integrative approach* (pp. 15–43). New York: Plenum.

Shmotkin, D., & Lomranz, J. (1998). Subjective well-being among Holocaust survivors: An examination of overlooked differentiations. *Journal of Personality and Social Psychology, 75,* 141–155.

Singer, B., Ryff, C. D., Carr, D., & Magee, W. J. (1998). Linking life histories and mental health: A person-centered strategy. *Sociological Methodology, 28,* 1–51.

Soldo, B. J., Hurd, M. D., Rodgers, W. L., & Wallace, R. B. (1997). Asset and health dynamics among the oldest old: An overview of the AHEAD study. *Journal of Gerontology, 52B* (Special Issue), 1–20.

Solkoff, N. (1992). Children of survivors of the Nazi Holocaust: A critical review of the literature. *American Journal of Orthopsychiatry, 62,* 342–358.

Solomon, Z. (1995). From denial to recognition: Attitudes toward Holocaust survivors from World War II to the present. *Journal of Traumatic Stress, 8,* 215–228.

Solomon, Z., & Prager, E. (1992). Elderly Israeli Holocaust survivors during the Persian Gulf War: A study of psychological stress. *American Journal of Psychiatry, 149,* 1707–1710.

Suedfeld, P. (2000). Reverberations of the Holocaust fifty years later: Psychology's contributions to understanding persecution and genocide. *Canadian Psychology, 41*, 1–9.

Turner, R. J., & Lloyd, D. A. (1995). Lifetime traumas and mental health: The significance of cumulative adversity. *Journal of Health and Social Behavior, 36*, 360–376.

Walter-Ginzburg, A., Blumstein, T., Chetrit, A., Gindin, J., & Modan, B. (1999). A longitudinal study of characteristics and predictors of perceived instrumental and emotional support among the old-old in Israel. *International Journal of Aging and Human Development, 48*, 279–299.

Walter-Ginzburg, A., Chetrit, A., Medina, C., Blumstein, T., Gindin, J., & Modan, B. (2001). Physician visits, emergency room utilization, and overnight hospitalization in the old-old in Israel: The Cross-Sectional and Longitudinal Aging Study (CALAS). *Journal of the American Geriatrics Society, 49*, 549–556.

Walter-Ginzburg, A., Guralnik, J. M., Blumstein, T., Gindin, J., & Modan, B. (2001). Assistance with personal care activities among the old-old in Israel: A national epidemiological study. *Journal of the American Geriatrics Society, 49*, 1176–1184.

Weinfeld, M., Sigal, J. J., & Eaton, W. W. (1981). Long-term effects of the Holocaust on selected social attitudes and behaviors of survivors: A cautionary note. *Social Forces, 60*, 1–19.

Winship, C., & Radbill, L. (1994). Sampling weights and regression analysis. *Sociological Methods and Research, 23*, 230–257.

Yaari, A., Eisenberg, E., Adler, R., & Birkhan, J. (1999). Chronic pain in Holocaust survivors. *Journal of Pain and Symptom Management, 17*, 181–1 87.

Yehuda, R., Kahana, B., Schmeidler, J., Southwick, S. M., Wilson, S., & Giller, E. L. (1995). Impact of cumulative lifetime trauma and recent stress on current posttraumatic stress disorder symptoms in Holocaust survivors. *American Journal of Psychiatry, 152*, 1815–1818.

Yehuda, R., Schmeidler, J., Siever, L. J., Binder-Brynes, K., & Elkin, A. (1997). Individual differences in posttraumatic stress disorder symptom profiles in Holocaust survivors in concentration camps or in hiding. *Journal of Traumatic Stress, 10*, 453–463.

Zautra, A. J., & Reich, J. W. (1983). Life events and perceptions of life quality: Developments in a two-factor approach. *Journal of Community Psychology, 11*, 121–132.

Elderly Israeli Holocaust Survivors During The Persian Gulf War: A Study of Psychological Distress

Zahava Solomon, Ph.D., and Edward Prager, Ph.D.

ABSTRACT: *Objective*: The aim of the current study was to systematically assess the psychological effects of the Persian Gulf War on a nonclinical group of elderly Israeli civilians with and without a Holocaust background. *Method*: Sixty-one elderly Holocaust survivors and 131 elderly civilians without a Holocaust background completed questionnaires in their homes. Measures included sense of safety, symptoms of psychological distress, and levels of state and trait anxiety. *Results*: Findings indicate that Holocaust survivors perceived higher levels of danger and reported more symptoms of acute distress than comparison subjects. In addition, they displayed higher levels of both state and trait anxiety. *Conclusions*: Findings do not support the notion that prior experience with extreme stress has an inoculating effect that leads to greater resilience in dealing with other forms of stress. On the contrary, Holocaust experience was found to render the elderly more vulnerable rather than less. These findings of greater vulnerability among Holocaust survivors are of particular significance since they stem from a nonclinical group.

Over a period of 6 weeks, from mid-January to the end of February 1991, the residents of Israel were exposed to a war in which 39 Iraqi Scud missiles, not aimed at military targets, fell in the heart of civilian residential areas. The citizens of Israel were required to equip themselves with masking tape, plastic sheeting, wet towels, and baking soda and were issued gas masks to protect themselves against the Iraqi threat to use biological and chemical weapons. Life in Israel carried on in what became known as the "emergency routine," that is, an ongoing series of emergency alerts separated by hours or days of relative calm. Some places, primarily those providing vital services, remained open in the mornings, but social and cultural activities were almost completely curtailed so as to avoid large gatherings. In the late afternoon, most people retired to their homes, close to their sealed rooms and gas masks, and nervously readied themselves for nighttime, when the missiles would fall.

Despite the fact that millions of people around the globe have been exposed in this century to the horrors of war, and although there have been many studies of war-induced stress, relatively few have focused on civilians. There are a few pioneering works (1, 2), but these have primarily been either impressionistic or based on small samples. Research on high-risk segments of the population are particularly lacking. The present study examined the responses of one group that was identified during the war as being at high risk for psychological distress: the elderly.

Approximately 10% of the population of Israel is over age 60, and in the greater Tel Aviv area (the area that sustained the most missile attacks during the war), the elderly constitute around 14% of the population. While many younger people left the city during the war in search of safer areas, most of the elderly remained at home. Certain aspects of the war were especially distressing for the elderly: community support activities were drastically curtailed during the war and senior citizens' centers were closed, since people refrained from leaving home when not absolutely necessary. Protective devices such as gas masks, which require a certain amount of manual dexterity, also posed problems for many of the elderly. For those with impaired vision or hearing, seclusion in the sealed room often aggravated their sense of isolation from the outer world. Fear of not hearing the warning sirens or difficulty in understanding the emergency instructions broadcast over the media distressed and worried many. These difficulties were especially severe among those who lived alone; their loneliness was exacerbated during the war.

While the war was stressful for all the elderly in Israel, there was one group in particular whose prior life experiences might be expected to affect their responses to the current crisis: Holocaust survivors. Many of this group who immigrated to Israel after World War II seemed, at least outwardly, to have overcome the horrors of their past. Most have raised families and have led productive and full lives. Some of them, however, are haunted by the past and remain scarred by posttraumatic stress (3). The literature is divided with regard to the extent and depth of long-range impairment resulting from the Holocaust. On the one hand, some claim that the Holocaust left a permanent mark and that a large percentage of survivors suffer from severe and debilitating disorders such as chronic anxiety and depression (4) or personality constriction (5). On the other hand, others believe that severe disorders are to be found only among a minority and that most survivors do not manifest serious psychological impairment. On the contrary, most of them lead productive lives despite their ordeal (6).

There is, however, consistent evidence that people who undergo extreme stress are left more vulnerable and more sensitive to *future* adversity (7). Moreover, even people who have seemingly overcome their traumatic experiences may suffer from heightened vulnerability in the future (8) and in extreme cases from reactivation of acute stress responses following exposure to stimuli that symbolize or recall the original traumatic experience (9). The work of Christenson and colleagues (10) is especially relevant in this regard. They examined reactivation of posttraumatic reactions among the elderly. In their work they found that life events such as retirement, children leaving home, death of a loved one, and other stressful events served as triggers that accelerated and unmasked latent posttraumatic stress disorder (PTSD) among American World War II combat veterans.

Clinical impressions indicate that while the Persian Gulf War was stressful for all the population of Israel, it was an especially painful reminder for the Holocaust survivors. The feeling of being "sitting ducks," the sense of impending doom, the threat to use gas (purchased in Germany), and the rows of decontamination showers positioned at the entrance to every hospital (which reminded the survivors of the entrance to the gas chambers in the concentration camps) all made the war particularly stressful for the Holocaust survivors.

The aim of the current study was to systematically assess the psychological effects of the Persian Gulf War on elderly civilians with and without a Holocaust background. Specifically, we examined sense of safety, symptoms of psychological distress, and levels of state and trait anxiety.

Method

Subjects

A total of 192 subjects participated in this study. Sixty-one (31.8%) were Holocaust survivors and 131 (68.2%) did not have this background. In the Holocaust group, the mean age was 68.3 (SD=7.2) and 33.3% (N=20) were men. In the non-Holocaust group, the mean age was 72.9 (SD=7.5) and 38.5% (N=50) were men. Thirty-six percent of the subjects lived in kibbutzim (communal settlements), and the remaining 64% resided in cities in the center of Israel. Five percent of the subjects were born in Israel, and the remainder were of European origin. Seventeen percent of the respondents had completed elementary school, 53% had finished high school, and 30% had studied beyond high school. Fifty-seven percent were married at the time of the study, 37% were widowed, 2% were divorced, and 4% had never married. Sixty-six percent of the respondents described themselves as secular, 26% as traditional, and 8% as orthodox. Twelve percent were residents of an urban community home for the aged; the remainder lived in their own homes, whether in kibbutzim or in cities.

Procedure

In each community, a local social worker who was well acquainted with the elderly residents of the area and experienced in working with this population was recruited to administer questionnaires. The social worker approached potential subjects and requested their consent to participate in the study. Subjects completed the questionnaires in the presence of the social workers, who answered questions as necessary.

Subjects were first presented with a brief questionnaire inquiring about sociodemographic variables such as age, sex, education, religious observance, marital status, place of residence, country of origin, and current health status. Subjects were then queried in detail about prior traumatic experiences, such as internment in concentration camps during World War II, participation in wars, loss of loved ones, and personal life events. Subjects were also asked to note if they had experienced any event similar to the Persian Gulf War in the past.

Sense of safety. Subjects were asked to rate their level of personal safety during the war in a number of different areas on a scale ranging from 1 (not at all) to 5 (very much). Internal validity of the nine-item questionnaire was examined through factor analysis with varimax rotation. This analysis yielded three principal factors (eigen value greater than 1) that explained 62.6% of the variance.

In the current study, we employed only the first factor, which explained 31.0% of the variance and related to the subjects' perceptions of danger. This factor includes questions such as "To what degree do you feel that your life is in danger?" "To what degree do you assess that the country of Israel is in danger of being annihilated?" and "To what degree do you think that your family is in danger?"

State-Trait Anxiety Inventory. This questionnaire (11) is a standardized measure of anxiety that has been used frequently in studies of traumatic stress throughout the world, particularly with civilian populations, thus allowing for comparisons with other samples (2). It is composed of two 20-item scales. The State Anxiety scale assesses the person's *current* or transitory emotional state, and the Trait Anxiety scale examines the way the subject *generally* feels.

Psychological Distress in Wartime. This self-report measure, devised for the current study, comprises 19 items all of which examine typical responses to extreme stress. Unfortunately, no standardized criteria for assessment of acute stress reactions are currently available, and even the most recent diagnostic and statistic manual, *DSM-III-R,* does not include a relevant category. The closest and most relevant nosological category in *DSM-III-R* is that of PTSD. The symptoms required for diagnosis of PTSD (e.g., distancing from others, nightmares, startle response, hypervigilance) were, therefore, chosen as the basis for most of the items in this questionnaire. Since this assessment was conducted *during* rather than after the exposure to the stressor, however, not all of the *DSM* criteria were appropriate, and, of course, the criterion of 1-month duration could not be met. For this reason, no attempt was made to address the issue of diagnosis. Subjects were asked to rate the presence of each symptom in the past week on a 4-point scale ranging from 1 (not at all) to 4 (very often). The mean score on this scale was 36.4 (SD=11.7). In order to examine internal consistency, Cronbach's alpha was calculated and was found to be high (0.90).

Results

In order to examine differences between subjects with and without a Holocaust background, a multivariate analysis of the four dependent variables was conducted. The analysis indicated a large and significant effect (F=8.14, df=4, 109, p<0.001). All four dependent variables were significantly different between the two groups (all p values were <0.001); elderly Holocaust survivors perceived significantly higher levels of danger, experienced more emotional distress, and had higher levels of both state and trait anxiety than subjects without a Holocaust background.

In order to examine whether there were differences in background variables between the two groups, a multivariate analysis of variance (MANOVA) was performed with the sociodemographic characteristics (age, sex, education, religiosity, health status, and proximity to bomb sites) as independent variables and Holocaust background as the dependent variable. This analysis yielded a significant main effect (F=10.19, df=6, 173, p<0.001) because of the fact that the Holocaust survivors were significantly younger (F=21.51, df=1, 179, p<0.001), less educated (F=14.37, df=1, 79, p<0.001), and more religious than the other subjects (F=12.88, df=1, 179, p<0.001) and were closer to the bomb sites (F=16.00, df=1, 179, p<0.001). It was therefore decided to perform the MANOVA on the dependent variable with the background variables as covariates. Table 1 presents the means and standard deviations of the four dependent variables separately for Holocaust survivors and the other respondents and the results of the multivariate analysis, covarying for the background variables.

TABLE 1. Psychological Ratings During the Persian Gulf War for Elderly Israeli Survivors of the Holocaust and Other Elderly Subjects[a]

	Holocaust Survivors (N = 61)		Other Subjects (N = 131)		F
Measure	Mean	SD	Mean	SD	df = 1, 100
Perception of Danger	-0.2	0.9	0.5	1.1	2.29
Psychological Distress	42.9	11.9	33.0	10.1	6.20
State Anxiety	47.4	13.2	36.5	13.0	6.27
Trait Anxiety	50.3	10.4	41.5	7.4	7.53b

[a]A multivariate analysis of covariance was performed with age, sex, education, religiosity, health, and proximity to bomb sites as covariates. Overall F=2.43, df=4, 97, p<0.05;
[b]p<0.05, with Bonferroni correction (12) for multiple comparisons.

As can be seen in table 1, the effect of the Holocaust was marginally significant (p<0.05) after the effects of the background variables were removed. When the structure of the relationships was examined with univariate analyses, we found that perception of danger was not significantly different between the two groups. In univariate analyses of variance we found that state anxiety and psychological distress were different between the two groups (p<0.05). These significance tests should be interpreted cautiously because multiple comparisons were performed. We therefore performed a more conservative estimate of the significance level, using the Bonferroni correction (12), and found that the two groups did not differ significantly. Trait anxiety was significantly different between the two groups after the background variables were covaried (p<0.05, with Bonferroni correction).

In sum, results show that even after a wide range of background variables were controlled, there were still marginally significant differences between the Holocaust survivors and the other elderly civilians, with the Holocaust survivors experiencing more difficulties than the other subjects.

Discussion

The findings of this study indicate that elderly survivors of the Holocaust suffered considerable emotional distress during the Persian Gulf War. It should be noted that differences between the Holocaust survivors and the other elderly subjects were evident even when a most conservative analysis of the data was conducted that controlled for a wide range of background variables, some of which may themselves have been a function of Holocaust experiences (e.g., health status).

These findings do not support the notion that prior experience with extreme stress has an inoculating effect that leads to greater resilience in dealing with other forms of stress. Norris and Murrell (13), for example, studied a large sample of elderly flood victims and found evidence for both direct tolerance (exposure to a particular stressor reduces the subsequent impact of the *same* stressor) and cross-tolerance (exposure to one type of stressor lowers the pathogenicity of a *different* stressor). In the current study, however, there were no such effects. On the contrary, Holocaust experience was found to render the elderly *more* vulnerable rather than less. In fact, using a cutoff point of 44 on the Trait Anxiety scale, as suggested by Himmelfarb and Murrell (14), we found that a large proportion of the Holocaust survivors (51%) were at risk for a "degree of psychological distress that would require intervention" (14, p. 162). Moreover, the proportion of Holocaust survivors with Trait Anxiety scale scores above the cutoff point was more than *double* that of the other subjects (24%).

These findings are consistent with those of prior studies that have demonstrated greater vulnerability to stress among trauma victims. Prior studies by this group (9), for example, have found that the greater the similarity between two traumatic events, the greater the chance for a reactivation of the original stress response after the second event. It should be kept in mind, however, that even a very different stressor may lead to reactivation of an earlier stress response among the elderly (10).

There is some controversy in the literature with regard to the long-term effects of the Holocaust on survivors. Titchener (15, 16) has suggested that a process of posttraumatic decline may take place in the years after exposure to a traumatic event and that permanent characterological effects of the trauma may be observed, particularly in terms of proneness to anxiety reactions. Niederland (4) has characterized the "survivor syndrome" as a chronic state of anxious bland depression. One major limitation of most reports on Holocaust survivors has been that formulations of the survivor's adjustment during and after internment have been based primarily on analysis of individuals who were seeking help for emotional problems. Few studies have used normal samples. Researchers such as Leon and colleagues (6) have claimed that generalizations about survivors as a group were based on the analysis of clinical cases and have questioned the generality of these findings. In fact, community studies have often failed to uncover significant pathology among Holocaust survivors. The current findings of both acute stress and higher levels of state (acute) and trait (characterological) anxiety are, therefore, of significance, since we used a normal group as well as a comparison group of the same ethnic and cultural background as the survivors.

Supported in part by a grant from the Chief Scientist's Committee, Israel Ministry of Health.

References

1. Rachman SJ: Fear and Courage, 2nd ed. New York, WH Freeman, 1990
2. Saigh PA: An experimental analysis of delayed posttraumatic stress. Behav Res Ther 1984; 22:679-682
3. Nadler A: Forty years later: long term consequences of massive traumatization as manifested by Holocaust survivors from the city and the Kibbutz. J Consult Clin Psychol 1989; 57:287-293
4. Niederland WG: The problem of the survivor, in Massive Psychic Trauma. Edited by Krystal H. New York, International Universities Press, 1969
5. Dor-Shav NK: On the long-range effects of concentration camp internment of Nazi victims: 25 years later. J Consult Clin Psychol 1978; 46:1-11
6. Leon GR, Butcher JN, Kleinman M, Goldberg A, Almagor M: Survivors of the Holocaust and their children: current status and adjustment. J Pets Soc Psychol 1981; 41:503-516

7. Silver RL, Wortman CB: Coping with undesirable events, in Human Helplessness: Theory and Application. Edited by Garber J, Seligman ME. New York, Academic Press, 1980

8. Solomon Z, Oppenheimer B, Elizur Y, Waysman M: Exposure to recurrent combat stress: can successful coping in a second war heal combat-related PTSD from the past? J Anxiety Disorders 1990; 4:141-145

9. Solomon Z, Garb R, Bleich A, Grupper D: Reactivation of combat-related posttraumatic stress disorder. Am J Psychiatry 1987; 144:51-55

10. Christenson RM, Walker JI, Ross DR, Maltbie AA: Reactivation of traumatic conflicts. Am J Psychiatry 1981; 138:984-985

11. Spielberger CD, Gorsuch RL, Lushene RD: STAI Manual. Palo Alto, Calif, Consulting Psychologists Press, 1970

12. Miller RG: Simultaneous Statistical Inference. New York, Springer-Verlag, 1981

13. Norris FH, Murrell SA: Prior experience as a moderator of disaster impact on anxiety symptoms in older adults. Am J Community Psychol 1988; 16:665-683

14. Himmelfarb S, Murrell SA: The prevalence and correlates of anxiety symptoms in older adults. J Psychol 1984; 116:159-167

15. Titchener JL, Ross WO: Acute and chronic stress as determinants of behavior, character, and neurosis, in Adult Clinical Psychiatry: American Handbook of Psychiatry, 2nd ed, vol III. Edited by Arieti S, Brody EB; Arieti S, editor-in-chief. New York, Basic Books, 1974

16. Titchener JL: Post traumatic decline: a consequence of unresolved destructive drives, in Trauma and Its Wake, vol II: Traumatic Stress Theory, Research, and Intervention. Edited by Figley CF. New York, Brunner/Mazel, 1986

Permissions

The articles in the anthology appear with the permission of the authors or publishers of the journals in which the articles originally appeared. The original citations are as follows:

Avi Bleich, Marc Gelkopf, Yuval Melamed and Zahava Solomon. (2006). Mental health and resiliency following 44 months of terrorism: A survey of an Israeli national representative sample. *BMC Medicine 4*:21, doi:10.1186/1741-7015-4-21. (© 2006 Bleich et al; licensee BioMed Central Ltd. This is an Open Access article distributed under the terms of the Creative Commons Attribution License hhttp://creativecommons.org/licenses/by/2.0), which permits unrestricted use, distribution, and reproduction in any medium, provided the original work is properly cited.

P. S. Curran. (1988). Psychiatric aspects of terrorist violence: Northern Ireland 1969-1987. *Br J Psychiatry, 153*, 470-5.

Sandro Galea, Jennifer Ahern, Heidi Resnick, Dean Kilpatrick, Michael Bucuvalas, Joel Gold and David Vlahov. (2002). Psychological sequelae of the September 11 terrorist attacks in New York City. *New England Journal of Medicine, 346*, 982-987. Copyright © 2002, Massachusetts Medical Society. All rights reserved.

Behzad Hassani. (2005). Trauma and terrorism: How do humans respond? *University of Toronto Medical Journal, 83*(1), 58-62.

J. D. Kinzie, J. K. Boehnlein, C, Riley, and L. Sparr. (2002). The effects of September 11 on traumatized refugees: Reactivation of posttraumatic stress disorder. *Journal of Nervous & Mental Disease. 190*(7):437-441, July.

G. James Rubin, Chris R. Brewin, Neil Greenberg, John Simpson and Simon Wessely. (2005). Psychological and behavioural reactions to the bombings in London on 7 July 2005: Cross sectional survey of a representative sample of Londoners. *British Medical Journal, 331*:606-612.

Joel Sadavoy (1997). Survivors: A review of late-life effects of prior psychological trauma. *American Journal of Geriatric Psychiatry, 5*(4), 287-301.

Nadežda Savjak. (2003). Multiple traumatisation as a risk factor of post-traumatic stress disorder. *PSIHOLOGIJA, 36* (1-2), 59-71.

Mark A. Schuster, Bradley D. Stein, Lisa H. Jaycox, Rebecca L. Collins, Grant N. Marshall, Marc N. Elliott, Annie J. Zhou, David E. Kanouse, Janina L. Morrison and Sandra H. Berry. (2001). A national survey of stress reactions after the September 11, 2001, terrorist attacks. *New England Journal of Medicine, 345,* 1507-1512. Copyright © 2001, Massachusetts Medical Society. All rights reserved.

Arieh Y. Shalev, Rivka Tuval, Sarah Frenkiel-Fishman, Hilit Hadar, and Spencer Eth. (2006). Psychological responses to continuous terror: A study of two communities in Israel. *American Journal of Psychiatry, 164*(4), 667-673.

Dov Shmotkin, Tzvia Blumstein and Baruch Modan. (2003). Tracing long-term effects of early trauma: A broad-scope view of holocaust survivors in late life. *Journal of Consulting and Clinical Psychology, 71*(2), 223-234. Copyright © 2003 by the American Psychological Association. Reprinted with permission.

Zahava Solomon and Edward Prager. (1992). Elderly Israeli Holocaust survivors during the Persian Gulf War. *American Journal of Psychiatry, 149*(12), 1707-1710.

Brian Trappler, Jeffrey W. Braunstein, George Moskowitz and Steven Friedman. (2002). Holocaust survivors in a primary care setting: Fifty years later. *Psychological Reports, 91,* 545-552. © Psychological Reports 2002.

Brian Trappler and Steven Friedman. (1996). Posttraumatic stress disorder in survivors of the Brooklyn Bridge shooting. *The American Journal of Psychiatry, 153*(5), 705-707.

Carmelo Vázquez, Pau Pérez-Sales and Georg Matt. (2006). Post-traumatic stress reactions following the March 11, 2004 terrorist attacks in a Madrid community sample: A cautionary note about the measurement of psychological trauma. *The Spanish Journal of Psychology, 99*(1), 61-74.